Social Movements and the New State

Social Movements and the New State

The Fate of Pro-Democracy Organizations
When Democracy Is Won

Brian K. Grodsky

Stanford University Press
Stanford, California

Stanford University Press
Stanford, California

Printed in the United States of America on acid-free, archival-quality paper

Library of Congress Cataloging-in-Publication Data

Grodsky, Brian K., 1974– author.
   Social movements and the new state : the fate of pro-democracy organizations when democracy is won / Brian K. Grodsky.
      pages cm
   Includes bibliographical references and index.
   ISBN 978-0-8047-8231-9 (cloth : alk. paper)—ISBN 978-0-8047-8232-6 (pbk. : alk. paper)
   1. Social movements—Political aspects—Case studies.
   2. Democratization—Case studies.   3. Democracy—Case studies.   I. Title.
   HM881.G76 2012
   303.48'4—dc23
                                                              2012009556

Typeset by Westchester Book Group in 11/13.5 Adobe Garamond

I would like to dedicate this book to Maya and Ania,
whose incredible patience made it all come together.

Contents

Acknowledgments

I WANT TO USE THE OPENING LINES OF THIS BOOK to thank most of all the approximately 150 interviewees on whose words much of this study is based. Many of these individuals gave hours of their time recalling sometimes personally painful experiences. Without their willingness to tell these stories, this book would have been impossible to write.

I would also like to thank several outstanding scholars who proved extremely helpful during various stages of this manuscript. I reserve a special thank-you for Doug McAdam, whose *Freedom Summer* was one of the inspirations for this work. Doug generously took the time to sit down with this manuscript and provide me with invaluable insights that resulted in a much stronger book. I am also indebted to Doug for his kind advice in steering this manuscript through the publishing process.

Early on, I had the great fortune and pleasure to participate in CUNY's Politics and Protest Workshop (September 2010), where I received excellent feedback from participants, especially organizer Jim Jasper and Vince Boudreau. This workshop was an enormous asset, and I hope to someday be able to repay those who made it so illuminating for me. I am also very grateful to Valerie Bunce, Ron Aminzade, David Meyer, Sidney Tarrow, Graeme Robertson, Anna Grzymala-Busse, Lincoln Mitchell, Scott Radnitz, Tsveta Petrova, Clifford Bob, Brian Loveman, and Philip Oxhorn for their tremendously helpful comments on various chapters and early feedback on methodological issues, as well as the two anonymous reviewers from Stanford University Press. And I am thankful for the research assistance of Matthew Czekaj.

A study of this sort necessitates both extensive travel and a significant amount of detective work to locate long-lost activists, and I was fortunate to have assistance in Poland, where I owe an enormous debt to Joanna Posmyk, whose help in tracking down contact information about Solidarity leaders from the most recent to the distant past was indispensable. For the research I conducted in Georgia, I am grateful to Alexander Rondeli, president of the Georgian Foundation for Strategic and International Studies, for opening his doors to me during my stay in country. In addition, I thank the University of Maryland, Baltimore County, whose support—in the form of a Summer Faculty Fellowship and a Special Research Assistantship/Initiative Support award—made this research possible.

1

Introduction
How Many Lives Does a Social Movement Have?

IT WAS A SHOW OF EPIC PROPORTIONS: Hundreds of thousands of Egyptians in early 2011 took to the streets of Cairo, demanding an end to strongman Hosni Mubarak's thirty-year grip on power. They followed the newest pro-democracy, social-movement script almost to the letter: Motivated by their own mix of economic and political grievances and inspired by events next door, the mostly youthful protesters turned their grumbling into action that attracted the participation of longtime regime opponents, who sometimes adopted the lead role. The sparks of the Arab Spring were struck in Tunisia, but its fires roared through Egypt before singeing other countries in the region. From the news satellites orbiting overhead, the characteristic order of the Middle East gave way to immense and chaotic billows of smoke. In both Tunisia and Egypt the resolution occurred shockingly fast; the movements were victorious.

But on the ground, in Egypt's Tahrir Square, the picture was anything but clear. In the immediate aftermath of victory some activists decided it was time to take to the newly opened political stage in order to institutionalize all that the movement had stood for. "We made the Republic of Tahrir," said one youth leader who had quit his job on the stock exchange to enter the political arena. "Now let us make Egypt" (Worth 2011). Others lingered on the square, wondering whether it was really time to throw away the signs they had hastily crafted when the movement got under way just weeks before. Again, the Egyptians were on cue, their movement splitting into those who would move on to power and those who would remain behind. For the latter, promised changes could not come fast enough, and, as disappointment quickly spread, activists returned to the square and employed their now familiar, contentious methods against the new state.

For the casual observer, the plight of these activists was a function of a quirk in the Egyptian democratization story: Unlike in most episodes of revolutionary democratic breakthrough, where new elites transition into the state en masse, in Egypt a military caretaker government linked to Mubarak had temporarily assumed power. Those movement activists who turned political, from this perspective, never even reached positions of power as the movement mobilized for another round of the fight. In fact, this Egyptian aberration merely shortened the time it took for tensions to boil over between activists and those who left for the political arena. Just across the border in Tunisia, young protesters had predictably turned against their own government, angry that their economic grievances remained unaddressed. As the fates of social movements from northern Europe to southern Africa indicate, the split was practically inevitable. And, as this book demonstrates, it was systematic.

Movement activists, who are typically jolted from the wilderness of dissidence and exclusion into the frenzy of mass-based action and then the euphoria of victory, rarely have time for soul searching in the early period after democratic breakthrough. From the activists' perspective, those organization leaders who then depart for the state are invariably an asset. What better way to influence the new regime and secure the revolutionary transition than to inject into the state's highest echelons those who blazed the path to democratic breakthrough in the first place? These organization leaders, on the one hand, personify the ideals of the movement and, on the other hand, will be tied by personal bonds to those remaining behind. The combination of identity and peer pressure, it seems, will be enough for those activists who remain in the organization to keep their old friends, who are now at the policy helm, true to the movement's agenda.

Yet within two years of regime change, activists in the three culturally and geographically disparate cases analyzed in this book—Poland, South Africa, and Georgia—all felt profoundly disempowered and bitterly cheated by their ex-comrades, who were now running the postbreakthrough show. Identity became a contested stage on which actors on each side of the state divide accused those on the other of betrayal. Moreover, personal networks built up during the years of struggle mutated from what some thought would be ties of influence into something more reminiscent of a noose. Activists in all three states were left reeling by the shocking answer to the critical question of how social-movement leaders behave when they move into positions of power.

From Social Movements to the State

This is a study of social movements, broadly understood as challenges to "existing arrangements of power and distribution by people with common purposes and solidarity, in sustained interaction with elites, opponents, and authorities" (Meyer and Tarrow 1998, 4). These movements, ranging from massive grassroots organizations to small "principled" groups (Sikkink 1993, 411) acting "on behalf of largely silent constituencies" (Ottaway and Chung 1999, 107), are all bound by the contentious activities they pursue to achieve a common, collective good. Regardless of their most immediate demands, these movements invariably necessitate extensive political changes as the lynchpin of their success.

They are also bound in their postmovement trajectory. It is the rule rather than the exception that upon victory some leaders of social-movement organizations take to the state. They are by nature embedded in the political process, linked by mission (and sometimes personnel) to opposition political parties. In fact, oftentimes these organizations would not exist but for the political dissidents who create them as, in Bratton's words, "the refuge of last resort for partisan opposition groupings" (Bratton 1994, 64). During the struggle, actors on both sides of the political/civil line frequently converge for strategy deliberations or protests and thus develop a symbiotic relationship as any previously existing boundaries fade.

It is of little surprise that the pro-democracy cases explored in the following chapters are therefore only the tip of the iceberg; the postdemocratic breakthrough migration from this most vocal sector of civil society to the state has occurred in many places around the world, from Africa (including Kenya, Nigeria, and the Democratic Republic of the Congo) and Asia (the Philippines) to Europe (Serbia, Czechoslovakia) and Latin America (Chile, Brazil).[1] The same phenomenon has proven true for activists in other social-movement spheres that demanded greater levels of inclusion, from feminists and civil-rights leaders to environmentalist and leftist organizers. It is these new political elites, buoyant after their hard-earned victory and confident as a result of the societal enthusiasm that catapulted them to power, who are the focus of this study. What happens to those "principled" organizations that participate in a pro-democracy movement when their members are subsequently drawn into the new, democratic government? In what ways do they benefit or suffer from the new relationship?

These questions have enormous import not only for citizens in postbreakthrough states but also for U.S. policymakers engaged in overseas assistance. In 2009 the United States spent $2.7 billion on democratization around the world, including $482 million on civil-society promotion alone; the State Department's 2011 budget request was for $3.3 billion. According to USAID's mission statement, the purpose of this assistance was to "help transform non-democratic countries" in the short term and "represent citizens' concerns and ensure transparency and good governance" in the long term (USAID 2010). External assistance, including monetary and diplomatic support, for key elements of civil society has helped fuel movements credited with ending illiberal regimes around the world. However, we have significantly less understanding of how these pro-democracy, social-movement organizations, envisioned by external backers as both the vanguard and then guardian of democracy, actually function as their leaders take to the state.

The fact is, those who observe their movement-era colleagues depart for the state tend to feel assured of the advantage their departure will bring. Apart from their enormous level of faith based on personal and interpersonal arguments mentioned earlier, there is another important reason these movement leaders are at times surprised when their state-bound colleagues act inconsistently with their expectations. While scholars and policymakers have accumulated a wealth of information on the rise and maintenance of social movements, the "what next?" question has been largely pushed to the side. Predictably, foreign-policy officials involved in these processes have neither the time nor the occupational incentive to stop and take a closer look at the "what next?" (Grodsky 2009). As one democracy specialist at USAID conceded, "People in the field are so busy they just don't have the time to look at lessons learned" (USAID 2007). Academics, focused primarily on the important issue of mobilization, have also been largely uninterested in this topic. As a result, activists (and everyone else for that matter) have very little empirical evidence to point them in the right direction.

There are a few important exceptions, including McAdam's (1988) fascinating study of the civil-rights generation more than a decade after the struggle concluded; Banaszak's (2009) intriguing work on the inclusion of feminist-movement activists in various branches of the U.S. government; and Mische's (2008) analysis of student-activist networks in Brazil. However, although these studies alternatively demonstrate the long-term impact of social-movement identities and personal networks or the policy impact of activists in their new institutional shells, they do not explicitly look at the role of friendships and identities in creating state–movement bridges.

The approach to this study is therefore rather unusual. Rather than analyzing existing theories (which are generally absent, given the relative dearth of research on this subject), I create arguments that extend out of the rich, multidisciplinary literature on the rise and maintenance of social movements, as well as the nascent demobilization and postmovement literature. I focus on key elements of mobilization and organization activities that seem likely to have a long-term impact and emphasize the role of movement identities, social networks, and institutional structures. It is important to stress that these arguments are not mutually exclusive. In fact, as I explain in the next chapter, they frequently overlap and may as a collective enhance our understanding of the processes that occur in newly democratizing states.

The first argument to emerge from this literature, the group-identity argument, projects the empowerment of organizations whose members have taken state positions, based on the notion that former activists remain attached to the principles and demands they long advocated and govern in accordance with these ideas. Group identities form around a "cognitive, moral, and emotional connection with a broader community, category, practice, or institution" (Polletta and Jasper 2001, 285). They involve strong norms of behavior that organizations both create and serve to enforce through positive and negative incentives. Institutions that develop around or within these networks, including formal rituals and everyday interactions, reinforce and further transform group understandings and solidify belief systems. The output should be principled organization activists with a heightened sense of purpose and belonging. As Polletta and Jasper note, "participation usually transforms activists' subsequent biographies, marking their personal identities even after the movement ends" (Polletta and Jasper 2001, 296). Evidence from the scant postmovement literature suggests that ideologies formed during movement years are indeed durable.

The second social-network argument similarly suggests that activists who have left their organizations for the state remain bound by social ties to those presiding over their former organizations, empowering these associations through mechanisms such as access and peer pressure. This argument is grounded in part in the numerous analyses of how preexisting social networks (friends, colleagues, kin, etc.) can contribute to the rise of social movements. Others have found that the very process of mobilization creates new ties. Over the course of the movement, activists become emotionally fused with their organizations, which become "a goal in themselves" (Melucci, Keane, and Mier 1989, 60). The emerging networks elicit strong emotions such as loyalty and obligation that serve to further strengthen groups and might be expected to survive after the struggle ends. Whereas the identity argument is based on the strength of ideas to hold former and ongoing activists together in the postbreakthrough period, the network argument focuses more on a human aversion to ostracism.

The third institutional argument that I put forward holds that although previously established identities and social networks can create new opportunities, they can also be undermined by institutional constraints and the new walls built between former colleagues and friends. This argument emerges from the political-science institutional perspective, which emphasizes the influence of organizational structures and responsibilities in determining actors' preferences. It also builds on social-movement work that explains how activists struggle to integrate various expectations and pressures emanating from the diverse structures in which they are immersed (from formal organizations and institutions to family). Where institutionally structured preferences yield somewhat similar policy priorities among groups, previous ties should prove an asset. However, where these preferences diverge, particularly in broad policy areas, personal aspects will create more intense conflict than if no personal ties had existed beforehand. Incorporation can be either a blessing (by providing new opportunities to long-excluded social-movement organizations) or a curse (by setting the stage for tension, animosity, and personal vitriol).

The institutional argument accounts for an array of internal and external pressures that are overlooked in identity and network arguments. Internally, old friends may be watching new state leaders, but so are millions of voters who are eager to see their long-standing grievances addressed. These individuals tend to see liberty not as a goal but as a means to prosperity. As the Greek playwright Aeschylus said nearly 2,500 years before these most recent revolutions, "Only when man's life comes to its end in prosperity can one call that man happy." For state leaders, movement demands may no longer be their most pressing concerns. Externally, these actors face constraints generated by neoliberal global pressures, meaning that the dominant sources of outside assistance, which are often critical to bringing citizens the economic uplift they demand, are bound in policy chains. New political elites discover in the process of rebuilding their economy that everything from advising to enticing new foreign investment and trade relations involves bending to the dominant and, at least in the short term, domestically painful, neoliberal rules of the game.

This losing scenario can be the one that prompts despair and demobilization of the broader movement after "victory." This prospect is all the more likely given that most movements are, beneath their most basic tenets, quite heterogeneous, which sets the stage for a fragmentation of such coalitions over time.

Yet some movement leaders clearly find it in their interest, whether out of political strategy or in the pursuit of both tangible and intangible rewards, to maintain their organizations despite apparent victory. These leaders frequently adapt to the new environment by transforming their organizations into bureaucratic and formalized units more capable of everyday interaction with new state institutions and external donors. Since engaging in conventional politics normally means being more pragmatic and less idealistic, the result can be alienation or a backlash further down in the organization and, in turn, pressure on more senior leaders to stand their ground on long-held principles and policies. Just as ex-movement leaders in the state face significant institutional constraints, so do those who remain behind. One of the main lessons that Egyptian, Tunisian, and other activists should learn from this new line of research is that contradicting institutional pressures work to sever long-held bonds and make them toxic.

Organization of This Book

In the next chapter I explain how, based on the social-movement literature, rational and emotionally driven social-movement activists in all of these cases might rightly have expected their colleagues' moves to the state to be an organizational advantage. I then detail my institutional theory, according to which previous bonds play only a limited role in the new relationship. Throughout this chapter I introduce each of my cases and explain how these various arguments relate to them.

My first country study, Poland, focuses on the fate of Solidarność (herein referred to as Solidarity), the umbrella union organization turned social movement that forced the first transition of a communist state. In this chapter (3) I analyze the relationship between Solidarity and the state at two stages: first, in the early 1990s, when leaders of the broad Solidarity social movement took positions in the state, and second, in the late 1990s, when leaders of Solidarity, which had already become a more typical labor union, made a similar transition. I find that in both cases organization leaders and their political colleagues soon became profoundly estranged despite their continued cooperation on low-level issues.

While the Poland chapter describes how different movement cohorts face the same basic dilemma over time, the South Africa chapter (4) demonstrates how two quite different organizations can face the same fate. In this chapter I analyze the evolving relationship between former and ongoing leaders of the Congress of South African Trade Unions (COSATU) and the South African National Civic Organization (SANCO, a federation of neighborhood organizations) since they began a series of transitions to the state after 1994. I find that, although there is some variation based on organization type, in both instances organization leaders and their former colleagues fell into a highly contentious relationship. Georgia's Rose Revolution (2003), the first of three recent "color revolutions" in the post-Soviet space, differs in many ways from the previous two cases, especially in the prominent role played by small, elite nongovernmental organizations. In Chapter 5 I look at how the relationships between these various organizations and their ex-colleagues differ and find that this depends in part on the degree to which organizations moderated their agendas and tactics. Organization leaders who made demands of their state-bound ex-colleagues that were similar to those they had made during the previous regime found that personal relationships became a burden. This was not the case for those who had no former colleagues in the state.

Finally, in the concluding chapter I present a cross-state analysis that identifies patterns and divergences, and I explore the policy implications of this study.

Summary

Scholars and policymakers who focus on democratization have accumulated a wealth of information on how social movements arise. The question of "what next?" has, however, been largely pushed to the side. If activists and policymakers are intent on avoiding the "morning after" (McAdam 1988, 200) stories that emerge from unfulfilled promises and expectations, this oversight must be addressed. This is particularly important in the context of democratization, where the stakes are so high. In the pages that follow I move from a detailed theoretical analysis of this issue to a practical and qualitatively compelling examination of the dilemmas these individuals face.

2

From Mobilization to Victory
Democratization and the Fate of Social-Movement Organizations

WHEN THE DOMINOES OF COMMUNISM BEGAN TO FALL with Poland's first semifree elections in 1989, something peculiar happened: Solidarity leaders who had long fought against the state suddenly joined it. Some went into parliament, some took cabinet posts, and others took seats in the highest courts. The puzzle was not so much that these leaders initiated what would be just the first of several migratory waves from social movement to the state; social-movement activists, after all, are naturally inclined to participate in the political process. The oddity was that members of Solidarity, facing what was in effect a form of decapitation, actually supported their colleagues' exodus. They were not, of course, suicidal. Rather, they had clear expectations that the expansion of Solidarity leaders into the state would bring the social movement–based union a new degree of influence over the country's new course.

Solidarity was neither the first nor the last pro-democracy organization to see its leaders off to the state following a democratic breakthrough. A few years later and thousands of miles to the south, the same process played out in South Africa, where the two largest antiapartheid organizations, the Congress of South African Trade Unions (COSATU) and the South African National Civic Organization (SANCO), delegated their leaders to national and local government positions. And nearly a decade after this, a different set of pro-democracy organizations in post-Soviet Georgia, where mobilization occurred on the backs of small nongovernmental organizations (NGOs) rather than mass-based ones, followed a similar pattern.

In each of these cases, movement members and leaders kept to the same calculus that countless others have in what has become an almost expected, if largely undocumented, postbreakthrough pattern of abandoning civil society for public service: that close friends and colleagues, who had for years been held together by shared principals and a passion for justice, would realize their organization's ideals at the state level. Moreover, in each case activists were soon struck by a profound sense of disappointment when, as they put it, their aspirations were devoured by ex-colleagues who revealed themselves to be nothing more than power-hungry politicians in waiting. "Power changes people—and they changed," one former Georgian NGO leader summed up this sentiment (Zurabish-vili 2007).

The easy explanation for this phenomenon is that there was a selection effect: Those who left the social-movement organizations for the state were, by nature, the most moderate. It is therefore important to note from the start that these individuals were not inherently different, except perhaps in the high-level positions they vacated. They were not, at least in the cases investigated here, older or younger, more or less educated, or—worth emphasizing—more radical or more moderate than their former peers.[1] Nor were they far removed from their old peers as theories about the rise of microcohorts might suggest; in each of these cases they were less than a year or two out of the organizations before they began to press for policies their organizations opposed. Often new state leaders assumed power holding closely the ties they had formed during the struggle but with a new sense of mission and responsibility that pulled their policies in an unexpected (to both them and their former colleagues) direction. Institutions became the wedge that divided activists from ex-activists. In addition, when old comrades, who expected their friends to follow organization policy prescriptions, attacked these political elites for being unfaithful, power holders, who similarly expected their friends' understanding and support, lashed back at them, setting the stage for a cycle of recriminations.

On the individual level, this is a study of loyalty and betrayal, a melodrama that, sadly, has real consequences for the effectiveness of key civil-society organizations following democratic breakthrough. In the chapters that follow I use the perceptions of individual actors to analyze hopes and disappointments of those empowered and those who remained outside formal power structures after transition. More broadly, this is an analysis of how new elites manage the burdens of governance that arise in the face of conflicting internal and external policy demands. Despite the array of organizations and transitions covered in this book, the cacophonous outcome is predictably the same in each case.

Identities, Networks, and Empty Promises

At first glance, we find no reason to suspect that activists in the three disparate cases studied here should become so quickly and so similarly disillusioned in their victories. The struggles, which range from the most brutal and enduring to the relatively mild and fleeting, and the movements, from all-inclusive to highly elitist, are seemingly incomparable: a union-cum-social-movement toppling communism in Poland; an alliance of unions and neighborhood associations leading to the fall of apartheid in South Africa; and a set of extremely elite, Western-backed, pro-democracy nongovernmental organizations declaring victory over post–Soviet style competitive authoritarianism in Georgia.

What ties these very different cases together is the overwhelming euphoria, tinged with a nagging sense of unease, that enveloped movement leaders upon victory. As Napoleon noted more than a century and a half earlier, "the most dangerous moment comes with victory," and leaders of these pro-democracy movements were eager to ensure that they would continue to influence the postbreakthrough situation. In every case, senior organization leaders took to the state in an effort to implement the goals of the struggle. As one former activist in South Africa put it, "Where else can you do that other than in government?" (Mkhize 2008).

It seemed perfectly logical that the best way to maximize one's organizational influence would be to inject into state structures persons who embodied the organization. This logic is an extension of two important areas of the social-movement literature, identities and networks. On a personal level, according to this literature, collective identities formed through the struggle were critical to maintaining organizational strength and frequently bled into one's own sense of self. On an interpersonal level, regardless of the strength of these identities, individuals' commitments to their comrades-in-struggle were themselves sufficient to, whether through internal feelings of loyalty or peer pressure, keep organizations alive and active. If identities and networks could serve as the engines of mobilization during the long, hard push against the former regime, they surely could be used to merely steer the way after victory, when, it seemed, the road was all downhill.

It is important to at first differentiate these arguments, which were so important to the decision-making process across the states studied. Identity is, by definition, an emotional attachment based on one's feelings about a set of principles or persons. In the social-movement context, such identities—which may exist prior to group entry—are largely based on shared norms and values that dominate within a group but can also emerge and strengthen through the very transformative experience of activism, especially where opposition groups collectively challenge existing societal rules and boundaries. Identities congeal over the course of struggle as members are socialized into their organizations through activities, traditions, and patterns of behavior particular to the social movement. At the same time, these collective identities become deeply ingrained in one's sense of self.

For veteran activists, assuming their colleagues embodied the aims of their movement was not particularly brash. Identity had been the flame that kept many organizations alive for years, including Poland's Solidarity and South Africa's civics, during periods of harsh repression and apparent inactivity. Evidence in the (albeit underdeveloped) literature provides some support for the premise that identities formed during a movement's peak should continue to affect individuals' political sympathies, occupational trajectories, and likelihood of renewed activism long after the social movement has achieved its goals. In her valuable study of feminist-movement activists, for example, Banaszak found not only that did some of those leaders who transitioned to the state continue to identify with the movement they left, but also that they actually pursued movement goals from their new state positions (Banaszak 2009, 27).

Other studies of leftist and civil-rights movements have similarly found that one-time activists remained oriented toward movement goals in the long term, well after leaving the organizations, precisely because of the collective identity established during the period of movement participation. As Giugni points out, there is a "powerful and enduring impact of participation in movement activities on the biographies of participants" (Giugni 2004, 494). "You must remember that a lot of these people came from working-class communities," one South African activist from the pro-democracy struggle explained of his former colleagues in the state. "The issues we were raising were very close to their hearts" (Coleman 2008).

According to the first hypothesis, following from this work on collective identities, we should find that across cases former and ongoing movement actors should remain bound by their movement-era identities, which should result in broad agreement between state and social-movement organization actors over policy direction; newly empowered leaders from pro-democracy organizations should carry their missions to the state. Even if yesterday's and today's organization leaders do not formally work together, new state actors should appear to be following the same agenda that their organizations pursue (to the degree that this agenda has not significantly changed in the postbreakthrough period), and relations between the two groups should be generally positive.

Yet it was not only movement identity that created a sense of trust among movement activists. It was also the feeling that those leaving the organization for the state were emotionally bound to networks of peers, many of whom they had known since before the movement even began. "All our friends were there (in government)," explained the former owner of the independent Rustavi 2 TV station, which was so instrumental in orchestrating Georgia's Rose Revolution (Kitsmarishvili 2007). These interpersonal networks were apparently quite strong. Some were rooted in preexisting personal connections, frequently developed by particular life experiences, that brought activists together in particular organizations, but others emerged during the movement stage, when ties created social pressures, including the carrot of inclusion and the stick of ostracism, which spur intraorganizational loyalty and obligation. For movement colleagues, activism could be so powerful as to eclipse the initial motivating ideals of the movement with affective ties. Activists did not come to COSATU marches simply to protest hikes in transportation costs, for example; they also came to show their solidarity with friends and colleagues with whom they routinely interacted. Cohorts and network ties have been instrumental in the rise and persistence of everything from communist revolutionaries to civil-rights groups and anticommunists. Network analysts have highlighted the important role of interpersonal relationships in human behavior. From this perspective, activists, especially organization leaders, in South Africa, Poland, and Georgia should have felt united by strong friendships and a powerful sense of belonging. Unfortunately, we know relatively little about how personal relationships forged within movements can be translated into policy influence since scholarship has tended to look more at the role of broad and impersonal social bonds on decision-making processes. The available evidence suggests that the inclinations of these various activists were backed up by theory: People tend to "perceive friendship networks in organizations as small worlds" and place a priority on keeping them intact (Kilduff and Krackhardt 2008, 25). These ties, which facilitate communication among former comrades, can be enduring.

Activists who watched their colleagues transition to the state thus felt they had both identity and networks on their side—and in many ways these are mutually reinforcing. Through movement participation, the combination of ideas and friendships merge into a powerful tool as individual and group interests become inseparable and ensconced in participants' memories. In the short term, this benefits organizations by raising the cost of free riding and encouraging active participation. In the long term it creates high expectations for future cooperation. As Hunt and Benford explain, social movements change participants in "not only the way they see themselves, but also the way they view the world, the occupations they pursue, their consumption patterns, and the friends they make" (Hunt and Benford 2004, 449).

Given the significance these factors acquire over the course of a struggle, we have little reason to believe they would dissipate upon victory. Therefore, according to the second hypothesis, based on personal networks, former and ongoing movement actors should remain bound by movement-era networks, which should result in broad agreement between state and social-movement organization actors over policy direction. Personal bonds created during the struggle, based on affective emotions such as trust and respect, tend to be enduring. Furthermore, just as the previous movement provided the activists with a sense of collectivity during the struggle, these actors subsequently find solidarity through their "collective memory" (Eyerman 2005, 46) of the previous period. This is all the more likely since ties that emerge while participating in a massive social endeavor, according to Eyerman, are built on a process of collective change, making them particularly profound (Eyerman 2005, 45).

Although we should expect to see the same phenomena play out in all of the cases presented here, on an intercase basis we might differentiate outcomes based on the intensity and duration of the particular struggle under consideration. Again, given a dearth of literature on this subject, this hypothesis depends on a degree of extrapolation from current studies. However, if oppositional space is a breeding ground for new belief systems, the more isolated this space is, the more adherents should feed off each others' convictions. Confrontation by the "other" (the oppressive state, for pro-democracy movements) is known to mobilize activists and reinforce what Levite and Tarrow refer to as "intense subcultural solidarity"[2] (Levite and Tarrow 1983, 298). Organizational space not only brings together like-minded people and intensifies their beliefs but also strengthens the units themselves. Intensity and thus durability of movement identities and networks can be a function of severity of repression and movement duration, with longer-lived movements functioning in more repressive conditions having the strongest identities and networks.

Although this argument is somewhat tentative, given the scarcity of research, it appears to be present in the minds of at least some activists. As one Solidarity leader who continued to function in the underground commented, "We felt very connected to Solidarity because we grew up in Solidarity" (Pietrzyk 2009). From an identity perspective, group identities developed during the repressive, predemocratic period should survive well into the period after democratic breakthrough. From a personal-network perspective, circles that might start out as a rational calculation of interests can transform into more durable and meaningful networks as members become emotionally fused with them, and one might expect social networks to be denser and more salient where the struggle was longer and more intense (Andrews 1991, 29).

In practical terms, this means that activists throughout these states might have expected their alliances with and influence on former colleagues to be strong. However, from a theoretical standpoint we should expect these ties to be more formidable in one state than another. In particular, identity and networks should be strongest in South Africa, where the movement lasted more than a decade and faced a particularly brutal regime, followed by Poland, where the regime was less violent and the movement of shorter duration. The impact should be weakest in Georgia, the state with the briefest movement against the most moderate state. I return to this question in the cross-case analysis in Chapter 6.

In summary, we can differentiate identity and network arguments in that the latter are based on powerful and enduring feelings of trust and respect, whereas, according to identity arguments "the well-trained conscience is the best policeman" (Chong 1991, 69).[3] In both cases, actors find cohesion in their collective memory of the previous period and expect those who go to the state to function essentially like "institutional nomads," more loyal to their personal cliques than to the offices they are placed in (Wedel 1998, 106).[4] These arguments also assume that affective emotions toward fellow activists create powerful "commitments or investments" that structure one's "orientation toward the world" (Goodwin, Jasper, and Polletta 2004, 418). According to this view, reciprocal emotions (between oneself and others in the group) and shared emotions (common feelings about people, situations, and institutions outside the group) are mutually reinforcing and promote powerful feelings of solidarity and identification with the movement.

From Activist to Power Broker: The Role of Institutions

Those are the rosy assessments that seem to have dominated as activists celebrated victory in the heady days following democratic breakthrough. They not only had the power to shake the foundations of the old system but would have the influence to mold the new one as well. Clearly, however, something went wrong.

In Poland, the first of these cases, Solidarity came to power not once but twice, and disappointment followed each time. During the first years, 1989–1993, the movement quickly regained the shape of a typical trade union and watched in horror as former colleagues embarked on an economic course that directly reduced their membership and threatened their credibility. Poland's shock-therapy, free-market economic program was intended to quickly bring the country out of a moribund socialist economy. In practice, it meant the disappearance of many unionists' jobs and financial havoc for hundreds of thousands more. When a new crop of Solidarity leaders, ostensibly more radical unionists, took to the state from 1997 to 2001, they promised to "finish the revolution" by introducing a comprehensive and, it turned out, painful set of social reforms ranging from social security to health care. By the end of their term, these state leaders were similarly estranged from their organization, which officially renounced direct participation in politics.

COSATU and SANCO activists had no more luck, watching their most socialist revolutionaries make an about-face in the postdemocratic breakthrough period to demand neoliberal policies that many cynically said left members of the nonwhite majority in the same sad economic state they had struggled so hard to overcome during the previous apart- heid regime. COSATU leaders not only took ministerial positions at the national level but also assumed an awkward and often cantankerous place in the governing political alliance led by the African National Congress (ANC). Some SANCO leaders also reached national levels, thanks in part to their organization's junior position in the ANC-led alliance. How- ever, given their focus on local issues, they were more often deployed to senior provincial and municipal positions. Even at the local level they were frequently targets of derision from ex-colleagues, who claimed that they had turned away from the pro-poor policies they had once espoused. Years after the start of the postapartheid transition, COSATU remained impotent in the face of continued neoliberal policies, and SANCO vir- tually imploded.

Soon after Georgia's Rose Revolution, NGO activists berated one-time pro-democracy leaders and former colleagues for having compro- mised their principles in the name of power. Rather than economic charges, Georgian activists hurled political accusations at President

Mikhail Saakashvili's government, accusing its members (and their own former fellow activists) of centralizing power and, in the process, trampling on citizens' rights. Veterans of the so-called revolution, backed by international observers, lamented that critical democratic institutions, from the media to the judiciary, had actually suffered in the years following what had been billed as a democratic breakthrough. Meanwhile, state leaders who during the struggle saw nongovernmental watchdogs as loyal allies now condemned them as grant grubbers and saboteurs of progress.

So what happened? How were the arguments that the movement veterans subscribed to, so intuitive and consistent with the implications from the academic literature, faulty? The answer is that identities and personal networks did, in fact, provide some access, but they also created enormous (and enormously unrealistic) expectations in both activists and former activists in the state, who each expected the support of the other. Both sides considered themselves true guardians of the movement identity and believed that this, coupled with their personal networks, would help bring the other on board. However, in the new democratic morass, where each group sought to adjust to the demands of its (new) constituents under fundamentally new conditions, these individuals no longer saw eye to eye. An institutional perspective is critical to understanding how identities and networks became a liability for pro-democracy organizations in each of these cases.

Institutions, including formal rules and standard modes of operation, affect actors' power, as well as their interests, which become a function of responsibilities and relationships with other actors and units. There are two basic ways to understand how state institutions might affect activists who assume power: Former activists could actively construct the institutions in ways that maximize their goals (agency-centered approach), or they could be dropped into organizations that function as constraints rather than opportunities for these actors (structure-centered approach). In either case, endogenization of preferences, according to historical institutionalists, occurs as institutionally defined rules become virtually taken for granted and gradually alter definitions of self-interest, with actors operating under the logic of appropriateness, their actions (or output) based largely on "roles, routines, rights, obligations, standard operating procedures and practices" (March and Olsen 1996, 249).[5] This process can be indirect, allowing institutions to create new perspectives by shaping the degree to which internal and external actors have access to state elites. Activists remain rational actors, according to these accounts, but what precisely is in their best interest begins to change.

Institutional accounts are quite compelling in the context of these democratic transitions. As one Georgian NGO leader sympathetic to his ex-colleagues in the state acknowledged, "When you come to the government, you take on huge responsibility. This changes people" (Salamadze 2007). Furthermore, even though new state leaders may seek to build fundamentally new institutions (in an agency-centered approach), the reality is that they must do so by means of yesterday's apparatus. New actors with a democratic mandate may be able to do some institution molding but are constrained by their new institution's previously existing mission, composition, and procedures. For instance, the new head of a security apparatus that historically targeted domestic dissent might alter the mission (e.g., targeting foreign rather than domestic threats), but the organization remains responsible for monitoring the population; the new director might replace some personnel but will need the expertise (hinging on old modes of operation) of most. The new head makes a dent in the organization, but the organization also makes a dent in its new leader, who must in large part rely on information from and judgments of those lower down. In the process, the director's perceptions of what can and should be done drift away from those of the movement community the director left.

The dilemma facing the security head may be by institutional design, but it is rooted in the identity- and network-based social-movement phenomenon of "multiple embeddedness," where actors must bring about a balance among different groups of peers and objectives (Kilduff and Krackhardt 2008, 19; Jasper 2006, 67; McAdam and Paulson 1993, 641). Spending one's days facing new colleagues and engaged in tasks related to the new organization can gradually erode the standing of the previous cohort as, Jasper explains, "we come to feel solidarity with a different group" (Jasper 2006, 66). Yet is it not possible that a state leader who spent years in the pro-democracy trenches could emerge from that period with a deep-seated identity and bonds that could at least provide resistance to the strong institutional tug? Institutional approaches have moved far beyond the black-and-white bureaucratic arguments that preceded them, but they still seem to pay inadequate attention to the balance that former activists must consciously make between institutional pressures and "preexisting mind-sets" (Art 1973, 471).[6]

A basic tenet of this institutional approach is that former movement leaders will likely hold on to some prior beliefs and friendships, but these connections are overshadowed by the burdens of governance. Intra- and extraorganizational constituent pressures, budgetary constraints, and new perceptions propel state leaders from the ideal to the feasible, but previously formed identities and networks should continue to have some influence. Balance is the operative word. As Searing notes, "politicians are purposive actors who pursue their individual preferences or goals. They calculate and they compromise as they adapt to the situations" (Searing 1991, 1241). Ex-activists in the state are in an unenviable position as a result of having to struggle to appease their colleagues in the new institutions without alienating former movement peers or betraying their internal sense of what is right. Moreover, as illustrated earlier, perceptions of what must be done are altered as a result of their new roles and institutions. Under what conditions, then, should former activists expect conflict rather than cooperation?

Conflict, I argue, is a function of high mutual expectations of support based on former beliefs and bonds that fit awkwardly in the new institutional context. The larger the potential field of contention, the more we should expect these bonds to snap and even backfire. In particular, this should occur where (a) organizational demands concern broad policy goals; (b) ex-colleagues are placed in very influential positions with respect to their former organization's locus of activity and interest; and (c) movement organizations continue to rely on contentious activities to force their agenda. Under these conditions, leaders on both sides of the state/nonstate line become aggressive as they perceive their credibility to be challenged by former, nonloyal comrades. This sets the stage for a cycle of animosity that can even make previous ties a liability rather than an advantage.

Given the institutionally defined differences outlined earlier, ex-activists in the state will be most likely to resist postbreakthrough organizations that continue to struggle for broad policy goals since these former activists' new (regular) constituents, peers, and organizational mandates should trigger a preference adjustment. By *broad policy goals* as opposed to *finite goals* (described later) I mean objectives that are national or regional in scope and complex in nature; a broad policy must be applicable to a wide swath of the country and involve an array of derivative policies. One example of a broad policy is sweeping health-care reform, which could necessitate legislation that controls a variety of subissues from insurance regulation to infrastructure creation. Another is an effort to support judicial independence, which might involve everything from the appointment and impeachment process to salary formulas for judges. These are wide-ranging reforms that demand change on a number of dimensions.

According to this argument, once in power, a movement leader is likely to see these broad policies differently than colleagues who remain outside. In Poland, for instance, Solidarity demanded a fundamental purging of former functionaries who under communism had been used to repress political activists. Former Solidarity activists in power from 1989 to 1991 would have been faced with a national policy of considerable complexity: establishing procedures to discipline the array of officials (from security services to judges) involved in the previous system, while ensuring continuous function of these institutions. The strategy ultimately took the shape of a series of policies, each dealing with a different institution. In each case, parliamentarians and government officials who had only recently left that movement organization took a much more moderate approach than movement activists because they feared that too "thorough" a reckoning would cripple Poland's intelligence and counterintelligence capabilities (Kozłowski 2004). Thus, the first stage of the Interior Ministry purges, which were relegated to the local level, where Solidarity activists played a significant role, led to numerous firings, which central authorities, to the chagrin of grassroots activists, subsequently reversed (Jachowicz 1990).

In this example, new political elites were under pressure domestically not only from their former movement organizations but also from an array of formal and informal pressure groups who together formed, and were able to inform, their electoral constituency. Those in state institutions intent on bringing about change must balance the demands of these various actors as well since their fate is ultimately in the hands of the voters. Finally, they must be sure their policies are sound and will work to the advantage of the greatest number possible. This balancing act is daunting; movements might be good at winning elections, but the people they empower—usually with no previous experience—do not necessarily have the requisite skills to run a country.

This lack of experience, coupled with the tendency of nondemocracies to pursue economic programs that disproportionately favor a relative few, leaves leaders of new democracies in a bind when it comes to delivering economic goods. On the one hand, they need to restructure their economies to convince voters they are delivering on their promises of a better life rather than just the "rhetoric of democracy." On the other hand, they need help—from expertise and capital to trading partners and investors—to make this happen. It is in this context that new state leaders find that they face not only the significant domestic pressures noted earlier but also international ones. The third wave of democratization has largely dovetailed with the dominance of neoliberalism, meaning that those in policymaking institutions seek assistance from and are pressured by outside state, interstate (e.g., World Bank, International Monetary Fund), and nonstate (including multinational corporations) actors. As one deputy premier of Serbia starkly portrayed his feeling immediately following democratic breakthrough, "We didn't have electricity when we came to power, and we weren't professional politicians" (Korac 2005). The assistance of outsiders frequently came with painful conditions, but without this assistance new state leaders felt they had little chance of success. Unlike their ideologically motivated counterparts back in the social-movement organizations, ex-activists were left with little choice but to engage in pragmatic compromise.

Institutional position matters as well but in ways not predicted by those activists who watched hopefully as their colleagues took high-ranking positions in institutions most pertinent to them. Movement leaders who accept senior positions in institutions directly related to their movement organization's missions face especially high outside expectations and demands for broad reform. In fact, the notion of mutuality applies here: Both movement activists and the new state leader will expect loyalty and, subsequently, the ability to influence each other. The former have found the golden egg—a senior state leader who, as "one of us," will implement the array of broad policy goals the movement has long espoused. The latter, conversely, accepts new powers and duties of the position and has confidence that movement activists will trust and support him as he presses for the most optimal—and feasible—policies.

From a distance, it is clear that movement leaders and state leaders have almost inevitably conflicting roles. Those who remain in movement organizations must continue to mobilize in order to demonstrate to (potential) adherents both their rationale for existence and their power. Those who govern, by contrast, must take responsibility for their actions, which usually trump any manifestos they might issue. Given institutional considerations, the new leader's choices will almost certainly conflict with demands from below, thereby breeding distrust and cries of betrayal.

Polish interior minister Krzysztof Kozłowski, responsible for the administrative cleansing described earlier, found this out the hard way. A Solidarity leader who had served for decades as the deputy editor in chief of the church-based opposition magazine *Tygodnik Powszechny*, Kozłowski suddenly found himself having to moderate movement-based calls for justice, which amounted to demands for a wholesale purging of security-service personnel. As a result, Kozłowski recalled being perpetually vilified "as the one who saved them" (Kozłowski 2004). In many other cases, the recriminations ran both ways: State elites claimed to be true to their old identities and lashed out at their former movement colleagues for failing to understand the necessities of governance. "I am still idealistic," one Georgian government official summarized this sentiment. "Of course, I have more information now" (GOG 2007). Similar mindsets were evident as former Solidarity activists pushed for highly unpopular social-security reforms and South African elites resisted popular calls to regulate rising prices for food and electricity.

What is characteristic of these mutual recriminations is their very public nature. Organizations that react to disappointment by using the same contentious methods that contributed to their victory over the previous regime will elicit counterreactions from their ex-partners. A repertoire of political action that involves open and public criticism is inherently a challenge to the credibility of the targets, but it can also be seen as a breach of loyalty and ironically leave movements with ex-leaders in positions of power at a *disadvantage* relative to those who lack such connections. At the nexus of the conditions discussed here—where leaders of organization-relevant state institutions pursue broad policies that prompt contentious organization reactions—the emotional elements described earlier boil over, leaving previously established bridges burning. Organizations without close connections to power holders may engage in similarly contentious activities, but in the absence of power-holders' expectations of moderation, the fallout is unremarkable.

Of course, organizations make their own political opportunities, and having friends in high places can translate into access. The case for movement influence is conversely related to the earlier argument governing conflict. Influence should be reserved especially for those organizations that moderate both their activities and their demands. In the social-movement context, apparent victory typically leads to either a process of demobilization or institutionalization, neither of which has been sufficiently studied.[7] In the latter case, organization leaders, struggling to remain relevant in the new political context, transition from a high-mobilization modus operandi (difficult to maintain in the long term) to routinized forms of collective action more akin to activities of an interest group than to a stereotypical social-movement organization. This can involve professionalization, where grassroots activism is largely replaced by full-time, paid staff. However, it also involves strategic moderation, a movement away from the all-or-none demands typical during the social-movement days in exchange for access to mainstream institutions, where political exchange takes place. Deeper moderation can involve replacing some or all of an organization's watchdog responsibilities (e.g., street protests for free media) with service provision (e.g., providing technical assistance to media outlets).

Moderation reduces conflict by eliminating outright tensions, thereby allowing social-movement organizations to maintain personal ties with former colleagues. Even where organizations continue to engage in watchdog functions but do so less vocally than before, state actors have more wiggle room to find a middle ground in cases of potential conflict. By keeping the level of open conflict relatively low, organizations create space in which old identities and networks can continue to resonate, thus creating new access points to the state that organizations without this leadership bridge will lack.

The middle ground is easiest to find—and outside activists with connections to ruling elites can most expect to gain favor—with respect to finite policy requests. By *finite policies* I mean issues that are limited in scope (restricted to a particular location) and complexity (not involving significant ramifications for broader policy). They are, in other words, occasional exceptions rather than new rules. In contrast to the broader policies discussed earlier, examples of finite issues include individual matters (e.g., health or pay issues) or localized grievances (e.g., related to public-goods delivery to a particular area or limited to a particular work-place or behavior of a small group of functionaries). Even where former leaders dominate institutions critical to those organizations' missions, they might gain from such low-level favors. Because these issues are so specific, they can fly under the radar of—and may not even significantly run counter to—policymakers' new institutional pressures (Eaton 2003, 482). They provide an easy way for activists and ex-activists alike to remain loyal to their old friends without risking the ire of their current peers.

According to the hypothesis based on this institutional argument, the effect of social networks and identities will be in part a function of the new institutional walls built between former colleagues and friends who take positions on either side of the state line. Regardless of the length and intensity of the democratic struggle or the nature of the organizations that waged that fight, we should expect to find institutional constraints setting the parameters for relations. The personal dimension can help organizations on small issues by providing them new access and opportunities as they support their former colleagues. Nonetheless, personal ties can also spark a backlash where views and preferences conflict as a result of these institutional pressures, particularly with respect to broader issues and the refusal of organizations to moderate.

Unit of Analysis and Case Selection

I evaluate these arguments in states where various social-movement organizations have emerged from quite different repressive states: Poland, South Africa, and Georgia. The nature of my research question is highly conducive to a case-study approach rather than a large-N statistical analysis. Although the latter design might be useful for assessing patterns of state support for organizations (if such data were readily available in each of my cases), my goal is to unearth individual perceptions of how the relationship between state and organization has evolved. This objective involves gauging the underlying environment in which relations exist, a phenomenon that my research methods, described later, are particularly capable of performing.

My central research question concerns the relationship between prodemocracy organization leaders and their former leaders who attain high-level political and state positions. By *relationship* I mean the formal and informal interaction between these sets of actors. While these two types of interactions can in principle be distinct (one might get along splendidly with one's old colleague while sitting at the bar but disagree on policy conflicts in the public media), I assume that they tend to be interrelated. Just as a positive relationship between former colleagues in the formal sector may result in a positive one in the informal sector as well, a negative relationship in the formal sector is likely to lead to a negative one in the informal sector.

The unit of analysis for this book is individuals who are rooted in or have uprooted themselves from a social-movement organization. I focus on political elites, those who use their positions in key state or nonstate institutions or organizations that regularly influence political outcomes on a national scale. I include within the term *social-movement organization* a subsection of civil society, defined broadly as "the realm of organized life that is open, voluntary, self-generating, at least partially self-supporting, autonomous from the state, and bound by a legal order or set of shared rules" (Diamond 1999, 221). Civil-society actors are intermediaries between the private sphere and the state and include an array of distinct interests ranging from economic (labor unions) and cultural matters to developmental and issue-oriented concerns (e.g., women, consumers, people with disabilities). Groups that come together to challenge "existing arrangements of power and distribution by people with common purposes and solidarity, in sustained interaction with elites, opponents, and authorities" are known as social-movement organizations (Meyer and Tarrow 1998, 4).

My comparative analysis relies on a "most different systems" case-study approach. Cases differ with regard to three key independent variables that might be expected to impact on state/organization relations after breakthrough: movement type (from highly inclusive to highly exclusive), the duration of the movement, and the nature of the opposition-era struggle (varying by regime type and degree of repression). These variables were chosen since they should, according to a reading of the literature described in this and the preceding chapter, have an important effect on the strength of identities, networks, and available opportunities.

By *movement type* I mean the degree to which social-movement organizations sought to include and mobilize large numbers of citizens for their cause. Unlike Zald and Ash, who use inclusivity as a measure of membership requirements and demands of commitment, I define *highly inclusive organizations* as those that put extraordinary effort into bringing the community into social-movement activist circles and encouraging them to engage in regular, contentious political action (Zald and Ash 1966, 331). Examples of such organizations include the grassroots Chilean *pobladores* (slum dwellers) associations and the Philippine people's organizations. Groups with low levels of inclusion, such as professionalized nongovernmental organizations, might also occasionally seek to use broad swaths of the population for strategic means (such as protests). This was the case in Thailand, where various NGOs in the 1990s led protest movements over a range of issues, from the environment to HIV. Among the organizations that occupy a middle ground in this typology are membership-based groups with a naturally large but limited constituency. Labor unions fit this definition well because their large memberships are oriented toward a particular agenda that benefits workers first and foremost. In the cases in this book I focus on the primary mobilizers, the leading social-movement organization(s) in each case.

Movement duration can also vary, and in this book I categorize movements into short term (lasting less than five years), medium term (lasting more than five and less than ten years) and long term (lasting more than a decade). An example of the first type is the Serbian youth movement, Otpor, rooted in 1996 municipal-election protests, formally established in 1998, and able by 2000 to lead a pro-democracy movement that brought down the country's strong-arm president, Slobodan

Milosevic. Other movements have had to fight significantly longer and often incurred considerable costs as a result. The lives of these movement organizations can be better measured in generations than in years. The Indian National Congress, for instance, first formed in 1885 and eventually spent decades fighting for freedom from British colonial rule, finally emerging victorious in 1947, nearly thirty years after it had transformed itself into a mass-based organization.

Although movement duration can be an indicator of the difficulty facing activists, level of repression is a more direct measure. Serbia's Otpor faced a state low on this indicator, at least early on; Milosevic's Yugoslavia might be classified as a competitive electoral regime where opposition parties could contest and even win certain elections, though they faced an uphill battle (such as harassment and detention of activists, limited media access, and electoral fraud). Other movements, such as those led by pro-democracy organizations in Kenya, have historically faced more restrictive and repressive regimes, which declared activists' activities illegal and subjected organizations' members to long jail sentences or even occasionally torture and murder. Struggles against the most socially isolated regimes tend to involve the most blood given that the leaders utilize all of the tools at their disposal to eliminate signs of opposition. In these states, the imprisonment, torture, and judicial or extrajudicial murder of activists and their supporters is routine and systematic.

The first case of democratic breakthrough evaluated in this book, Poland (1989), has a moderate score along each of these dimensions. The most difficult to assess is inclusivity. Although Poland's Solidarity was a workers' organization turned mass-based social movement at the start of the 1980s, by the end of the decade it had lost much of its grassroots character. It resurfaced, in the final push for change in 1988, largely as a membership-based labor union fighting predominantly for workers' issues, though it was quickly brought back under the underground leadership, which comprised a worker-intellectual alliance of sorts. This resilient leadership embodied the staying power of Solidarity, which lasted nine years and survived the post-1981 martial-law period by utilizing underground networks and activities. Martial law was the most repressive period in Poland since the formal end of Stalinism in 1956 but was characterized by only moderate levels of repression. The state first negotiated with Solidarity activists and then imprisoned them, but even though leaders managed to exclude the opposition for decades, state terror was unusual. As one Polish activist who had the atypical experience of being imprisoned for five years in the post-Stalinist period recalled, "I was never beaten in jail. I was treated well" (Niesiołowski 2004).

In South Africa, by contrast, the 1994 elections marked a dramatic end to decades of extraordinarily harsh state oppression against the nonwhite majority. High on the repression index, South Africa's nonwhite activists (as well as many nonactivists) were subjected to severe limits on movement, economic disempowerment, and periodic police roundups and massacres that prompted the country's largest freedom party, the ANC, to declare an armed resistance in 1961. While the banned ANC was in exile, moderately inclusive labor unions (which eventually created an umbrella worker's organization called COSATU) allied with highly inclusive community organizations known as "civics" to lead the struggle at home. The unions initiated their struggle with the 1973 wave of strikes, and the civics first emerged in 1979. In reality, these were only the newest embodiment of a struggle many of these same activists had waged for decades through political organizations such as the ANC and the South African Communist Party.

Finally, in the most recent case of democratic breakthrough evaluated (2003), relatively noninclusive, highly professionalized nongovernmental organizations in Georgia spearheaded a movement (modeled partly on similar movements in Serbia, Croatia, and Slovakia) that used short-term popular mobilization to restore competitive democracy to a semidemocratic, corrupt regime left over from the communist period. Only mildly repressive, the regime itself was characterized by a relatively free media and civil society up against a strong presidential system and personalistic power structure. Key organizations involved in antiregime mobilization after the falsified 2003 elections, including the Liberty Institute and the Georgian Young Lawyers' Association (GYLA), had been in existence for years (Liberty was founded in 1996; GYLA in 1994), but their occasional mass-based, contentious political actions occurred only later in their existence. Thus, although the organizations had existed previously, they became social-movement organizations less than five years before democratic breakthrough.

TABLE 1 Divergence in Independent Variables

	Movement Type (inclusivity)	Duration	Struggle
Poland	moderate	moderate	moderate
South Africa (Unions/Civics)	moderate/high	high/high	high/high
Georgia	low	low	low

The degree to which these cases diverge is summarized in Table 1. What makes these cases highly comparable is the fact that, in each one, numerous leaders—often the seniormost—from the victorious pro-democracy organizations left their colleagues to take up formal positions in the newly democratizing state. As noted in the preceding chapter, the organizations they left behind neither disintegrated, as might be expected from the current social-mobilization literature, nor experienced an all-out personnel change. Instead, they remained active, demanding and in the hands of colleagues and friends of those now running the state.

Each of these dynamic cases is designed to be leveraged in ways that increase the total population and allow for microlevel, intrastate, "most similar systems" tests. In Poland, for example, I analyze two different periods in which Solidarity took power—1989–1993 and 1997–2001. In South Africa I discuss how two different organizational types (moderately inclusive unions and highly inclusive civics) vary in their relationship with incorporated leaders. And in Georgia I analyze organizations that vary according to their organizational connections to state leaders and the degree to which they moderated their tactics after breakthrough.

I want to emphasize that in all of these cases the new governments following breakthrough faced considerable international pressures to follow the Western-dominated pattern of neoliberal economic policies as they pursued domestic reforms—external pressures that helped shape the institutional incentives characteristic of the state bodies ex-activists entered. This means that international neoliberal pressures are essentially controlled for within my cases and most of the others that have occurred since the late 1980s. However, it also means that these cases may in some ways be different from those in which democratic breakthrough occurred before the late 1980s.

Summary

Much of the social-movement literature, not surprisingly, focuses on the activists' ability to create and maintain a social-movement organization. The process by which they do so bears on the research question posed here: What is the nature of the relations between social-movement organizations and the state once victory has been achieved? This book, atypically, looks not at theories that deal directly with this topic but at the implications of theories that can be logically extended to it. The most optimistic arguments for a social-movement organization stem from group identity and personal network arguments, each of which suggests that enduring ties will enable the leaders of social-movement organizations to have a significant influence on their former colleagues now in the state.

According to the institutional argument, by contrast, new structures and formal walls erected between one-time colleagues temper the advantages of having ex-colleagues in high places. While social-movement organizations that are willing to adapt may benefit to a limited degree under the new arrangements, especially where the nature of their demands is relatively low, these bridges should buckle where expectations are particularly high. Here, personal dimensions will extend the conflict beyond where it otherwise would be if organizations lacked personal ties to the state, resulting in a vicious circle of charges and countercharges.

Two important caveats are necessary. First, for many movement organizations long used to fighting for—and winning—much broader demands, the proposed (finite) rewards offered in exchange for organizational moderation are unlikely to be satisfying. These organizations continue to face their own constituent pressures for action (for example, from donors and active/latent supporters), the absence of which can drive these organizations into oblivion. When your former colleague curtails workplace dismissals in one factory but supports an economic program that will likely lead to that same factory's bankruptcy, the gain is nil. Second, and related, organizations and policymakers are not inevitably placed on a destructive trajectory. Where institutions are rebuilt from ashes or resources are plentiful, for instance, state leaders may choose to implement ambitious programs rooted in their former organizations. Nonetheless, given their diverging constituents and institutional missions, it seems likely they will have opposing preferences. Moreover, accustomed to broad goals and contentious tactics that yielded fruit only fairly recently, it also seems likely that organizations will continue along their previous trajectory (Bell and Keenan 2004, 346; Hipsher 1998, 161; Kubik 1998, 142; Segarra 1997, 493).

In all three of the cases examined in this book, longtime activists who remained in the organizations for the most part continued to make political and economic demands similar to the ones they had always made, occasionally reacting to new conditions and constituent demands to make moderate programmatic changes. In contrast, those activists who transitioned to the state were dropped into alien structures characterized by new constituents and missions that had a profound impact on how they viewed the world. In short, each side saw the other as a political opportunity. This clash of expectations, characteristic across states, often sabotaged relations between activists and the newly democratizing state. In the subsequent chapters I use the words of the participants themselves to explain how their respective stories played out.

3

From Solidarity to Isolation

How Poland's Pro-Democracy Movement
Lost in the Transition

WHEN LECH WAŁĘSA SCALED THE FENCE at the Gdańsk Shipyard in 1980, he became a legend. Wałęsa personified the Solidarity social movement, a ten-million-strong opposition composed of workers, intellectuals, and peasants that, for a brief and euphoric time, seemed able to finally shake the country's—and perhaps, to a certain degree, the entire region's—communist foundation. Solidarity also proved resilient when it survived a harsh government crackdown by morphing from a public spectacle into an underground phenomenon in which its army of activists, linked by tight personal networks and a profound allegiance to their organization's ideals, struggled to maintain the movement. By 1988, Solidarity had been reborn in a series of strikes that brought the government to the negotiating table and led to the country's first semifree elections in 1989. A year later Lech Wałęsa became Poland's first democratically elected president, when he received nearly 75 percent of the vote in recognition of his dominant role in the movement. "I killed off communism," Wałęsa recently claimed (Wałęsa 2009).

If Wałęsa came to power a hero in the Solidarity camp, he left political office in 1995 anything but. Solidarity activists had watched in disbelief as their longtime leader appeared to turn against his former organization on everything from economic reforms to the very existence of Solidarity, which he said should roll up its banner. Wałęsa's words rang of arrogance to those he formerly led. " 'Solidarity should involve itself in passing out parsley and carrots like unions did under communism,' " one organization leader interpreted Wałęsa's message. " 'We [political leaders] know what is good for Poland' " (Langer 2009). However, for Wałęsa, accusations of disloyalty and personal attacks from below missed the point. "I considered myself a worker, a union activist, but also the president. It wasn't easy to bring all this together," Wałęsa recently reflected. "Many people still wanted to see me just as a worker or a union activist."

Wałęsa's shift from being Solidarity's icon to its profound source of discomfort was not an exception. Rather, it was the rule. Throughout the first decade of Solidarity's victory over communism, members of the organization saw their successive leaders off to various state and government positions in the hope that ex-activists' empowerment would, thanks to the strength of interpersonal relationships and long-held movement identities, bring Solidarity access and pull. Instead, those who remained in Solidarity encountered a series of personal and organizational defeats that finally prompted them in 2001 to formally forsake a direct role in politics.

It took twelve years and three waves of leadership migration to the state for Solidarity's leaders to understand that friendships and loyalties would ultimately crumble under the weight of institutional pressures. The first wave occurred between 1989 and 1991, when the top ranks of Solidarity's historic leadership took to the state under the Solidarity banner and launched a series of painful economic reforms that left the movement reeling. Solidarity's leaders explained away their exclusion from influence as an aberration; those who had left for the state were disproportionately intellectuals, they said, which left the unionist core with little hope.

In 1991 they sought to remedy this by sending an explicitly unionist parliamentary club to the legislature. When that club proved ineffective and then fragmented into "pro" and "anti" union forces, organization leaders blamed the broader political disorder and a numerically insufficient representation. The broader public, by contrast, concluded after four years that Solidarity—a label numerous political parties led by former activists had ascribed to themselves—meant political incoherence and economic suffering. Postcommunists dominated the 1993 parliamentary elections, leaving Solidarity in the political wilderness for four more years.

The remedy, Solidarity leaders decided in the run-up to the 1997 parliamentary elections, involved not less union activism in the state but more. By uniting the Center-Right under the Solidarity Electoral Action (AWS) coalition, which would guarantee the organization a decisive role in a new government, Solidarity leaders hoped to "finish the revolution." Even with their organizational leader, Marian Krzaklewski, simultaneously at the helm of AWS, this final experiment in political influence (1997–2001) proved to be as disastrous as earlier ones, if not more so. The defeat would come at great organizational and personal cost to those who took part.

From Communism to Solidarity

Communism came to Poland, as to most of Central Europe, in the wake of enormous destruction. With a chaotic and violent history of interventions by neighboring countries, the Polish state had existed for only a little more than two decades, as a weak democracy, when it became the first victim of World War II. In 1939 the Germans and Soviets had split the country, leaving it occupied for what would, in effect, turn out to be decades. For when the Nazis were finally defeated in 1945, they were replaced by the Soviets and a legion of Polish communists who functioned as their subordinates. Poland was behind the Iron Curtain, where these local communists would rule over the country's political and most of its economic and social institutions until 1989.

Despite the communists' hold on power, Poland—an overwhelmingly agricultural state—never quite fit their mold. Bringing communism to Poland, Stalin once said, was like putting a saddle on a cow. Unlike farther east, the churches were not shuttered; the land was not wholly collectivized; and there was little effort to change a people beaming with national pride into anything like *Homo sovieticus*. Communism was forced to cohabitate with a unique and salient Polish identity, resulting in a system that was milder than in other parts of the communist bloc. And this meant there was more room for an opposition movement to eventually appear.

While sporadic resistance from armed partisans characterized the immediate postwar years in Poland, organized opposition was the most difficult during this period. As in other parts of the communist world, Stalinism, which lasted until the early 1950s, marked the worst era of rights abuses in Poland, when political imprisonment, torture, and state-sponsored killings occurred regularly. However, in the posttotalitarian period (after 1956), outright repression mutated into subtler forms of state control over society, including a strong police presence and large networks of informants to keep opposition in check. Scholars have referred to the posttotalitarian era throughout the region as "civilized violence" (Rupnik 1988, 277) or "selective repression" (Paczkowski 1999, 384), which ranged from workplace dismissals and bans on foreign travel to the destruction of property, as well as more occasional death threats aimed at, and abductions of, the regime's most feared opponents. State censorship of the media and culture was also used to prevent political discontents from gaining momentum.

Most citizens of post-Stalinist communist states such as Poland could usually, by keeping a low political profile, avoid harsh repression. The rights abuses witnessed by the masses were more akin to corruption than state violence. Communists restricted access to privileges, frequently making personal connections essential for professional opportunities and everyday necessities ranging from "luxuries" such as meat or liquor to more basic essentials such as an apartment. People's rights were abused in that they were forced into "preference falsification" or maintaining an outward appearance of support for a system they did not truly back (Kuran 1991). As di Palma notes, "protection was bought at the price of civil and political rights" (di Palma 1991, 61). Public acceptance, derived from outward expressions of support and widespread acquiescence to elite-imposed rules, was enough to keep a series of despotic leaders in power for decades. Václav Havel, a former Czech dissident and playwright, described how millions of Central and Eastern Europeans propped up the communist system through passive collaboration:

> [T]he overwhelming majority of shopkeepers never think about the [communist] slogans they put in their windows, nor do they use them to express their real opinions. . . . [The shopkeeper] puts them all into the window simply because it has been done that way for years, because everyone does it, and because that is the way it has to be. . . . It is one of the thousands of details

that guarantee him a relatively tranquil life "in harmony with society," as they say. (Havel 1985, 27)

Memories of Stalinism, which demonstrated the extent to which the system was capable of abuse in order to secure the status quo, may have played a role in tempering subsequent mass demands for change. These memories were reinforced by the occasional use of harsh repression reminiscent of the Stalinist period. The police and military were sporadically used to brutally repress those demanding change, and even the threat of direct Soviet intervention had an intimidating effect: "Driving a tank through the street was one highly effective means of sowing terror and panic in the population" (Bartosek 1999, 438). The omnipresent nature of the Communist Party, which was involved in everything from national politics to workplace and apartment administration, made the state monopoly visible and served as a clear reminder of one's position in society. As Sharman notes, "[P]eople had very little that could not be taken away with a minimum of effort by the state apparatus" (Sharman 2003, 15).

But Poland and other communist states were not constructed solely from sticks. Rather, their leaders balanced various forms of political repression with a variety of economic carrots designed to increase their legitimacy. As Rupnik explains, "from social control it is a short step to an implicit 'social contract' between the state and the citizen" (Rupnik 1988, 276). Citizens gave up certain individual and collective rights in exchange for economic goods. Communism's subjects were the beneficiaries of a sprawling state-controlled social-safety net, characterized by low unemployment and free (if substandard) social services, such as health care and education. But the communist system was also characterized by massive inefficiencies and economic bungling on the part of central planners. This left each communist regime across the region open to attack.

Early demands for change—in Hungary (1956), Czechoslovakia (1968), and repeatedly in Poland (1956, 1968, 1970, 1976, 1981)—challenged certain party policies, especially economic ones, but not the system of party rule. The events of Poznań 1956, when dozens of Poles were killed during the state's operation to end protests initiated by factory workers, marked the first and bloodiest period of rebellion in Poland and were met with concessions by the state. In fact, Polish leaders, who had no illusions of omnipotence, would make concessions after each brief but explosive manifestation of opposition.

The most serious threat to communism was the Solidarity movement, which would come to epitomize a populist notion of labor unions, bringing together a huge portion of the working population in support of fundamental change. The rise of Solidarity in 1980 was triggered by a range of events from state-subsidy cutbacks and long-term structural problems in the Polish economy to the inspiring visit of Pope John Paul II in 1979. Its immediate catalyst was a hike in food prices, and initial strikes were largely local and focused on particular grievances. At first glance, relatively few saw the wave of strikes, again by actors interested primarily in their own weakening economic conditions, as a grave threat to communism.

However, Solidarity had much deeper roots that had begun growing in the 1970s with the nascent opposition movement. One key organization in this movement was the Committee for the Defense of Workers (known by its Polish acronym, KOR), established in 1976 following the repression of striking workers in Radom and Ursus. KOR activists were intellectuals who supported workers by providing financial, legal, and advisory assistance to the repressed as part of a broader attack on the authoritarian order. These actors began building bridges that would help ensure that workers and dissidents would eventually no longer be subject to the authorities' divide-and-rule tactics. By the time Solidarity came to the surface, many of the workers involved had had experience with these intellectuals who would take on an active role after 1980, advising and assisting workers in articulating their demands.

So while Solidarity began as a more traditional union, it quickly became a larger, grassroots movement that numbered around ten million. At its first national congress in late 1981, Solidarity leaders referred to themselves as "the most powerful mass movement in the history of Poland" and one that "reflects the desires and aspirations of Polish society" (Solidarity 1982, 205). The universality of the movement was highlighted by Solidarity's use of national symbols. Solidarity had what one called an image of "the corporate body of the civil society" (Bielasiak 1985, 31). Extraordinarily heterogeneous, it included blue-collar workers, peasants, and intellectuals, populists and conservatives, liberals and radicals.[1] This diversity led to rifts among those who preferred to focus on social and economic struggles versus those who were more eager for a political confrontation. The normative principles around which Solidarity identified, however, allowed it to bridge these various divisions. Over time, Solidarity leaders came to realize that their primarily economic goals could not be met without political change as well. However, the organization—like smaller predecessor movements throughout the region—never in its first years adopted a revolutionary role but instead accepted the lead role of the Communist Party. Poland's communist regime met Solidarity's demands with a mix of repression and, as had become customary, promised reforms. After nearly a year and a half of tussling, Gen. Wojciech Jaruzelski finally implemented martial law in December 1981, arresting thousands of Solidarity activists. While Solidarity continued to function underground, it had little more than a skeleton presence in the workplace. Promised reforms were, without union pressure, never completely implemented.

It was during this underground period that former KOR members and intellectuals from other organizations such as the Helsinki Committee, the Movement for the Defense of Human and Civic Rights (ROPCIO), and the Commission for Intervention and Rule of Law (CIRL) NSZZ Solidarność once again took the lead role. By organizing educational groups, discussion clubs, publishing activities, and charity organizations, these activists helped Solidarity survive in the underground and later played a key role in the infamous "roundtable negotiations." Despite these activities, Solidarity's popularity declined during the underground period. Solidarity had already begun to lose its shine in the preclampdown days as the movement faced off against the authorities for not weeks or months but nearly a year and a half. Fatigue, coupled with Solidarity's virtual disappearance after 1981, left the number of Poles who identified themselves with Solidarity down from more than one-third in 1981 to slightly more than one-fifth in the mid-1980s (Wydra 2000, 144; Laba 1991, 113). At the end of the decade Solidarity's membership stood at just two million, and the union lacked a presence in the large factories that had once been its power base.

Yet relative to the communists in power, Solidarity still represented a formidable force. Two things had changed over the course of the decade.

First, in 1988 Soviet leader Mikhail Gorbachev, who had himself launched a process of economic restructuring and liberalization, declared that the Soviet military would no longer be used to support communists in neighboring states. Communist leaders throughout the region were thus deprived of the major force that had helped keep them in power for the previous four decades. Second, the country continued to face economic decay with no viable escape plan. It was clear to everyone that communism, at least in Poland, was dying. In addition, despite the fact that Solidarity's membership plummeted in the face of repression, thanks to its underground activities the organization maintained a heartbeat.

Solidarity's resurgence in 1988 was sparked when authorities implemented another stopgap measure designed to keep the state above water a bit longer. As in times past, the trigger was a series of price hikes that led to strikes in February of that year. Despite the fact that this newest wave of strikes was largely spontaneous and small in scale and involved a new leadership, the strikers drew on Solidarity's past experiences and claimed to act on behalf of the whole country. The new activists were unified by their loyalty to Solidarity's historical leader, Lech Wałęsa, and broader sentiment with regard to the Solidarity tradition. The strikes were welcomed by former Solidarity members, who quickly returned to the organization, with Wałęsa retaking the helm. The strikers came out again that August, as Solidarity's approval ratings suddenly rebounded. Despite actually representing a limited proportion of the population, having largely returned to its labor-union roots, Solidarity renewed its nonworker ties and enjoyed an enormous public following that lent it a grassroots character.

It became clear that an economic transformation was inevitable. Under pressure, authorities proposed a series of roundtable talks that would ultimately last eight weeks and accentuate divisions in the organization, especially between those older activists who favored negotiations and the younger ones, who demanded more radical action. Still, most of them came together to support the country's democratic alternative in its first semifree elections in mid-1989.

With just two months to mobilize, Solidarity's leaders scrambled to create an electoral list, running as the Civic Parliamentary Club (Obywatelski Klub Parlamentarny—OKP). As part of the settlement, former

Communists guaranteed for themselves (or members of their former satellite parties) a place in the new government and 65 percent of the seats in the powerful lower house of parliament (Sejm), while allowing Solidarity to freely contest the weaker upper house (Senat); the presidency initially remained uncontested and in the hands of General Jaruzelski, who had ruled Poland undemocratically during the 1980s. Solidarity delivered a crushing electoral blow to the communists by taking all of the available Sejm seats and 99 out of 100 Senat ones. This victory gave rise to the first post-Solidarity government of Tadeusz Mazowiecki and enormous expectations of change.

Take One: From Social Movement to the State

Those Solidarity leaders who had preached a movement toward "normalcy" in 1989 came to the state with a heavy burden, the first charged with transforming a communist state into a democratic, free-market one. Knowing firsthand what social movements were capable of, post-Solidarity leaders—somewhat ironically—backed a radical shock-therapy, economic-reform program in order to effect changes before interest groups could mobilize against them. As a social movement, Solidarity had throughout the 1980s preached egalitarianism; this message would be difficult to square with the market transition its former leaders in the state now planned and implemented.

Known as the Balcerowicz Plan, after its instigator, Finance Minister Leszek Balcerowicz, the rapid transformation to a capitalist economy was just as painful as predicted, resulting in an immediate devaluation of the currency and a sharp rise in unemployment. From a macroeconomic perspective, the reforms were soon considered a success: Inflation was quickly tempered, the currency stabilized, and the economy soon began to grow at an impressive pace. However, for a population suffering from double-digit unemployment, shock therapy was a disaster. The "myth of the market," one Polish sociologist wrote at the time, was quickly replaced by "shops full of goods and many empty wallets" (Kolarska-Bobinska 1994, 113).

Initially, state leaders benefited from their personal connection to organization leaders, who, in turn, believed their ex-colleagues would act in Solidarity's best interest and be receptive to calls for a change of course if reforms proved overly painful. Solidarity's "protective umbrella" over the reforms would, in the words of one, keep society from getting "in the way of the sensible direction of the changes" (Lewicka 2009). In keeping with the social-movement tradition, the umbrella was erected at Solidarity's own discretion rather than at the request of state-bound colleagues, in large part out of faith in the movement's former leaders. As one core activist recalled the feeling, "We looked at them like at Mother Mary. They were our representatives, from the union movement" (Borowczak 2009). "These were authority figures. I didn't reflect on whether it was smart or dumb," another regional leader said of the reforms (Mosiński 2009). There was a broad acceptance among movement leaders that the shift to a Western political-economic model would involve costs that simply had to be paid. Organization leaders throughout this period claim to have been acting in the name of "Poland" rather than in the name of the union itself, trying to shield the transformation by restraining their own. The level of overall strike activity subsequently fell from just under 900 in 1989 to only about 250 in 1990 (Ost 2001, 86; Levitsky and Way 1998, 178).

Throughout 1990 and 1991, as costs began to exceed expectations, Solidarity's protective umbrella gradually frayed. Organization leaders faced enormous pressures from below to change course, most evident during meetings in which thousands demanded that their leaders explain the debilitating costs of the Balcerowicz Plan and assuage their fears that things would only get worse. These institutional pressures were compounded by the decline in Solidarity's membership, which resulted from resignations by members who were angry at Solidarity's pro-reform politics or had simply lost jobs that these policies entailed. If Solidarity had coasted to power on a wave of enthusiasm in 1989, by 1991 it was thrown by an even greater "wave of reluctance" caused in part by the widespread belief that the organization was in charge through the tough period and had ceased to defend its workers (Pałubicki 2009). In the words of one union leader, "Yesterday's heroes stood at the gates without the means to live" (Rulewski 2009).

These bottom-up pressures took an enormous toll on union leaders, many of whom were already split between doing what they thought was best for the country and what they felt would be best for the workers they had long identified with. "I had this personal dissonance," recalled one regional union leader. "For us unionists, this was problematic" (Bartosz 2009). Interpersonal dimensions exacerbated this dilemma, as organization leaders were forced to disagree with and watch the dismissal of colleagues lower down in the ranks (Mozolewski 2009). The heads of Solidarity were accused of lying and profiting from the economic restructuring that wreaked havoc on society. "I was a traitor," said one leader (Bujak 2009). People would say, "Solidarity cheated us . . . the people in power are thieves," recalled another (Frasyniuk 2009). The fallout hit activists hard. As one former leader, then heading Solidarity's railway department, commented in reference to the initial reform period, "I was even ashamed of my role, calling up various railway workers and telling them not to strike" (Dubiński 2009). "I, as one of the holders of the umbrella, feel horrible," lamented another (Bujak 2009).

By 1991, having watched their representatives throughout the state continue to maintain a course so painful to their members' pocketbooks and the reputation of Solidarity itself, union leaders' patience had worn thin. "This was not the way the democratic system was supposed to come. Why does society, why do workers need to pay this price?" one regional leader described the prevailing sentiment (Mozolewski 2009). Organization leaders soon began to subscribe to the dominant rank-and-file view that their political ex-colleagues were neither true to Solidarity's identity nor receptive to their personal pleas.

The more organization principals spoke out against the reforms, the clearer it became that ex-Solidarity state and political leaders were functioning in ways shaped by their own institutional environment and willing to ignore their former colleagues who had supported their rise to power. Political elites' focus on the societal rather than the narrower union aspects of Solidarity helped to create a disconnect between those who departed for Warsaw and those who remained in Gdańsk. Having lived through this conflict, one MP concluded, "You can't be a little bit a unionist and a little bit a politician" (Smirnow 2009). When organization leaders began openly contesting the path of reforms, their ex-colleagues in various state institutions defended the path of change. Those in power recalled an atmosphere of determination. "We had a great feeling of unity," said OKP's vice chairman from the period of the economic reforms undertaken (Stelmachowski 2004). This feeling of unity was no longer shared with Solidarity leaders, who openly contested various elements of the reform program although to no avail.

Perhaps most troubling for activists was the fact that their own heroic leader of Solidarity, Lech Wałęsa, appeared to join this harsh reformer group after winning the presidential elections—partly by contesting the reforms—in 1990. Many of my interviewees expressed a reverence toward Wałęsa and a reluctance to criticize him directly. "He was our symbol. If we respect our symbol, we can't destroy it," explained one (Wojcik 2009). However, they also made clear their strong disappointment in his behavior after moving to the presidential palace, including pressing the union to accept painful reforms without strikes and promoting particular policies, such as salary caps, that unionists almost universally opposed. For Wałęsa, the decision to back tough reforms was a function of his office and came down to the basics of budgetary policy. "I am practical. Would the president—or premier—not want to give something if he had it?" Wałęsa asked. "There was nothing to give from. These are damn hard reforms" (Wałęsa 2009).

The result, in contrast to expectations arising from network and identity arguments, was an environment in which during the initial period former ties could provide only small advantages, such as ameliorating factory-specific and sometimes even branch-specific conflicts but did not translate into favor with respect to big-ticket items. As one parliamentarian from the period recalled of his organization colleagues, "Of course, they came with many issues that were impossible to do. What could be done I tried to do" (Jurczak 2009). Rather than providing Solidarity with influence in the fundamental policy debates taking place, networks meant narrow favors that were usually designed by state leaders to encourage the union to patiently sit out the fight, if only for long enough to make the reforms essentially irreversible.

These institutional pressures eventually created a rift between one-time colleagues. Those remaining in the organization were angered when ex-movement leaders shifted their positions with so little regard for their effects and their own protests. "We did everything so these [enterprises] wouldn't fall, and they did everything so they would crumble to the ground," as one longtime labor leader characterized the schism with reference to the privatization process (Pietrzyk 2009). Unionists' frustrations resulted in threats to stage localized and even national strikes in an effort to get the government's ear. "[Tadeusz] Mazowiecki, as premier, didn't have to think so hard about what this meant for others," recalled the head of Solidarity's representation at the Ursus tractor factory, an enormous Warsaw-based enterprise that faced large-scale job losses. "He didn't want to know what my situation was" (Bujak 2009).

Those in state positions, by contrast, were surprised that their colleagues could not see the writing on the wall and, in their view, had abandoned both the broad mission of Solidarity and their personal friends responsible for implementing the tough but necessary changes: "This is a difficult time; we should be in solidarity," Wałęsa said. Instead, he continued, Solidarity's leaders would still approach him, but "some were coming as colleagues, some out of necessity, some out of hatred" (Wałęsa 2009).

Although a national strike never materialized in the early period, the number and scale of strikes grew almost exponentially, from about 250 in 1990 to 6,350 strikes (some of which were massive) in 1992 (Langer 2009; Ost 2001, 86; Levitsky and Way 1998, 178). For leaders of the largest of these actions, such as Wacław Marszewski, they signified Solidarity's fragmentation along clearly institutional lines. As head of Solidarity's National Mining Committee, Marszewski led the massive 1991–1992 strike against mine closures, among the largest in Polish mining history (Marszewski 2009). Opposing the strike was Marszewski's predecessor, then vice minister of industry Andrzej Lipko, who just a year or so before was seen by his peers as a "very radical" union leader known for organizing local mining strikes to the ire of Solidarity's national authorities (Marszewski 2009; *Gazeta Wyborcza*, November 5, 1990). Now in the ministry, it was Lipko who accused his successor of radicalizing the mining sector. "The mining sector simply had to change," he explained from his new vantage point (Lipko 2009).

As the institutional schism widened, personal ties in the early period appear to have hurt rather than smoothed relations. For those who went to the state, it was evident that "the union wanted things that were not at all possible to implement, but they didn't understand this" (Pałubicki

2009). For those still in the trenches, the apparent policy reversals of their ex-colleagues wreaked of arrogance. "Now that he's on a higher rung of the social ladder, because he has this post, he doesn't care about them," said a regional Solidarity leader. "He says 'I am a lofty (*wielki*) politician' " (Marczak 2009). Another local leader related this to a similar phenomenon that he said occurred when Solidarity activists moved to management positions in an enterprise during that same period. "He was worse than the communists. He knew better, he *was* Solidarity" (Osiński 2009).

It was this attitude, perhaps even more than the reforms themselves, that strained relations. "This disappointment was especially based on the fact that this phenomenon began of '*we* know what is good for Poland,' " recalled Solidarity's national deputy chairman (Langer 2009). Under these circumstances, personal ties could actually be counterproductive. "We negotiated, and they were offended that we were pressuring them," recalled one organization leader, who would a decade later experience this dilemma himself (Komołowski 2009). "The labor union was always pushed in the corner and told to 'be quiet because we are doing very noble things,' " said a local leader in Warsaw. "You should just sit quietly and listen to us" (Dubiński 2009). Unionists were outraged that they had so little influence on the policies implemented under the Solidarity banner. "We were [held] responsible, but really we often did not have any influence on the decisions made," commented one regional leader (Denysiuk 2009).

Policy disagreements spilled over into conflicts over identity, in which both sides charged their ex-colleagues of not only abandoning the Solidarity identity but also perhaps never really having it in the first place. Those more senior personnel who went to work for the state, including more workers in 1991, claimed that other, more junior leaders who took their place—though often of the same generation—were substantively different. By turning their backs on the reforms the country needed to move forward, former leaders said, new organization leaders lost the universalist qualities that had once made the organization so great. This division became one of the "first Solidarity," a social movement with the goals of the entire country in mind, and the "second Solidarity," a classic labor union representing workers' narrower interests (Komołowski 2009; Mietlicka 2009). With the loss of key leadership and the purported radicalization of the union under the new guard, President Wałęsa declared the period of Solidarity over (Bujak 2009).

Those remaining in the union were indignant at accusations they were second- or third-rate representatives, adding that while they might not have been in the top leadership circles since 1980, they were longtime activists. "Which one am I? I've been here since day one," one regional leader said indignantly (Denysiuk 2009). "I am living, museum-like proof of the continuity [and] that there is no first and second Solidarity," added Marian Krzaklewski, Lech Wałęsa's successor as head of Solidarity (Krzaklewski 2009). And though they admit that the first few years after democratic breakthrough left their organization without the free assistance of advisers and therefore challenged on an analytical level, Solidarity's leaders deny that they were hurt by a lack of leadership. "We managed," commented Krazklewski (Krzaklewski 2009). From the perspective of these new leaders, those who departed to the state were, from the start, not true to Solidarity. Instead, these state leaders represented a narrow subset of Solidarity, having been disproportionately drawn from Solidarity's intelligentsia base. Even great worker leaders such as Wałęsa were written off as the typical dilemma of old activists falling in with the wrong crowd. "These tendencies were more those of the advisors of Solidarity than of Solidarity, the union," explained Solidarity's chaplain (Maj 2009). Thus, despite their disappointment with their colleagues in the first two years of the transition, Solidarity's leaders decided that they would create their own parliamentary club, which would be uniquely Solidarity, to contest the 1991 parliamentary elections.

Take Two: Back to Parliament (1991–1993)

Solidarity's decision to place its leaders on its own electoral list in the 1991 parliamentary elections was calculated to make amends for all the organization had lost in the first two years of the transition. According to one of the NSZZ Solidarść Parliamentary Club's (henceforth "club") initiators, the organization's inability to reach those of its leaders who had taken to politics in the first two years of the transition meant that at the legislative and governmental levels "the union was left all by itself" (Kulas 2009). Since 1989, unemployment and consumer prices had skyrocketed, while the value of earnings had fallen. Creating a parliamentary representation would ensure that the union could propose, analyze, and amend policy initiatives pertaining to social and economic legislation in order that Poland "would not have laws that look like eighteenth-century capitalism" (Tomaszewski 2009). It would be a way to have a voice in the halls of power, where it was nonetheless blamed for whatever happened. Moreover, this voice, union leaders reassured themselves, would this time be the true voice of Solidarity.

Having shed their "liberals" in the first phase of the transition, Solidarity activists would now send true union leaders to Warsaw to "take care of workers' issues," which had been pushed to the side (Rybicki 2009). Union leaders would be able to use their parliamentary seats not only to enact legislation but also to put pressure on the government. As an added bonus, parliamentary offices would give Solidarity the benefit of outside experts who had since the transition left the organization for better-paying jobs. In short, the cost of sending a group of union leaders to Warsaw to influence policy early in the process was seen to be significantly less than the cost of staging strikes after that process had passed them by.

In order to keep Solidarity's representation true to its base, in contrast to its experience from 1989 to 1991, Solidarity's governing body, the National Commission (KK), opted to support a "limited representation" rather than an all-out effort to win as many seats as possible. The decision to endorse a finite number of candidates was designed to give Solidarity a say in, without being responsible for, governance. In part, this numeric limitation was also meant to create a cohesive organization immune to the splinter political parties that had plagued OKP from 1989 to 1991. More important, the decision reflected a belief that a greater parliamentary victory would put Solidarity's representatives in government, surely a conflict of interest in a postcommunist country where the state was the primary employer. "The government was the chief opponent of the labor union," said one leader. "We would fight each other" (Pałubicki 2009). For these reasons, members of Solidarity's club would subsequently turn down government positions and avoid interparty alliances. Solidarity was, in the words of one club parliamentarian, "limited not only in the sense of numbers but also in the sense of aspirations" (Rulewski 2009).

While there were great expectations that the twenty-seven unionist parliamentarians (who took just 5 percent of the popular vote) would represent their organization well, this was based solely on the perception that union leaders on both sides of the newly formed line were bound by a common identity and strong personal networks. In the words of one unionist who departed for parliament, he and his colleagues shared "a certain catalogue of principles and values that we declared publicly" (Śniadek 2009). "We felt very connected to Solidarity because we grew up in Solidarity. We grew out of Solidarity," added another (Pietrzyk 2009). Solidarity would rely on faith rather than policies and procedures to manage relations with its political counterparts. There was subsequently a divergence in expectations: Many unionists expected their parliamentarians to serve as a "transmission belt" by converting KK resolutions into national legislation (Polmański 2009; Śniadek 2009), while parliamentarians felt they should have more input in how they represented union interests (Bartosz 2009). As the Solidarity club's leader put it, "We're not there to take demands" (Borusewicz 2009).

One way Solidarity leaders did seek to keep their parliamentary colleagues on the same policy page was to strengthen preexisting networks by keeping parliamentarians integrated in union functions. Most of them continued to participate (though not vote) in the KK, where they related what was happening in the legislature and listened to alternative perspectives. In addition, by locating their regional parliamentary offices in regional Solidarity offices, they maintained regular interactions with organization leaders lower down as well. "We were at almost every regional meeting," one MP recalled of the early relationship. "[It was] like a big family" (Kulas 2009). "There was constant cooperation," confirmed Solidarity's leader from that period (Krzaklewski 2009).

Yet again, in terms of effects, the institutional barriers proved formidable. While parliamentarians occasionally helped organization leaders with legal issues and budgetary items in their legislative initiatives, in reality very little legislation was cowritten by Solidarity leaders and their MPs. MPs charged that Solidarity activists simply lacked initiatives or the skills to put them forward, but Solidarity leaders felt increasingly estranged from their political counterparts, who, they believed, had, in their new institutional shells, moved beyond union interests. The physical proximity to former Solidarity colleagues failed to bridge the new boundaries that appeared. "There was little connection despite even those physically joint offices," recalled one MP. "Let's be honest: From the side of the union there was no understanding of our work, and we couldn't convince them" (Rulewski 2009). Even the most loyal "unionist" politicians side-stepped their organization colleagues to promote bills that Solidarity opposed when, in the words of one, "I decided they didn't understand" (Pietrzyk 2009).

In fact, by the time Prime Minister Jan Olszewski's government fell in mid-1992, the constraints of their new institution and a perceived inconsistency between what was good for the country and good for Solidarity prompted a split within Solidarity's parliamentary club. Club leader Bogdan Borusewicz recalled "numerous" votes in which he and his colleagues supported government programs, from transforming heavy industry to restructuring the mining sector, that they knew "would hit the unionists" (Borusewicz 2009). These MPs consulted not only with organization leaders at both the national and regional levels but also with the general public, to whom they ultimately owed their mandates. In the end, said Solidarity's parliamentary leader, they—like their predecessors from Solidarity's intelligentsia—sided with the latter: "We voted for Poland. We had to reform Poland" (Borusewicz 2009).

Such votes led to constant struggles between Borusewicz and his followers on the one hand and Wałęsa's successor as union head, Marian Krzaklewski, on the other. "This 'us' versus 'them' had formed," said one MP who was tied to Borusewicz. "The club began to split" (Rulewski 2009). To Borusewicz's followers, Solidarity's criticisms of the reform program were—once again—an indication that the organization was no longer the same social movement that had once defended all Poles but instead now promoted only a very narrow sliver of the population. "Radicalism was emerging on a scale never seen before," said one, echoing the voices of his 1989–1991 political predecessors. He added, "We wanted to bring about contemporary politics for Solidarity, for society" (Kulas 2009). However, to "unionist" MPs, Borusewicz and his followers betrayed the union cause by backing the same liberal reforms promoted by the first wave of Solidarity leaders. "It turned out that they were on the other side of the barricade," a regional union leader from the time recalled (Polmański 2009).

In spring 1993 this barricade, which was visible during a massive strike by teachers (prompted by inadequate pay raises), was built on institutional grounds. Krzaklewski faced pressures from lower down in the union ranks that boiled to the surface at the beginning of the midyear union leadership elections, in which he ran against a much more radical local union leader. However, for Solidarity activists the crisis primarily resulted from what they referred to as "the arrogance of the authorities" (Kurski, Rot, and Zaluska 1993, 1). Among these authorities was Jacek Kuron, one of Solidarity's longtime intellectual behemoths and then labor minister, who chided the union by proposing that "if we fired those teachers who are not working now, then the rest would have amazing salaries, and maybe the children would stop suffering" (Skipietrow 1993, 1). President Wałęsa, though more restrained, also expressed impatience at Solidarity's increasingly contentious tactics against its own former members now in power. "The protests are deserved, but they are not a way to solve the problems," Wałęsa said. "We need to be serious and solve these problems well so that it doesn't come to a tragedy in the country" (Koral 1993, 1).

Once supported by club MPs, some in the club now condemned the government of Prime Minister Hanna Suchocka when it continued to refuse wage increases for public-sector employees. Alojzy Pietrzyk, leader of the club's union faction, argued that the government "was practically against the labor union" (Pietrzyk 2009), and others similarly felt that continued support for Suchocka would drive the union into disrepute: "It wouldn't count. People wouldn't treat it as a responsible labor union" (Bartosz 2009). By that point, at least one club MP had suspended his Solidarity membership "until the union stops its politics of destruction" (Grzechowiak 1993, 2).

Solidarity's National Commission responded to the crisis by recalling its representatives to Gdańsk to participate in a special hearing on a motion of no confidence in the Suchocka government, a vote that would accentuate the divide in Solidarity's parliamentary club. In reality, according to one bitter parliamentarian attendee who supported Suchocka, MPs who were brought to Gdańsk "were ordered to fulfill a command" (Kulas

2009). Organization heads back in the KK, said one MP, "decided that we are also now 'them' [government enemies]" (Rulewski 2009). "Walking into the hall of the National Commission, we were greeted very coldly," said another (Bartosz 2009). MP opponents of the no-confidence measure sought to convince their colleagues that toppling the government would be counterproductive, but they believed that the decision was made long before their arrival. President Wałęsa claims to also have met unsuccessfully with the union's newest leaders. "People began to be more and more dissatisfied with politicians, with us, with me, with everybody," Wałęsa recalled of the institutional schism (Wałęsa 2009).

Club MPs returned to Warsaw and put forward the ballot that would, by a margin of just one vote (and with several club MPs opposing or abstaining), end their second brief experiment with political representation. About one-quarter of Solidarity's political representatives, including historical figures such as Jan Rulewski and Wojciech Arkuszewski, refused to abide by the KK's decision, having now come to see the country's needs in a new light. Moreover, there is evidence that even some who did vote in line with the KK did so not out of loyalty or personal influences but pragmatism. Borusewicz, for instance, sided with Solidarity on the vote in the belief that the alternative was large-scale strikes and increased state instability (Borusewicz 2009). In his new institutional position, that was his primary interest.

As in the preceding period, the combination of mutual disappointment, competing claims on identity, and emotionally charged personal connections led to increased tensions, which were most evident in the way leaders on both sides of the political divide interpreted the 1993 no-confidence vote. Harkening back to the first post-Solidarity political cohort in the Suchocka government, Krzaklewski recalled acrimoniously that "our colleagues were sure they would win the election and show us as a union where our place was" (Krzaklewski 2009). Others reserved their vitriol for the group within their own parliamentary club that, by not voting for the measure, treated their former union colleagues "as a mass of people who can be manipulated and steered" (Mosiński 2009). Frequently they alleged that these political traitors had merely used the union as a springboard to handsome salaries and prestige, "thinking of themselves, not about what's good for the masses of working people" (Kropiwnicki 2009).[2] When Solidarity club parliamentarians explained to unionists that their demands either could not be fulfilled or, if implemented, would bring great harm, "this irritated the unionists the most," said another activist (Pałubicki 2009).

Disappointment ran both ways as political leaders expressed resentment about being treated by their associates as personal enemies and were accused of "sabotaging the economy, of being traitors to the union" (Rulewski 2009). These leaders believed that the union was actually the group that was disregarding those who were, after all, their chosen representatives. "This really surprised and hurt me because it was precisely the union, our close colleagues, who suddenly demanded that we be this transmission belt," recalled another club MP. "We had what for me was this brutal policy." Interestingly, this particular parliamentarian decided to change his 1993 no-confidence vote for Suchocka, his personal preference, to a vote for Solidarity, explaining that "some sort of basic loyalty was always strongly encoded in me" (Kulas 2009). He subsequently ran on Solidarity's 1993 parliamentary ticket.

Given all of the problems encountered with the 1991–1993 Solidarity parliamentary representation, including its dramatic culmination, respondents in my study appear to have come out of the period with a realization that the union could not fight while numerically limited. "This was a very small group, and it couldn't do much," recalled one regional head who would go on to be a leader in Solidarity's next political rising (Komołowski 2009). They also claimed that, in retrospect, union leaders were unrealistic to expect the sorts of policies they hoped to see enacted at a time of economic crisis (Borowczak 2009; Marczak 2009; Pałubicki 2009). The lessons Solidarity carried forward from this period, as it witnessed the rise of its former communist nemesis, was that limits were a handicap. As one leader of the club's unionist faction put it, signing on to a limited representation was utopian to the point of naïveté (Smirnow 2009).

Take Three: The Rise of AWS and a "Solidarity" Government

Solidarity's leaders emerged from the first two episodes of political activity deeply scarred. Carrying its historical name, the union was blamed for all of Poland's problems, in large part because one-time leaders of and advisors to the organization who had moved on to the political arena continued to squeeze what little positive associations it could bring them. A wide range of post-Solidarity parties arose, each using the Solidarity banner. "Who was blamed? Not this or that political party but Solidarity," commented one regional leader, explaining an increase in strikes and the fall of the last of these "Solidarity" governments in 1993. "We realized we just had to say no" (Dubiński 2009). At the time the union demanded the end of the Suchocka pro-reform government, only one in six Poles felt the costs of the transition had been "worth bearing" (CBOS 1993a, 1993b).

Solidarity's early political experiences prompted a "large minority" within its National Commission to express consternation over the union's intention to contest the 1993 elections. Since many Solidarity activists supported or were even members of various post-Solidarity parties, this minority objected that any Solidarity party would split the organization. "Do I vote for my labor union's ticket or for the party that I'm also a member or sympathizer of?" asked one (Wojtczak 2009). Solidarity ultimately failed to breach the electoral threshold in the 1993 elections, while the postcommunists, through the Democratic Left Alliance (SLD), regained their hold on the state. "Thanks to us," said one 1991–1993 club MP with a dose of irony, "SLD took power" (Kulas 2009).

For leaders of the Right and Center-Right, the SLD's political resurrection in 1993 was a national tragedy for those who thought "communists would die a natural death" (Borowczak 2009). "You wanted to cry in a way. People gave their lives, sat in jail, suffered, and here they can't get through to each other," recalled one regional Solidarity leader of the Right's fragmentation. "And those who beat us in the streets . . . had come back to power" (Mozolewski 2009). When Wałęsa lost the presidential elections just two years later to SLD candidate Aleksander Kwaśniewski,

Solidarity's leadership was further shaken by the rise of the Left. "How could this have happened so fast?" asked Jacek Rybicki, Solidarity's vice chairman and the driving force behind AWS. "These two shocks made Solidarity think a bit differently" (Rybicki 2009). The very dominance of postcommunists presented a moral and political dilemma that Solidarity's leaders believed they had to fight on the political stage.

Beyond a general distaste for postcommunist politicians was a series of concrete grievances, particularly a perceived increase in corruption and unemployment associated with the ongoing privatization process. Activists saw that without a say in how they were governed, the union was stuck in a cycle of fruitless confrontation. Although Solidarity's actions were largely tied to economic policies, they also concerned social issues more characteristic of its social-movement past, including enhancing the constitutional role of the church, carrying out lustration (a purging of those affiliated with the communist-era secret police), and curtailing abortion rights. Moreover, Solidarity's leaders claimed that if SLD politicians continued to rule, they would leave Poland ill prepared to enter NATO and perhaps even the European Union (Janiak 2009; Rybicki 2009). Finally, even though the union continued to strike in the name of its members' economic interests, it also went far beyond traditional union activities by organizing petitions and even drafting its own constitutional project.

Solidarity leaders now felt not only that their country needed to continue fundamental reforms but also that they were the ones who were prepared to implement four necessary reforms: social security, health care, education, and territorial administration (Langer 2009). Since they had lost power in 1993, Solidarity elites had strengthened their organization, increased their expertise, and developed these key legislative initiatives, which would emerge at the top of the agenda once they took power. Despite seeing their membership decline throughout the process of economic transformation—to 1.7 million by 1993 and 1.29 million by 1998—Solidarity's leaders believed they had greater capacity to act in the name of the population (Orenstein 2001, 48; Millard 1999, 111). "By 1997, Solidarity and its bloc were prepared to govern," one AWS MP claimed (Kulas 2009). "We didn't have to think about what to do," added another; it had already been decided (Komołowski 2009).

If Solidarity hoped to regain a voice in the state, its leaders concluded, it would have to ally with and unify a disparate range of parties on the Right and the Center-Right (Langer 2009; Osiński 2009; Wojtczak 2009). The creation of the Solidarity Electoral Action (AWS) coalition was, in the words of one activist, "the only medicine" (Bartosz 2009). Leaders of more than thirty other parties concurred and, albeit sometimes reluctantly, fell into line (Mosiński 2009). By underwriting the unification of the Right, Solidarity once again took on the shape of an umbrella (Bartosz 2009; Śniadek 2009). Solidarity's leaders also saw AWS as a way to remedy two of its past political errors: First, unlike from 1991 to 1993, Solidarity would have a direct role in governing. And second, unlike after 1989, it wanted to ensure that real workers—and not those closer to the intelligentsia— were placed in power regardless of their lack of political experience.

Other parties were encouraged to ride the newest Solidarity wave but with the understanding that Solidarity would have the final say in coalition decisions. In return, Solidarity served as the backbone of the coalition's electoral drive by mobilizing its members and providing union resources for the political race. As one regional leader recalled, "Solidarity wasn't just the inspiration but also the infrastructure around it" (Bartosz 2009). Each of Solidarity's regional leaders became simultaneously the regional head of AWS, tasked by the KK with preparing candidate lists for the elections, and Solidarity offices doubled as AWS offices. The overlap created a frenzy of activity. "We were all going together and fighting for a new, better quality [of life] in Poland," commented one regional leader (Krauze 2009). The union was once again ascending, this time to "finish Solidarity's revolution" (Borowczak 2009).

The bid was an enormous success. AWS won nearly 34 percent of the popular vote, a situation that left Solidarity, which held about half of AWS's more than two hundred parliamentary slots, back in the political driver's seat. Despite the fact that the result of the 1997 elections left AWS with a share of the vote that necessitated partnering with other parties to create a government, expectations on the Right were enormous (Krzaklewski 2009; Wojcik 2009). Within the union, in particular, there was a feeling that "We'll take care of everything. After all, they are ours" (Kowalczyk 2009). In many ways, these feelings, based on network and identity arguments, were reminiscent of 1989, with all the "euphoria" (Wasiński

2009) and "pioneer spirit" (Lewicka 2009) of the first victory over communism. But Solidarity in its newest political manifestation faced an uphill battle. Not only did it come up against expected enemies from the outside, demonstrated by an upsurge in militancy from the left-wing labor union, All-Poland Alliance of Trade Unions (OPZZ), but it also confronted enemies on the inside, including breaks in the AWS coalition and tensions between Solidarity's delegates to power and the anchor organization in Gdańsk.

As with any movement that unifies around a common threat, AWS was a highly diverse political organization, a fact that became increasingly apparent over time. While many activists claim to have advocated for the AWS leadership (under Solidarity's Krzaklewski) to transform the coalition into a single party characterized by party discipline, leaders felt that the coalition was too fragile and that such a move could actually threaten the cohesion of a grouping whose support was necessary to govern. There was a realization that many AWS members were simply using the organization to jockey for positions within their own constituent parties, making them tenuous partners at best. Even if AWS could be united, some feared that Solidarity's leadership would have to relinquish control over the organization. This concern was heightened by the lack of experience among Solidarity's politicians, which led other AWS party officials to disparage the unionists as "naïve, second-rate" (Szwed 2009) "screwdrivers" (Krzaklewski 2009) and "a hammer in the factory" (Mozolewski 2009).

As a result, Solidarity's leaders were loath to withdraw from the coalition and simultaneously felt the need to solidify their own representation. Although the Polish constitution forbids unions from creating their own electoral committees, Ruch Społeczny AWS (Social Movement AWS; hereafter RS) became the "political representation of the union," and Krzaklewski was named its honorary leader (Krzaklewski 2009). Almost all AWS unionists joined and therefore numerically dominated RS, though others, including political leaders from local government, also signed up. In addition, it was understood that the union would become less directly involved in AWS as RS became the party representing Solidarity's interests. Those back in Solidarity's ranks who believed that this organization would better represent their particular interests, however, were wrong. "We outright didn't want this to be a typical unionist circle," said one RS MP. "We weren't supposed to deal with just union issues" (Szwed 2009).

From below, RS seemed like a godsend—an apparent institutionalization of the unique and advantageous relationship it held with unionists now in the state. Solidarity's leaders immediately declared their backing and simultaneously drafted a list of tasks for their representatives. Solidarity's political representation offered—at least in theory—a new way to get things done. "If we could resolve a problem through contacts with parliamentarians, a minister, then why get involved in a large-scale action which costs money, stops the factory?" explained one regional leader (Solidarity1 2009). Many politicians with a union pedigree claim that these personal and organizational ties were extremely beneficial for unionists because they "profited from the climate; they could call a minister, and he went and talked to them, negotiated with them" (Mosiński 2009). "At all times, day and night, someone from Solidarity could come to me," claimed the AWS labor minister (Komołowski 2009). Solidarity's leaders who held state positions in turn expected to be able to use their organizational relationships to facilitate AWS's policies.

Yet some who remained in the union trenches downplayed the significance of these relations, lamenting that most ministers, especially after the four key reforms were initiated after a year in office, "wouldn't recognize us. If you wanted to get an appointment, to talk, he'd say 'no,' he didn't have time; he wouldn't call back" (Dubiński 2009). Others said that while some senior officials still returned to the union to consult, "this doesn't at all mean that he always did what the union wanted" (Solidarity1 2009). The head of the union and AWS concurred with this assessment, recalling his frequent use of "uncensored words" to explain to recalcitrant unionists "the greater argument, that we have to do these things; otherwise, it will be even worse" (Krzaklewski 2009). Cooperation was best when unionists sought assistance with individual matters without challenging overall policy. As one union leader said, "With these little things they were always eager. They even came and asked how things were" (Dubiński 2009).

However, RS members had much bigger fish to fry. While AWS had notoriously poor discipline and provided only tepid support for government policies, according to the secretary of state charged with smoothing relations between the government and parliament, RS—and the unionists in particular—could generally be counted on to support the government line on broad reforms. At least in the initial period, senior unionists protected the government not only in the halls of parliament but also, as in the past, in the streets. With a large number of RS leaders who were simultaneously voting members in Solidarity's National Commission, said the regional Solidarity head who was also charged with organizing union strikes, the KK did not authorize a single national strike during the AWS government (Mosiński 2009). "There was practically no large-scale protest because this wasn't possible," said another, adding that Solidarity's leaders served on state commissions and various consultative bodies. "Most of the KK members were involved in the process" (Kulas 2009).

Although no national strikes occurred, Solidarity activists were uneasy with their ex-leaders almost from the start. In December 1997, for instance, unionists criticized longtime activist and now labor minister Longin Komołowski for failing to consult with them on energy price hikes, which, according to unionists, violated the labor law (GW 1997b). Komołowski replied in language characteristic of someone who was operating under new institutional constraints: The government was forced to act quickly and had no time for consultation. Despite this explanation, Solidarity remained patient, promising that there would be no protests since "The union has a strong enough means of pressure through the AWS parliamentary club" (GW 1997c, 4). In contrast, OPZZ promised to take the case to the Constitutional Court (GW 1997d). Similar stories were related in other sectors, such as when the education ministry, again without negotiations, violated its pledge to raise teachers' salaries to the level agreed upon earlier (GW 1998a). The highly politicized Ursus factory, mentioned earlier, was especially symbolic of the new situation. When management of the state factory announced a fundamental restructuring that would include layoffs of more than 15 percent, Solidarity openly supported the decision as its rival, OPZZ, pledged to fight (GW 1998b, 1998c). In all of these early cases, Solidarity was remarkably sanguine.

While Solidarity's cover for the AWS reforms was "a sort of public secret" (Kulas 2009) in the first year and a half, eventually the perception resurfaced within Solidarity that unionist politicians had forgotten their roots; they "don't represent our interests anymore" (Mietlicka 2009). Within two years there was no shortage of national protests and branch-specific strikes. Each of the four significant reforms that AWS had campaigned on and RS now promised to deliver involved high costs, from wage reductions to layoffs, that would be borne in part by union members and thus ran into significant opposition. To make matters worse, Solidarity politicians who needed partners who would support their reform agenda created a governing coalition with the liberal Freedom Union (UW), many of whose followers they had branded traitors over the preceding years.

Unionist leaders in power were not surprised at the violent reaction from below, claiming that when they were on the other side of the state line they had felt as their colleagues did now (Krauze 2009). "We didn't completely grasp, first, what the true situation was in the country and, second, what these changes would imply," recalled one MP (Szwed 2009). In their new institutions, political leaders made decisions they found distasteful but necessary. "Sometimes I was very unhappy that I had to, with hesitation, press that button," recalled one, referring to his voting pattern (Wojtczak 2009). Another recounted a particularly painful period when, as an AWS MP, he was asked to support one of the four large-scale AWS reforms that would redraw the country's administrative lines, reducing the number of provinces from forty-nine to just sixteen. The result would be a loss of status for the province and a decline in negotiating power for many unions, as well as jobs for those (many unionists) employed in the provincial administrations (Kerlin 2002, 6, 10). Yet again institutions trumped the personal identities and networks and stretched them to the breaking point. "I was one of those who voted for the liquidation of my own province (*wojewódstwo*)," one MP said (Denysiuk 2009). "Reality hits. You see more and more and begin to know what this budget is," concluded another RS MP. "I don't know if this changed everyone, but it changed me" (Wasiński 2009).

Solidarity's political leaders, especially those closer to the government, began to understand their role very broadly (Kulas 2009). "[AWS] was always realizing the interests of Solidarity, but [it was] Solidarity broadly understood as Solidarity of the whole society. It had this feeling that it had more to do than just protect workers," said one activist involved in Krzaklewski's presidential campaign (Mietlicka 2009). "I couldn't take narrow responsibility solely for workers' rights. I had to take responsibility for the whole," commented AWS's internal affairs minister. "And I made decisions, some of which were liked; others not" (Tomaszewski 2009). "I had to in some ways look at the entire country," concurred one of AWS's leaders. "You can't reconcile everyone's differences" (Rybicki 2009). This change of perspective meant that Solidarity's own political designees would sometimes ignore their loudest and closest critics. "If there's a Solidarity protest where one group wants to get something at the cost of everyone else, then I'd say at the moment, 'Sorry, but no'" (Wasiński 2009).

Those who were leaders of both the organization and its political offshoot struggled to reconcile the differences. This was arguably most dramatic in the case of Marian Krzaklewski, who, given his "exceptional" personal leadership, was allowed to serve simultaneously as leader of both Solidarity and the AWS coalition that created and dominated the government (GW 1997a). There are disagreements as to Krzaklewski's actual relationship to the government—but he was clearly influential, particularly in the first two years (Borowczak 2009; Janiak 2009; Krzaklewski 2009; Langer 2009; Polmański 2009; Solidarity1 2009). Facing enormous expectations from unionists squeezed by economic reforms, Krzaklewski began to deal with the inconsistencies of representing both a narrow interest group and a broad idea.

The fact that AWS, much less RS AWS (of which Krzaklewski was "honorary chairman"), lacked the votes to accomplish everything it wanted meant that sometimes Krzaklewski stood in opposition to his own government. In 1998 a large protest headed by the Silesian section of Solidarity took place in Warsaw, where participants demanded more pro-family legislation, including tax breaks and days off. Senior activists assumed that Krzaklewski would side with them against the government or risk being deposed from his union leadership role. Krzaklewski obliged, leading the demonstration to the steps of parliament, where his own parliamentary group dominated.

The irony of Krzaklewski's position was not lost on activists on both sides of the government/union divide. "Many people laughed, saying

in the morning he is the one in charge (*rządzący*), [and] in the afternoon
he is the one charging (*rządzający*)," said one activist and parliamentarian (Borowczak 2009). While Krzaklewski downplayed the meaning of
this event, others saw it as emblematic of a conflicted leadership and a
grave strategic error. One former parliamentarian characterized his leader
(times two) as schizophrenic and unable to convince either side to move.
"No one felt good about this" (Bartosz 2009). For those in government,
Krzaklewski's actions were counterproductive for everything they—and
he—were supposedly fighting for. "This was absurd," commented the
Solidarity-rooted vice minister of health-care reform. "This really made
it complicated for us" (Mańko 2009).

Krzaklewski's dilemma might have been an extreme case, but it
was mimicked at lower levels. Although there was apparently a general
sentiment that one should not continue to serve in both union positions
and as a parliamentarian or political leader, this rule was formalized only
for those holding government office. Parliamentarians who maintained
both roles were often verbally attacked at local union meetings. "I would
go to a [union] meeting, and at the start there would be pure mouthing
off (*pyskowanie*) and people beating up on each other," said one MP. "We
were attacked that we forgot them, that we weren't implementing Solidarity's programs" (Wasiński 2009). Another parliamentarian who gave
up his regional union leadership role several months into his parliamentary term recalled feeling a degree of relief upon doing so. "I no longer
had this internal split" (Wojtczak 2009). Such dissociation might have
alleviated formal pressures, but it did not fundamentally change the situation of MPs who routinely met with their Solidarity colleagues. "These
conflicts were constantly there," recalled one MP from the Mazowsze
province (Smirnow 2009).

For cabinet officials, who took direct responsibility for the painful reforms, the relationship with unionists was complicated by both
their personal fingerprints on the new policies and their strong determination that such measures were essential for the well-being of the
country. "I was so convinced that the reforms had to occur. I felt help-
less because I knew it would be better if there was more money," said
one AWS vice minister, mimicking President Wałęsa's sentiment a decade

earlier (Kamińska 2009). Senior government officials who emerged from Solidarity recalled having constant and direct contact with the unions, but this did not prevent them from acting in ways the union saw as negative. "I, of course, went and told them what was [going on] here, what I was doing, what I would do, what I wouldn't do, and why I wouldn't do it," as one former vice minister described the relationship (Mańko 2009). Another union politician reflecting on miners' criticism of him and his colleagues added that often negotiations with unionists were futile: "For them 'there is none' doesn't count; they wanted as much money as possible" (Denysiuk 2009).

The case of health care, one of the four key AWS reforms, dramatically illustrates this dilemma. This reform program involved moving from a centralized health-care system financed by the national budget to a "health insurance organization" system, which managed payments and contracted caregivers to provide service.[3] Activists complained that the budget was insufficient to support the reforms, and the already shoddy quality of care deteriorated further in certain areas. Facing pay cuts, nurses took to the streets. One parliamentarian recalled this episode as a "personal dilemma" (Bartosz 2009). "On the one hand I saw that nurses earned too little," he said. "On the other hand, I was also looking at the budget." The predicament was even more problematic for AWS vice minister Teresa Kamińska, who had under the previous administration led a month-long hunger strike that forced the SLD government to authorize a 5.5 percent wage increase for health-care workers. In her new position Kamińska realized that the state could not afford this concession. "Destiny is facetious," she commented. "When I came into government, I saw how it looked from the other side" (Kamińska 2009). When Kamińska agreed with the rest of the government to suspend the 5.5 percent raise she had fought so hard for, she was personally criticized, and her government was threatened with strikes.

Such personal attacks were a direct result of the polarizing effects caused by each side's institutional environment. High-level Solidarity leaders faced consistent demands from the broader union membership to push the government harder. "They were under this pressure—'It's your guys who are ruling. Go to your colleagues and take care of it,'" recalled one union politician who took a ministerial job. "So they came, friend to friend, saying 'Take care of this, that's what the union rank-and-file expect to happen'" (Komołowski 2009). Where union activists expected their colleagues to back down from particularly painful reforms, empowered activists were stimulated by new motivations. "The union is always there to defend the rights of the worker, and it can't abandon that," said one AWS vice minister. "But the government, in turn, has its obligations" (Kamińska 2009). As was the case before 1993, unionists often felt belittled by their ex-colleagues. "One would say 'Listen, if you had all the data that we have, you would look at this problem differently,'" said one regional leader. "There would be these comments that 'you have too little information'" (Solidarity1 2009).

Whether during negotiations or while attending union functions, Solidarity's political elites were berated for their decisions. "Those meetings with unionists were dramatic," said one RS AWS parliamentarian. "These were the sorts of meetings I had never been through. There was such an attack on us!" (Szwed 2009). Explanations, an AWS minister added, were easily dismissed. "A great many activists, especially at the lower level, didn't understand this at all," he said (Komołowski 2009). Solidarity's parliamentarians were greeted at the gates of parliament by friends and ex-colleagues, screaming "thieves!" (Borowczak 2009) and "traitors!" (Lewicka 2009). One longtime unionist claimed that the "soda water" consumed in government and parliamentary circles had made many of his ex-colleagues lose their sense of direction (Solidarity1 2009). Well-established social networks frayed under the pressure. "I knew that our roads were dividing," said one AWS government official (Mańko 2009).

This name-calling, as well as the protests and strikes that accompanied it, offended and angered those in power. Reasoning that their former colleagues had unrealistically high expectations of them, political leaders sometimes decided it was simpler dealing with perennial enemies, such as the communist-era labor union, OPZZ. "With them it was easier," explained AWS's labor minister. "For them it was just a big deal that I sat down with them, drove over to them, talked to them" (Komołowski 2009). Unionist parliamentarians, who were only indirectly responsible for ensuring the reforms, were less likely to go this route, and some even moved away from the unpopular government stance after Krzaklewski's miserable showing in the 2000 presidential elections and in the period before their own 2001 parliamentary elections. The result was a virtual implosion of AWS, where once-dependable RS unionists increasingly asked, "Why should we agree to these things?" (Wojtczak 2009). "Not all survived this psychologically," the head of Prime Minister Buzek's political section commented in exasperation. "They felt how good it was to be a parliamentarian. It was comfortable. They wanted to come back again, and so they took that road" (Kamińska 2009).

Facing miserable public-opinion statistics, the Solidarity union formally distanced itself from politics at its national meeting in spring 2001. Those who participated in the AWS parliament and government look back on those years with pride, believing they made the difficult decisions Poland needed to move ahead and achieve further integration into the West. "This is responsibility. Show me a parliament, a government that would take on such hard reforms in one term," said one parliamentarian (Mozolewski 2009). "They risked the reputation, the position of the union, [and] their own positions in order to do something," added another. "There was an understanding that we could lose on this" (Wojtczak 2009). Indeed, in the 2001 parliamentary elections AWS failed to reach the 6 percent threshold, leaving it blocked from power as the postcommunists once again took control. Solidarity's third—and many say its last—political experiment again ended in disappointment and pain for the union.

Summary

After years of experience, longtime union activists in Poland have become convinced that institutional considerations will outweigh any amount of trust and friendship they may have in their ruling partners. Identities and networks that had failed to create political opportunities for Solidarity during the early postbreakthrough period were explained away as a function of the dominance of Solidarity's intellectual advisors (rather than true workers) in politics (1989–1991) and the numeric and aspirational limitations set for the Solidarity club (1991–1993). By putting true unionists in a governing coalition and in government itself, AWS was designed to remedy these shortfalls. As predicted by the institutional argument, however, Solidarity's third try at politics was another strike.

The leaders did not purposely purge themselves of long-held identities and interpersonal networks but rather held on to them to the degree that they were compatible with their new, institutionally structured views and goals. Those who moved into politics felt a responsibility to those ideas and friends, which made difficult governing decisions even harder. Krzaklewski, as leader of an ostensibly radicalized union and pro-reform governing coalition, exemplifies this complicated relationship, having become a believer in measures he felt were in the interests of his organization—as a representative of Poland writ large—even while so many in that organization opposed them. "For me the most painful thing was not the effects of the reforms but that they were connected . . . to Solidarity, the union" (Krzaklewski 2009).

In each of the periods examined, Solidarity's leaders in the political sphere apparently believed that they were acting in the greater good and in the name of the ideals the union espoused. They took pains to maintain collegial relations and to provide what they felt they could without dramatically breaking with the new institutions in which they served. This created some opportunities for Solidarity's activists, though they were apparently no more advantaged with respect to bigger issues even while they worked to shore up grassroots support for the government. The result was a Solidarity union that on the national level acquired some crumbs but lost the loaf.

This has left pro-democracy organizations seeking a role in governance in a bind. On the one hand, they see that placing their leaders in power can actually hurt them, as those who went on to work for the state become the natural enemies of those who sought to check it. "The worst thing is to have a part in governing," one regional leader concluded (Kropiwnicki 2009). On the other hand, it is also clear that any organization that wants to continue to play a significant, hands-on role in postbreakthrough transitions must engage with the state in various ways. "In public life one can't be apolitical," said another, who recently left his regional union leadership position for politics (Szwed 2009). In the next chapter I analyze how relationships have played out in South Africa, where two massive groups within the pro-democracy movement have since 1994 followed different paths in their quest to achieve influence in the postapartheid democracy.

4

From Elation to Frustration
The Tale of South Africa's Two Organizational Giants

FOR THE FOURTEEN YEARS BEFORE DEMOCRACY came to South Africa, Johnny Copelyn was an avowed "workerist" and leader of the Southern African Clothing and Textile Workers' Union (SACTWU). As a powerful voice of labor, Copelyn found himself and twenty-two other union leaders selected as delegates from the Congress of South African Trade Unions (COSATU) to the African National Congress's (ANC) historic 1994 electoral list. He and the others, three of whom would accept ministerial jobs, hoped to transform a brutally divided country and elevate the status of workers to a level never seen before. "We went off to parliament with all the joy and enthusiasm imaginable," Copelyn recently recalled (Copelyn 2008).

Within weeks of moving into his government office, Copelyn realized his new home was "stultifying," a "deathbed" on both a personal and an organizational level. COSATU's delegated leaders were subsumed into the ANC's agenda and cut off from their former colleagues. "People were not particularly interested in what the unions had to say in parliament," he explained. "The feeling was that the national liberation movement is our government, and they are going to solve everything." COSATU officials, said Copelyn and others, made little effort to formally hold their delegates to account, instead hoping that the biographies of those who had gone to the state, as well as their personal networks outside the state, would keep them in the union's orbit.

What COSATU leaders failed to account for was the enormity of their institutional shift. "Once you come to power or come close to coming to power, a whole lot of issues just don't seem sensible anymore," Copelyn said. "The notion that you would still feel like we were underneath it all . . . a labor group, that is impossible." As Copelyn's policy preferences were tested, his occupational path veered sharply away from the union career he had known up until the democratic breakthrough. Within three years, Copelyn had left the political sphere to pursue his own private business, in which his shares were already valued at more than $3 million (Valpy 1997).

Copelyn's saga has been replicated repeatedly over the last decade and a half. Since South Africa's transition began in 1994, several waves of liberation fighters have taken up state positions. As in Poland, those who left and those who remained behind in movement organizations have consistently hoped that their long-held identities and strong personal networks would be sufficient to guarantee the support of their partners on the other side of the state line. However, just as Solidarity's leaders found out thousands of miles to the north, institutional pressures left former bonds severely strained and former friends dubious of one another's true motivations.

From Movement to Power

Those who came to power in 1994 reigned over the remnants of the white-run apartheid regime, which had created an essentially bipolar state. For the tiny white minority, which composed less than 15 percent of the population, apartheid-era South Africa had all the trappings of a procedural democracy, characterized by competitive elections, multiple parties, and generally independent courts. Not only did South African whites have all of the privileges of citizenship that their cousins in Western Europe had, but they also shared a fairly high level of development; in fact, many of the white-dominated cities were as modern and clean as their northern counterparts. It would be a mistake, however, to think of white South Africans as simply colonizing Europeans. Rather, they had developed a unique African identity and felt that the southern tip of Africa was now their homeland. This was particularly true of the Afrikaners, who held a slight majority relative to the British component of the white population and had run the state since 1948 via the National Party. It was this group, whose Dutch forebears had come to South Africa in the mid-seventeenth century and gradually established their own localized language and culture, that was the primary beneficiary of apartheid, having enjoyed a sort of affirmative action in both the bureaucracy and the enormous state sector of the economy.

For those with slightly more pigment in their skin, South African apartheid was disempowering, humiliating, and potentially lethal. Just two years after coming to power, the National Party had passed a series of laws that would make race the primary determinant of political and economic security. Building on social Darwinism and its more recent Nazi incarnation, the 1950 Population Registration Act established a racial hierarchy: whites at the top, "coloreds" (those who were of mixed race) in the middle, and Africans (those natives with the darkest skin) at the bottom. The Group Areas Act, passed that same year, ensured that regions were racialized; the whites would inhabit the well-endowed cities and immediate suburbs, and coloreds (as well as Indians, who were added to the Population Registration Act later) would buffer them from Africans, who lived far outside the towns. The law also created Bantustans, homelands based on African ethnic groups that were purposely designed to divide the African population. These homelands were placed in the most desolate and resource-poor areas, making them (much like Native American reservations in the United States) isolated pockets of deprivation and despair. They also made Africans essentially visitors in their own country inasmuch as they were allowed to move about outside their assigned territories only with special identity cards and permission (known as the pass system).

Although the apartheid regime did not formally exist until the National Party came to power in 1948, it had begun showing its face in 1910, when Great Britain created the Union of South Africa and granted it independence. Just two years later, a group of prominent individuals, including chiefs and religious leaders, established the African National Congress to contest the oppressive and racist conditions. The organization became increasingly frustrated and aggressive throughout the 1940s, with the rise of a new generation of leaders in its youth movement. In the mid-1950s, the ANC approved its Freedom Charter, a sort of policy blueprint calling for a South Africa in which all races would be treated equally. This policy, while appealing to non-Africans and members of the South African Communist Party, splintered the opposition; subsequently, black-power supporters departed to found their own, much smaller organization, the Pan-Africanist Congress (PAC). There was, however, cooperation across these political lines, and when a 1960 PAC-organized campaign to protest the pass system ended in a massacre by police in Sharpville, the period of relying on peaceful protest ended. The ANC, like the PAC, was banned, and its leaders either were arrested or went into exile. The following year the ANC created its own military wing, Umkhonto we Sizwe.

While the ANC was in exile, sympathetic local groups took up the domestic fight against apartheid. The strongest of these were the unions and the civics. Union activism spiked in a series of strikes in 1973, and by 1985 thirty-three unions, with almost half a million members, came together in the formalized, membership-based Congress of South African Trade Unions. COSATU was long split between "workerists" (who focused on narrow economic issues) and "populists" (whose focus on community issues was seen by opponents as leaving unaddressed shop-floor issues). Despite the bifurcation, this union movement, like others around the world, eventually became deeply involved in community issues with the understanding that "it was impossible to separate struggles on the shopfloor from the wider struggle against apartheid" (Habib and Valodia 2006, 228). COSATU was simultaneously seen as a crucial ally and a potential challenge to the highly popular opposition ANC in exile, but within just a few years of its founding COSATU had adopted the ANC's Freedom Charter.

COSATU's relatively exclusive membership, based on regular workers, left large segments of the population, including the rural poor and unemployed, outside the organization. The more informal and inclusive civic movement was launched in 1979, first in Soweto and Port Elizabeth, as township dwellers demanded improved living conditions, and by the time of COSATU's birth the civics had established a presence in most urban townships. Civics were essentially residential associations set up as watchdog and mobilizing forces for local nonwhite communities. On the face of it, civics were overwhelmingly focused on specific grievances, but their leaders, many of whom were loyal to the banned ANC, also hoped to connect these struggles to much more general political and economic issues. Civic leaders all signed on to the belief that the formal, white-sanctioned local community councils (or local government structures) were illegitimate and should be purposely undermined. As crisis gripped the apartheid state in the mid-1980s many civics usurped various state functions of these councils, such as supervising pension payments, providing health care and sanitation services, assisting in dispute settlement, and even policing.

While there was initially a degree of aloofness between the unions and civics, the two organizations were in numerous ways complementary. The latter included many nonworkers who had been left out of COSATU and focused on local issues to create a national opposition that crossed ideological and class boundaries. They converted pleas for clothespins into demands for freedom. The organizations were closely linked in their tactics, including protests, work stay-aways, consumer boycotts, and non-payment campaigns, but also frequently in membership. During the day, union activists toiled for a white-run economy; late in the evening, and with the realization that shop-floor fights were inseparable from the wider antiapartheid struggle, many of these unionists returned to their townships to take part in the local civic organizations. Activists in both organizations were overwhelmingly loyal to the ANC and became the engine behind the party's calls to make the country ungovernable. Both civics and unions demonstrated to South Africans the ability of the masses to mobilize and press for change.

By the mid-1980s these organizations were formally allied in the United Democratic Front (and later the Mass Democratic Movement), an amalgam of groups opposed to the incumbent regime and allegiant to (though, in the case of the civics, not a direct signer of) the ANC's Freedom Charter. They were also joined by much smaller NGOs such as Black Sash and the End Conscription Campaign.

In South Africa, as in Poland, successive apartheid governments took a two-pronged approach to the significant opposition movement based in the unions and civics, alternating between brutality and symbolic concessions. A government crackdown following union and student unrest in the 1970s proved economically painful and only fueled the growth of the ANC's armed wing. By the end of that decade, a reformist faction of the governing National Party had come to power and was pursuing piecemeal reforms, including legalization of trade unions and relaxation of pass laws, that might appease urban blacks. Instead, the reforms strengthened the opposition's urban support base, which coordinated a boycott of the 1983 tricameral parliament and launched a rebellion through the mid- and late 1980s that led to the detentions of approximately fifty thousand people and the deaths of five thousand (MacKinnon 2004, 253; Taylor 2002, 69; Glaser 2001, 171; Eades 1999, 80–81). Still, although many organizations, especially the civics, were crippled by the national state of emergency in the mid-1980s, COSATU was able to use its central position in production to escape state crackdowns.

By working to withhold state legitimacy in areas they controlled (including most townships), civics and unions frustrated national policymaking, brought about increased international diplomatic and economic pressure, and prompted various domestic white groups, from the clergy and media to businesses, to seek their own way out of crisis. Mass mobilization ultimately forced the government to recognize that apartheid was unsustainable. By mid-1990, President F. W. de Klerk had released ANC president Nelson Mandela and promised to negotiate a new constitution. The ANC, in turn, ended its armed struggle and, to the consternation of many unionists, sought compromise by backing down from its historically socialist program. Despite this, the popular movement continued to use strikes, boycotts, work stay-aways, and occupations involving millions of workers to shape the outcome of the negotiations. The country's first free elections occurred in 1994, when the ANC bounded to power, carrying 63 percent of the vote, and made Nelson Mandela South Africa's first nonwhite president.

During the 1994 elections the ANC could not ignore the political might of the unions and civics. COSATU numbered nearly a million and a half members, and the civics, which had begun to rebound in both 1989 and 1992, came together in an awkward unitary structure known as the South African National Civics Organization (SANCO), whose members numbered six million. Both organizations had demonstrated their ability to contest a highly repressive regime for decades, and both organizations carried enormous emotive value in society, where their names were nearly synonymous with the liberation struggle. COSATU was made a formal partner in the ANC-dominated governing Tripartite Alliance, and SANCO, having historically disavowed politics and claimed to be a nonpartisan, mass-based watchdog organization, became a junior one.

It is little surprise that South African activists had such high hopes for their state-bound comrades. From both an identity and a network perspective, the belief that their ex-colleagues would remain true to the movement, as well as the personal connections forged during a struggle that had lasted decades, was not much of a gamble. Those who won ANC positions on the backs of the unions and civics were hardened leaders from the struggle, long sympathetic to—and often members of—the ANC. It seemed, however, that they were first and foremost leaders of colossal organizations that they had helped build and navigate through decades of oppression, during which many ANC leaders had essentially stood on the sidelines. Despite their close formal and informal relationships to the new state, both union and civic leaders claim to have suffered, not profited, since the democratization process began.

COSATU's Rise to Power

With democratic breakthrough in 1994, activists in COSATU and its affiliates celebrated the exodus of about eighty high-level officials to parliament and various ministries. Apart from its parliamentarians, some of whom took key leadership positions in the legislature, COSATU saw a handful of its top officials, including its general secretary since inception, Jay Naidoo, and the former general secretary of the first trade union federation, Alexander (Alec) Erwin, take ministerial jobs. Other government officials who were not formally unionists, including Finance Minister Trevor Manuel, were major United Democratic Front (UDF) players who, one former union leader explained with respect to Manuel, had "always come out of the same school as the people who run our union" (Copelyn 2008). Unionists and close associates who had helped topple the former system were poised to make their mark on the new one, and COSATU promised to "do all in our power" to support the new government's economic program, known as the Reconstruction and Development Program (RDP) (BBC 1994).

At least for parliamentarians, as Copelyn mentioned earlier, the move was sobering since ANC leaders quickly made it clear that the unionists' role in parliament was to support the party. Regardless of their pedigree, parliamentarians on the ANC ticket were government backbenchers with "nothing to say about anything" (Copelyn 2008). As COSATU parliamentarians explained to their comrades outside power, "when in parliament I'm accountable to the ANC" (Rustin 2008). Most unionist parliamentarians acknowledged that the most they could do in support of the union agenda was to occasionally raise unionist positions in committee or party meetings: "When that matter is on the table, we fight and fight. Then the majority wins. All of us become religious and preach that decision" (Godongwana 2008). Those who remained behind had an even more pessimistic view: "Once they go in there, they will not speak for us. They will speak generally as an ANC person," COSATU's deputy general secretary said of policy debates (Ntshalintshali 2008).

For their part, COSATU leaders on the outside were initially weakened by the (common) fact that many of their top colleagues had left for the state, an exodus that initially led to at least mild skill deficits in everything from operations to negotiations. They were also hamstrung by the sudden disappearance of many experts who during the struggle had provided advice for free. The combination, as the director of COSATU's in-house think tank commented, meant that before that unit was set up in the late 1990s the organization had difficulty responding "in a more proactive manner to issues" (Dicks 2008).

However, COSATU's leaders, having expected their ex-colleagues to stand up for them as a result of personal and interpersonal loyalties, also simply appear to have been unprepared to actively shape this relationship. As one former COSATU national leader said, "Surely people would vote for those [ideals] they had known during the struggle from the union movement" (Ehrenreich 2008). In retrospect, said another, this assumption was shortsighted. "We said, 'You have to take the interest of workers into account.' What the bloody hell does that mean?" (Dicks 2008). No formal checks were placed on these leaders (Banda 2008). Instead, said one parliamentarian who had headed the National Union of Metalworkers of South Africa (NUMSA), "COSATU said 'Go, you know what you have to do'" (Mayekiso 2008). Rather than press their old colleagues to stand up for them, COSATU's leaders tried to directly influence the party, which many from the get-go suspected might abandon the workers' cause.

COSATU's leaders also hoped that they could cement their position in the new state through two mechanisms. First, they became key participants in a neocorporatist bargaining forum known as the National Economic Development and Labor Council (NEDLAC), created in 1995 as a forum through which the state would meet with representatives of labor, business, and the community. Even more important, CO-SATU (along with the South African Communist Party) became a full member of the ANC's governing alliance.

This strategy showed its weaknesses from the start, as evidenced by COSATU's loss of the RDP program. The RDP, an extraordinarily ambitious economic program, was initially designed by COSATU's leaders and subsequently negotiated into an ANC policy program before the 1994 elections. It was, in the words of one civic activist, a form of "welfarism based on kick-starting development and meeting the people's basic needs" (Dor 2008). In the words of a historian, it was a "populist manifesto" (Lodge 1994, 32). Regardless of what COSATU intended it to be, the ANC altered the program to give it a neoliberal bent, which made it more palatable to outside investors and lenders and rendered it less of a budgetary burden. COSATU's leaders grimaced at the slimmed-down RDP budget released in 1994, characterizing it as a "holding budget" and demanding that the next one "reflect a more definite RDP-orientation" (Chiledi 1994). In addition, they issued a warning: "We have sacrificed our leaders to the ANC and it is time to repay that debt" (AFP 1994).

For those now ensconced in their new policymaking institutions, this was no longer the debt that concerned them. Although in 1994 CO-SATU demanded that the new government allow one-time "extraordinary" spending to boost state services, the ANC's leaders had pledged to international backers, including the IMF, that they would not allow the budget deficit to exceed 6 percent of GDP (Fine 1994). COSATU's long-time general secretary, Jay Naidoo, who had become the minister responsible for the RDP's implementation after 1994, found he could no longer pick up his COSATU ax. "I am not representing COSATU when I am in government," Naidoo said, adding that he and others were left accountable to the ANC alone (Mahlatsane 2008; Majadibodu 2008; Naidoo 2008). "I must abide with the [ANC] majority decision," concurred a longtime unionist who also took on senior regional and national posts (Godongwana 2008).

If RDP implementation was disappointing, so was NEDLAC. According to NEDLAC's first executive director (1995–1998), state leaders quickly began to "get more confident and want to do more on their own" (Naidoo 2008). Going against the spirit of the council, President Thabo Mbeki frequently refused to seriously discuss many broad (especially fiscal) policies at this level and either bypassed the council entirely or rushed the deliberations so that COSATU had too little time to poll its affiliates for their views on particular issues (Masemula 2008; Ronnie 2008; Unionist5 2008; Ensor 1998). Often, a subsequent NEDLAC executive director added, the forum was site of tense negotiations between former comrades who had clearly followed different paths (Mkhize 2008).

The willingness of ANC leaders to disregard NEDLAC and its labor allies became abundantly clear when the government in March 1996 launched its new macroeconomic Growth, Employment, and Redistribution (GEAR) program. Designed to attract foreign investment and subsequently increase GDP and job growth, GEAR scuttled COSATU's own RDP and led to the appointment of COSATU's former RDP director as, ironically, the minister responsible for privatizing South Africa's telecom industry. In his place, two union-backed leaders, Alec Erwin and Trevor Manuel, took the country's economic helm. Despite this, GEAR—derisively referred to within union circles as the ANC's 1996 "class project"—amounted to a profound realignment of the economy from heavy state involvement to neoliberalism. Manuel, once known for his revolutionary calls and Che Guevara T-shirts, shocked labor leaders by tearing down trade barriers at an even greater rate than international treaties obliged and by threatening the workers he had once championed. The institutionally based schism could not have been more graphic.

GEAR marked a transition from relative patience on the part of workers to a period of marked labor unrest. Interestingly, and as in Poland, it was less the policies than the unilateral method of policy adoption and implementation that set the stage for confrontation between former allies. According to NEDLAC's then head, Manuel came to each of NEDLAC's constituent partners individually, and "he said it is not negotiable, and then he stuck to that" (Naidoo 2008). Press reports from the time confirm that Manuel, realizing the difficulties in pushing GEAR on "all of our colleagues" lower down, promised to keep "a firm hand on the tiller" (AFP 1996). Not only did Manuel make the GEAR program out to be a patriotic duty, but, according to one member of NEDLAC's union delegation and thanks in part to his unionist credentials, "he sold the thing so well" (Mkhize 2008). Only months later did unionists realize what a disaster GEAR was at the workplace level and openly reject it. "Basically, it looked like a model, it talked like a model, [and] walked like a model, but it is a duck. So it was really a big load of crap," Naidoo said (Naidoo 2008).

That summer COSATU's leaders openly spoke out against the program and maintained that "there is no way the government will succeed in simply pushing its framework down our throats" (Hirschler 1996). Unionists "took to the streets" in resentment, relying on the contentious methods they knew best (Mahlatsane 2008; Mkhize 2008). COSATU had employed these methods on occasion even before GEAR, threatening strikes over a host of issues, from a major labor bill to privatization, but contestation had now gone from being the exception to the rule (Mosunkutu 2008; BBC 1995a, 1995b). With a renewed unionist militancy, the initial period of " 'Look, let's give the government a chance' " (Rustin 2008) was now over (MacKinnon 2004, 284). As in Poland, it had lasted less than two years.

COSATU's Return to Opposition

Unionists in the state responded to COSATU's cries of treason by saying that they were now obliged to "take care of many constituencies" (Essop 2008). Contradictions between unionists and broader society were inevitable, one former minister said, adding that as a government official he would "not hesitate to act in the interest of society where it is necessary" (Naidoo 2008). Beyond the question of constituencies lay the issue of pragmatism. Naidoo, who resented his RDP office's closing as "completely undemocratic," acknowledged that the GEAR program in fact addressed the "fundamental challenges we faced in a very fragile international environment." If South Africa was to secure foreign investment and a share of foreign markets, new government leaders decided, it could not follow the course championed by social movements on the outside.

Those remaining in the unions felt that such attitudes could only be the result of the brainwashing of their ex-colleagues by Western neoliberal institutions, which provided them with training abroad. According to COSATU's deputy general secretary, "People were overwhelmed and swallowed into a new thinking" (Ntshalintshali 2008). This meant no one to stand up for the unions in the state. Although some of the unionists left the state to pursue private business, as did Naidoo and Copelyn, practically none left in protest or on principle. Asked whether as a unionist MP he had ever opposed measures based on ideological grounds that took root during his time in the union movement, Copelyn responded, "Nope, it never crossed my mind" (Copelyn 2008). From the trenches, this conversion was dramatic. "Some of them became ultraconservative," said a COSATU representative. "Some of them tried very hard to forget their bloody roots" (Dicks 2008).

At first, COSATU's leaders (like Solidarity's heads) chalked their failures up to a generational shift, where that microcohort of unionists "who saw themselves as part of the liberation movement" left to take jobs with the state in 1994 and those "who saw themselves first and foremost as union members" created a more activist union (Unionist5 2008). As the years rolled by and new elections came and went, COSATU found that the majority in each successive group of these ostensibly harder-core activists that went to the state also conformed to the governing ANC's program. Most commonly, unionists believed that their ex-colleagues had betrayed their former friends and ideals in order to maintain both the ANC's good graces and the high pensions and prestige that accompanied their new state positions (Banda 2008; Majadibodu 2008; Makwayiba 2008; Ronnie 2008; Unionist5 2008).

The greatest benefit from the transfer of organization leaders to the state has been access to high-ranking state leaders, something most helpful with respect to those substantive issues "not in contradiction with the party line," one union leader explained (Mahlatsane 2008).[1] In cases of greater conflict, unionists might still expect low-level victories with no bearing on broader policy direction. "We might get one or two small concessions of a tactical nature, but [with respect to] the strategic orientation, things are going to stay pretty much the same," said Ronnie (Ronnie 2008). Beyond that, ex-unionists in the state can in the best of circumstances be counted on to do little more than express sympathy. More typically, they warily explain to one-time comrades that "the responsibilities of government means [sic] that we've got to take some additional steps. We can't just implement the views that we had in the unions'" (Ehrenreich 2008). After years of witnessing this, one provincial union leader realized that "it basically means that we are on our own" (Unionist6 2008). Another unionist, interviewed on his way to a Cape Town protest against rising food and energy prices, drew a similar conclusion: "You kind of get demoralized and think, 'Okay, the best thing is to continue waging struggles on the streets'—like we're doing today" (Masemula 2008).

Former COSATU officials and friends in the state came to resent COSATU's aggressive stance. One of COSATU's hardest-hitting actions, its two-day general strike against privatization in August 2001, led to harsh counterattacks from the government and ANC. Known as the 2001 ANC "briefing notes," the party condemned unionists as "counterrevolutionaries" in a document that amounted, according to one COSATU representative, to "the peak of tensions within the Alliance" (Coleman 2008). One concluded from this and other episodes that, although many ANC leaders behaved like trade unionists during the struggle, after taking power "the age of militancy, the age of serious robust engagement were lost on them" (Majadibodu 2008). COSATU's Ehrenreich recalled meeting with Minister of Trade and Industry Alec Erwin after these strikes: "Alec said, 'Look, you've thrown your worst at us. You've gone on national strike, and this is really your key weapon. And we're unaffected by it here in government. We're just going to go ahead with our program'" (Ehrenreich 2008). Ehrenreich continued, "People were pissed at him! That he's so bold that he could say that."

This bold attitude seemed to emerge from frustration felt by ex-unionists in the state upon realizing that their former colleagues did not understand the realities they were facing. For these actors, long-held identities had not been cast aside but were instead shaped by the new constraints they encountered. "It's not necessarily an ideological shift. It's an exposure to the reality of how the system functions," said one provincial minister. "Other than [Venezuelan president Hugo] Chávez, everyone—when he goes into government—understands the realities," explained another labor leader who was a major government critic before accepting regional and then national ministerial positions (Godongwana 2008). As another regional minister put it, referring to a dance from the struggle in which participants waved an imaginary machine gun, "I might not be Toy-Toying in the streets or marching with COSATU comrades, but what you do when you have power is to actually look at how you implement those things that you fought for" (Essop 2008).

In this transformed context, personal experiences with and knowledge of their ex-comrades could actually hurt the unions. COSATU's longtime parliamentary coordinator claimed that, although he could recognize no strong trend, his organization found that "some of the problematic people from our point of view had a history in the trade union movement" (Coleman 2008). In fact, according to others, it was precisely those who came from the unions who turned hardest against them in order to prove their own loyalty to the ANC leadership and compete for positions there. "To get political deployment they must be seen to be dealing ruthlessly with the [COSATU] federation," said one unionist (Wayile 2008). "Some people that we trusted would defend COSATU . . . [and] our working-class views in the government . . . began to attack CO-SATU," added another (Majadibodu 2008). As a result, current union leaders say, their former colleagues sometimes reacted to requests for assistance with antagonism (Makwayiba 2008).

Respondents who have achieved more senior state positions in which they have felt compelled to moderate their stances experienced the greatest personal conflicts resulting from previous relationships. "You're selling out, you sold out there," the head of NEDLAC has been told by "really mad" union friends (Mkhize 2008). One respondent discussed an incident in which his former union colleagues marched around town carrying a symbolic coffin containing the "leftist spirit of Trevor" Manuel. The architect of South Africa's neoliberal policies was, the respondent said, "too upset for words" (Copelyn 2008). Another former unionist and provincial government minister recalled that the attacks from those she personally knew were particularly vicious (Essop 2008). "[If] you talk privatization, you're a sellout. [If] you use the word *GEAR*, you're a sellout. [If] you talk about tight deficit control, you're a sellout," Tasneem Essop, former provincial minister of environment, planning and economic development in the Western Cape, said of her relationship with former colleagues from COSATU. "I'll tell you that the relationship in the province with COSATU has been just purely antagonistic. I don't want to say COSATU. [It was] really an individual." Illustrating how this dilemma can have broader consequences, Essop went on, "Eventually I reached a point where I saw COSATU letterhead come into my office, and I would tell them 'Please, I don't want this'" (Essop 2008).

Despite these obvious tensions and much talk of withdrawing from the ANC, COSATU has maintained its place in the ANC-led governing Alliance for several reasons. First, the emotional strength of the liberation movement continues to be connected to the "ANC brand" (Ntshalint- shali 2008), making it simpler to explain away policy failure as an issue of capacity rather than direction or of individuals rather than governments (Madisha 2008; Ntshalintshali 2008; Sambatha 2008). Those who go against the ANC, said one unionist, run the risk of being labeled "coun- terrevolutionaries" (Madisha 2008; Wayile 2008). Moreover, COSATU and the ANC share much of the same constituency, and most COSATU members prefer to remain in the Alliance. Despite having two million members a decade after the fall of apartheid, COSATU has an extraor- dinarily high membership overlap with the ANC (80 percent), leaving COSATU's leaders with the feeling that they have no choice but to re- main in Alliance structures (Coleman 2008; Masemula 2008; Ballard, Habib, and Valodia 2006, 15; Habib and Valodia 2006; Habib 2005, 49; Torres 2005, 68). "There is a sober realism," said one policy analyst within COSATU, "that the best chance we have of struggling for social democ- racy is being within the ANC" (Ndungu 2008).

COSATU's experience since democratization has been one of rela- tive weakness. The organization has managed to stay active in politics but has failed to win in the large policy arena, even with colleagues in power. COSATU's leaders acknowledge that they remain in "an abusive relationship" with the ANC a decade and a half after changes began (Ntshalintshali 2008). Having headed the struggle that brought the ANC to power, they believe that they have no choice but to continue along the same path. As one unionist concluded, "The ANC remains the movement that brought freedom in the minds of many. I think COSATU would be foolhardy even to contemplate [splitting from the ANC]" (Ndungu 2008). COSATU has therefore continued to support the ANC in every election since 1994, while marching against it in the interim (McKinley 2001, 199).

SANCO's Fall from Grace

Whereas COSATU was established as a federation to bring various antiapartheid unions together during the peak of the struggle, the civics were a series of independent organizations with no coordinating body until the period of liberalization in the early 1990s. The process of consolidation was gradual, though not smooth, beginning with a federation of fifteen regional civics that emerged in 1990 and then SANCO's launch in 1992. SANCO was initially formed as a unitary structure to convert the country's various civic organizations into an efficient pressure group in support of the ANC agenda. In the process, the relative homogeneity of neighborhood organizations gave way to a much more heterogeneous association in terms of everything from racial composition and demographic layout to level of militancy.

For the civics, which had historically focused on local community issues, the idea of creating a top-down unitary structure initially encountered some resistance since it seemed to run counter to the very local, bread-and-butter issues that they long fought for. For those organizations that did join—as many as 4,300—the organization they entered was characterized by paradoxes. For one, SANCO promised to be an organization of equals, yet it placed the civics under a hierarchical structure (Zuern 2006, 182). Unlike unions, which could continue to represent workers' interests against capital, the civics were far more heterogeneous, including different classes, ideologies, and community concerns, which made local, and especially national, representation tricky. Some regional federations, including the Southern Transvaal, rejected this centralized organizational structure immediately, while others feared that too loose a structure could allow the still-governing white National Party to employ easy divide-and-rule tactics.

Another problem was that SANCO came into being at a time when civic leaders, many of whom simultaneously viewed themselves as loyal members of the ANC, whose banishment had recently been lifted, wondered what the future role of their organization would be. Many civic leaders felt the role of the organization was over as soon as the ANC came to formally represent the community in newly legitimized local and national institutions, but others—including many who went on to the state—claimed that the civics maintained a special representative function.

In the end, the majority of civics did come into the SANCO fold, and the ANC was left with little choice but to incorporate the organization, which represented six million and had proved its mobilization capacity, as a junior partner in the ANC-led Alliance. As one provincial minister and former civic leader bluntly recalled, "The debate was, do you want someone inside your tent pissing outside or someone outside pissing inside? The idea was to keep them in the tent with you" (Hlongwa 2008). Like COSATU, SANCO saw many of its leaders depart in 1994 to take various state jobs at the provincial and national levels and a year later, still others moved to municipal posts. By one count, as many as 70 percent of SANCO's leaders began working for the state in 1994 and were followed by even more in 1995 (Lodge 2003, 207). Unlike COSATU, the remaining SANCO leaders were left with two critical questions to answer: Who would continue to guide the organization, and, even more important, how would SANCO's mission change after democratic breakthrough?

One way to deal with the leadership exodus in such a loosely structured grassroots organization was to allow those who moved on to the state to maintain their civic leadership positions. With an already existing, widely acknowledged overlap between the ANC and civics, a wave of civic leaders began moving into ANC positions when the party, in need of grassroots organizational experience, had its banishment lifted in 1990. "The civic and the ANC branch were actually almost one," said the leader of one civic in a generally less pro-ANC area (Doidge 2008). Thus, between 1990 and the run-up to the 1994 elections, some civics were simply collapsed into ANC structures (Hlongwa 2008; Mogase 2008; Sonto 2008). With formal democratization in 1994, SANCO adopted a policy forcing those moving to government to leave their SANCO office but in practice abandoned this policy in mid-1996 in the face of this leadership crisis.

The "two-hat" policy (in which SANCO's leaders served simultaneously in the organization and state) complicated the profound philosophical and even existential transformation being debated within SANCO. As noted earlier, many civic leaders, especially those who simultaneously viewed themselves as loyal members of the recently unbanned ANC, questioned whether their organization had any future role at all. Rather than concede that the civics were superfluous, in 1994 organization officials adopted the catchy slogan "from resistance to reconstruction," though they failed to clearly conceptualize what this phrase actually meant in practice (Williams 2008). The answer might have been confusing, but the question hanging over SANCO was clear: Should it continue to oppose the state, as it had historically done, or begin to partner with it? With so many leaders transitioning into provincial and national structures, there developed a somewhat muddied consensus that SANCO should be something akin to a loyal watchdog, sympathetic to, but willing to check, governing elites.

These leadership and mission choices were intended to create a more influential organization that would enjoy a comparative advantage over other civil-society organizations. "If we are to be a barking watchdog, we should be represented in the corridors of power," recalled a SANCO parliamentarian. Deploying civic representatives "everywhere in the ANC structures," the argument went, would give SANCO a chance to shape debates and policies from within (Sonto 2008). "Why do you want to bark from the outside instead of getting in there and making things happen?" Moses Mayekiso, SANCO's general secretary and simultaneously head of a large union, recalled the spirit of debate. "Go in there and make it happen" (Mngomezulu 2008). From this perspective, SANCO's new role was to delicately push the ANC, and its own ex-colleagues, to fulfill community expectations.

Like their COSATU counterparts, SANCO's officials recalled being sent off to the government with much fanfare. In response to a memo to lower-ranking SANCO leaders asking whether he should go into parliament, one SANCO parliamentarian said the response was overwhelmingly positive. "The majority of them said, 'Who on earth do you think is going to be doing what we've been doing all along? Go in there and do your job!'" Such parliamentarians remain confident that they did this satisfactorily by voicing SANCO's demands, or at least its sentiments, in policy debates: "We brought to bear in those discussions very important perspectives from our experience as civic leaders" (Tsenoli 2008). Others who went into the state felt the same way, claiming to have represented their organization with zeal even when other ANC leaders condemned the civics for excessive watchdogging. "I would challenge the ANC and say, 'If you say these [civic] people are troublemakers, let's discuss that and look at the facts,'" said one (Sonto 2008). Yet these leaders also admit that in their new institutions they were forced to answer to a broader constituency than just the civics since "there are certain formalities in government that require you to operate in a certain manner. You have to operate across interests" (Tsenoli 2008).

Among these interests were those of the party, meaning that SANCO leaders, just like their COSATU counterparts, were forced into policy adjustments based on new institutional incentives. "Because SANCO was my organization, I would agree with them," explained one municipal councilor and former SANCO officer. "But then agreeing with them didn't mean I must go in there and fight on their ticket. I had to toe the line of the African National Congress" (Leader 2008). "Once in, we are not accounting to COSATU or SANCO. We account to the ANC structures," said another longtime municipal councilor and national SANCO officer. "The ANC will act against us if we are doing it not according to what the movement wants" (Mali 2008).

Institutions did not just create formal obstacles to cooperation between one-time activists. They also erected informal ones that resulted from a new flow of information that put policies into a new perspective and left ex-civic activists in the state feeling torn by their new institutions. Thus, on the one hand, these new state leaders consistently claim to have brought their civic identity with them into their new positions. "What I brought in was some of the demands, some of the interests that I knew people would like to see in the legislation that would emerge," said one SANCO MP (Tsenoli 2008). On the other hand, new constraints created less-than-ideal policy output. One official who returned to direct SANCO after a several-year break used his own interim job as deputy municipal manager (1997–2003) to illustrate this dilemma (Mngomezulu 2008). When confronted with budgetary limitations, the official said, he was forced to go back to his communities with bad news. "You sit there and say, 'Well, possibly I need to go back and convince people I've been working with in the communities,'" he said. "You go back and speak that language, and people are beginning to doubt that you take their interests into account."

The situation sometimes turned ugly. For instance, after trying unsuccessfully to convince local residents they had to pay more for trash collection, a basic service that was at the heart of civics' demands, this official began a legal process that led to court summonses and the forced removal of nonpayers' assets. "It sparked war," he said, recalling how a local ANC councilor's home was ransacked by an angry mob in the community. "You're put into a very precarious situation." This relationship prompted this official to leave SANCO in 2000 (before returning after his municipal job ended). "When you get on the other side," he concluded, "you do realize, 'Damn, things are not as easy as when you look at them from the other end!'"

Not surprisingly, those civic activists who hoped that after 1994 "government would maintain some of its roots and its labor orientation" state that they were just as disappointed as their union counterparts (Dor 2008). They also used nearly identical language to describe the scenario. "They got swallowed up by the system," said one (Dor 2008). Another social-movement leader active in the apartheid-era struggle agreed that many who have moved on to the state have lost their identity with the struggle-era organization: "When I meet with them, I always try to remind them, 'Look, where are you?'" (Cassiem 2008). In addition, as civic leaders assigned precedence to their ANC roles, SANCO at certain levels began having trouble engaging in the watchdog activities it had assigned the organization. As one former SANCO official said, "That sense of being able to debate the issues started to disappear" (Dor 2008).

The dilemmas were exacerbated by the fact that those who moved on to the state generally did so with the understanding that their former colleagues would support them and be understanding of the new situation their longtime friends would face. From this perspective, opposition was anathema to the goals of both groups. As one former civic organizer in Soweto explained, contrasting pre- and postapartheid periods, "If our civics were purely based on protesting illegitimate policies, now we are setting democratic policies in place, so are you going to be in opposition to yourself?" (Hlongwa 2008). Yet this is precisely what happened, say those ex-civic members in the state who recall frequently encountering local civic opposition to the ANC policies that they felt compelled—by party discipline—to support (Councilor2 2008).

Thus, those remaining in the trenches were from the start left wondering how best to mix support and opposition functions. According to some activists from the time, the opaque nature of the civics' relationship to the ANC (especially its designation as a junior Alliance partner), coupled with a lack of direction from the top, made the watchdog function difficult to fulfill after the national liberation in 1994 and, even more so, the local one in 1995 (when the first free local elections were held). "The role of watchdog was not defined. What are you watching for and how do you do that?" asked one civic activist (Councilor3 2008).

Understandings of this role were fundamentally shaped by the new institutional divide. Some civic leaders who had transitioned to the state interpreted the watchdog role as based less on contentious action and more along the lines of a trip wire. According to this model, the civics would serve as another set of eyes on the local community, letting the ANC government know what services were being insufficiently provided. The civics were not there to shove against deliberate ANC actions but to nudge in the occurrence of inadvertent ANC omissions. As one municipal councilor and former civic activist summarized it, "Some SANCO people, like me, were going in and did not want to be watched" (Ngwane 2008). By contrast, many activists outside the state opted for a more aggressive approach to both delineate themselves from the authorities and defend their local citizens' interests. Often these activists were simultaneously ANC members who noted that, although they supported the ANC, they were not synonymous with it and subsequently demanded an independent civic movement that would not melt away. "Some of the members, they are not members of the ANC. They are just residents concerned about services," said one (Ngwedzeni 2008).

SANCO was left with a difficult balancing act, made even more complicated by its two-hat policy. Ex-civic leaders in the state frequently came to believe that they were the organization's true representatives, leaving SANCO redundant, and that they and their colleagues were automatically "fighting for the same thing" (Councilor2 2008). With "the same leaders on both sides," these actors said, civics "no longer had a role to play" (Doidge 2008). With the institutional capacity to act, ex-civic leaders in the state felt they embodied the organization. "I knew the issues of [my constituency] New Brighton just as well as anyone who represented the civic there," commented one former civic activist who accepted a local councilor position on the ANC ticket. "I knew the quality of infrastructure, I knew the areas with no running water, etc." (Goduka 2008). Within only a few years, said another former senior civic activist who had become an ANC parliamentarian, it was the ANC that represented the streets and community (Mosunkutu 2008).

Those activists who were leading the civics at national and local levels complained that this attitude was stifling, all the more so since many entrenched in this mindset were actually in charge of organizational branches. Even as the ANC came to formally represent the community in newly legitimized local and national institutions, activists said, the civics maintained a uniquely grassroots representative function. Those who maintained their positions in the civics actively fought to demonstrate their continued relevance. The watchdog function was crucial from this perspective. For instance, when one local council ordered that a thousand shacks on municipal property be destroyed for safety reasons, SANCO's leaders attacked authorities for failing to resolve the housing crisis and accused them of "dishing out worse treatment than apartheid-era councilors" (Eveleth 1997). With such outbursts, SANCO posed a threat to the legitimacy of the ANC and the party's own belief that it was the true representative of the people.

The ANC aggressively fought this threat through two mechanisms. The first involved usurping civic community functions and placing them in the hands of the state. Increased executive (mayoral) powers in 2000 pushed the civics out of their place in what one called the "collective leadership" at the local level—formal and informal structures that gave SANCO input into policy (Councilor 2008). That year the ANC also established ward committees, in which communities would appoint someone to consult with their councilor, a mechanism that allowed various groups—representing youth, women, businesses, and others—to maintain close contact with their ANC representative. "Where is the civic going to come in now and say these people have not been consulted? There is not a gap here for them to play any role," said an ANC councilor who emerged from the civic movement (Goduka 2008). Whoever wanted to play by the rules of the new game, it seemed, had to join the ANC's team.

The second mechanism amounted to a form of cooptation. The ANC offered political positions and slots on its election tickets in exchange for civic subservience. In a country where unemployment has unofficially hovered around 40 percent (and officially at about 25 percent), this policy severely tested the value of activism. Interviewees across the spectrum felt that SANCO over time had become a tool to pursue political positions, and many people acknowledged that one of SANCO's allures was the prospect, at least in the long run, of material betterment. "There's a perception that people have come into SANCO and gotten rich," said one SANCO official (Williams 2008). "We went into power from a background of poverty," another explained. "Your status has changed dramatically since you've become a councilor . . . Then the state becomes a struggle for resources because people are saying that's how you access resources, by getting to the state. . . . People were beginning to see the virtues of government" (Godongwana 2008). Given South Africa's dire economic state and that of SANCO itself, this phenomenon has been difficult to curtail.

SANCO's financial woes began in 1994, when those activists who were accustomed to receiving aid "from all over the world" saw their donor funding redirected to support the new government's Reconstruction and Development Program (Mtanga 2008). SANCO also found it difficult to get government funding since such resources went through local ward committees, where SANCO was just one of many groups requesting cash. Membership drives proved fruitless, and the occasional government contracts that did come in remained at the local rather than the provincial or national level. SANCO was so strapped for cash that it sometimes lacked the resources even to hold meetings to hear what its community members had to say.

The answer, according to SANCO's then secretary general, Moses Mayekiso, was SANCO Investment Holdings (SIH). Formed by Mayekiso in the mid-1990s, the idea behind SIH was to develop an internal income source that would get the civics directly involved in local projects, such as health and education. Some claimed that SANCO's own investment projects were less about strengthening the organization than about lining the leaders' pockets (Dor 2008). Money and the question of who was profiting from SANCO's investment arm played a key role in intraorganizational conflict. Within just a few years SANCO's investment arm had mysteriously failed, and many people were left wondering where the profits had gone. One longtime SANCO official said that SIH "created more problems than it did solutions" (Williams 2008). Getting in bed with the ANC was frequently seen as the only viable ticket out of the country's and the organization's poverty.

The ANC's efforts to invade SANCO's terrain and poach its leaders produced a schizophrenic organization, which spent the years after 1994 alternating between protesting ANC policies and backing the ANC against similar actions staged by other organizations. This dynamic was vivid in the context of the massive antiprivatization unrest that peaked less than a decade after democratic breakthrough. In 2001 SANCO's leaders stood by COSATU in its two-day stay-away to protest government sell-offs of state assets, during which time the organization's president made it clear that SANCO would not fold and that civic constituents would even be encouraged to boycott payments to state companies if the privatization process continued (AN 2001; BBC 2001). It was in this context that SANCO drafted a policy document that explained various potential directions for the civic movement, including one option that transformed the purportedly loyal civics into a "revolutionary social movement" (Williams 2008).

These assertive policies were enough to get the ANC's attention and convince its leaders to press for a closer relationship with SANCO. One year later the fruits of this policy were on display as SANCO suddenly did an about-face from its long-held position by opposing renewed antiprivatization strikes by COSATU, ostensibly because of its concerns that COSATU was more interested in threatening the ANC's leadership in the governing alliance (Zuern 2006). In reality, the decision appears to have been a strategic calculation by SANCO leaders that they had more to gain by cooperating with the ANC than working against it. In return for its decision, SANCO was brought closer into the ANC fold and received promises from President Mbeki of a more prominent position in the Alliance and the designation of two high-level ANC leaders—Minister of Public Enterprises Jeff Radebe and Deputy Minister of Minerals and Energy Susan Shabangu—to leadership positions in SANCO.

These contacts proved priceless to SANCO as it showcased its new role in the sprawling and politically valuable Soweto township, where tens of thousands of people were threatened with electricity cutoffs from the state-owned electric company, Escom. When Escom, with R1 billion (approximately US[2011]$1,238,000) in unpaid electric bills, began cutting off services to delinquent customers, SANCO and other organizations threatened mass action. However, with new allies in the political sphere, SANCO over the next year functioned more as an intermediary between state and society than as a contentious social movement. Its leaders soon victoriously announced that Escom would write off R1.4 billion in arrears and that the flow of electricity would continue (AN 2003). One SANCO official credited the organization's name recognition and personal contacts to Radebe, who had been instrumental in brokering this deal. "If we didn't have that type of network, it would have been very difficult" (Williams 2008).

The apparent success of personal networks, however, was an aberration. In this case, it was not longtime SANCO activists who went to the state and behaved as former associates would have expected. Instead, it was a case of the ANC doing a favor for an organization whose logo it hoped to have during the next elections. Moreover, one SANCO official discussing this incident added, this positive impact of networks was really more the exception than the rule (Williams 2008). According to national parliamentarians from the civic movement, SANCO contacts have not generally provided influence in and of themselves but rather given the organization access to knowledge about how one might influence the system via institutional means (Mogase 2008; Tsenoli 2008). Having colleagues in power "didn't help SANCO," another former SANCO official plainly put it (Jack 2008).

Instead, the institutional divide created cleavages among one-time partners as those leaving for the state turned away from civic demands. From the beginning, said one regional SANCO leader and longtime civic activist, "We were fighting with our own comrades. That was the dilemma we found ourselves in" (Mtanga 2008). Those who were once critical of the state in the name of democracy or in their own fight for legitimacy sometimes turned against the civics, perhaps in a defensive move, upon reaching power (Tsenoli 2008). This feeling that the ANC was watching over those transitioning to the state ensured a continuity of this conflict (Councilor2 2008). However, SANCO also became internally conflicted as those closer to the top of the organization, tempted by government favors, faced their own incentives, which were divorced from the rest of the organization. Former civic activists claim that, as a result, SANCO's head office often executes decisions made by the ANC. They are, said another social-movement leader, "policy promoters" (Cassiem 2008). "SANCO became redundant . . . [Its] agenda became the government agenda," said SANCO's former general secretary, who had himself gone into politics (Mayekiso 2008).

The Escom and privatization examples demonstrate that SANCO's leaders had become pawns in a much larger political game, in which favors were exchanged as quid pro quos. From the ANC's perspective, SANCO served as a counterbalance to COSATU, which had proved to be a difficult Alliance partner. SANCO's leaders could earn points from the ANC by attacking the labor organization for its antirevolutionary stance and by lending the party a logo that continues to elicit positive associations and legitimacy. "It is an important name, and it is respected by the Alliance," said SANCO's former president (Mayekiso 2008). At least one hopeful SANCO official argued that this name recognition still has real meaning. "SANCO may not be able to mobilize people, maybe because of resources, maybe because of untrusting leadership," he said. "But I guarantee you if SANCO says, 'Do not vote for,' you will get media coverage, you will have people saying this" (Williams 2008).

SANCO's leaders were a cheap alternative to COSATU in terms of acquiring at least the appearance of grassroots legitimacy. For while COSATU demanded policy changes (albeit in vain) in return for its support, SANCO was actually thriving on the legitimacy that its ANC counterparts heaped back on them. For example, by serving as the primary community representative in NEDLAC, SANCO's leaders could continue to claim the title of grassroots representatives they had held under apartheid. "We are representing the voiceless," this line goes (Goduka 2008). In reality, NEDLAC officials and others acknowledge that the civics have sometimes been charged by others with claiming representation on an issue without actually carrying out a consultative process in their communities (Mkhize 2008). Thanks to its relationship with the governing party, however, SANCO continues to receive such status-conferring privileges.

In addition, SANCO's leaders receive more than just status. As they "interact with government at the highest level," they find new opportunities for personal growth, whether in business or politics (Mngomezulu 2008; Zuern 2006; AN 2003). "SANCO's clearly being used as a stepping-stone" for individuals interested in more lucrative career opportunities, said the organization's general secretary (Mngomezulu 2008). SANCO structures that lie dormant for months and even years suddenly become active around election time as civic leaders fight for ANC positions in the local council. As one unionist put it, "there's been a tendency for turning structures of SANCO into fiefdoms" (Masemula 2008). Former civic leaders condemn the many who today use SANCO as a "field of contestation" among aspiring political leaders (Mogase 2008), but many in the ANC also keep their former civic hat on in order to enhance their own status and political capital.

Interestingly, this element of cooptation has left the ANC open to attacks from SANCO leaders, especially whenever they begin to feel their support is being taken for granted or insufficiently rewarded. Under these circumstances, civic leaders at various levels have attacked government programs to regain the ANC's attention. "I don't think the friction was about policies," said one in reference to the periodic conflicts. "But they would say the people that are in government are not delivering. It is a question of power" (Ngwedzeni 2008). Emerging civic leaders, who had replaced their now government ex-colleagues, sometimes created conflict in order to accentuate their own leadership qualities and encourage the ANC to incorporate them in the next election. Many who are still operating within the civics "because they have not made it [themselves]

try to discredit serving [ANC municipal] councilors and present themselves as an alternative who will be more accountable" (Hlongwa 2008).
This has led to factionalism within the civic movement. For
example, when the ANC failed to finalize its electoral list with SANCO
activists ahead of the local government elections in 2000, SANCO's provincial representation in the Eastern Cape decided to run candidates on
an independent ticket (Dickson 2000). SANCO's national leadership,
facing pressure from the ANC, in turn pledged to discipline those regional leaders who were disloyal to the party (Mvoko 2000). Typical of
the clientelistic patter the ANC has resorted to, SANCO's winning inde-
pendents were not disciplined but were instead allowed to assume their
new positions as ANC councilors (Williams 2008). In several regions the
race for ANC positions has led to the emergence of parallel civic structures, each claiming to be the only legitimate one. "It is not an ideological
problem, it is not political differences, it is economic," one activist explained. "Everyone wants a position to be closer to the resources" (Mali
2008).

With no money, its role unclear, and its ex-leaders showing little to
no allegiance to the organization they helped create, SANCO, unsur-
prisingly, has declined in the fifteen years since South Africa's transition
began. Despite claims by some officials that SANCO is still a "really,
really exceptionally popular instrument and form of mobilizing" (Williams 2008), former and current civic activists refer to the organization
in morbid terms, calling it "dead" (Mayekiso 2008) or "a dead horse"
(Mngomezulu 2008) that has "died a natural death" (Ngwedzeni 2008).
SANCO's membership is difficult to estimate, given organizational weakness, but may be around two hundred thousand, just a fraction of the
millions it once claimed (Mngomezulu 2008). These estimates may also
be high since many local branches consider one a member based on "the
mere fact you are a resident" (Councilor3 2008). Other social-movement
leaders agree. "SANCO is there. I can show you where the SANCO
building is, but as far as membership [goes], that is all fictitious," said one,
whose mother was once a civic activist (Cassiem 2008). Although there
are pockets of activity lower down, provincial and especially national
structures are essentially defunct (Mali 2008; Mayekiso 2008; Mngomezulu 2008; Mosunkutu 2008). The national office finally closed its doors

in 2005 (Williams 2008). Even over the most controversial issues today, a former regional president of SANCO said, "you don't find much voice in SANCO" (Councilor2 2008).

SANCO's 2006 conference highlighted the organization's miserable state. Its president had tried to prevent the conference from taking place for fear of being voted out, but its general secretary insisted the conference go on so that he himself could resign (Mngomezulu 2008). Several provinces sent two sets of delegates, each claiming to be the legitimate representatives. When a referendum on dissolving the leadership structures passed, SANCO's president declared it invalid because the organization lacked funds to hire an independent company to conduct the vote. The conference ended with a sudden adjournment by the president (who refused to give up his position) and chairs flying. "Some of us hold [that] we are no longer members of the leadership," General Secretary Mngomezulu sighed, adding that the president maintains, however, that they are (Mngomezulu 2008).

According to SANCO's general secretary, ANC leaders seem to have decided that this weakness is in their own best interest because it shields civic-cum-ANC leaders from potentially embarrassing facts about their upward moves. "There are those who want SANCO to disappear or just stay as weak as it is, confused, so it doesn't take account for what people have done both in terms of leadership and in terms of managing resources" (Mngomezulu 2008). Other interviewees from the civic movement claim that another important reason for keeping SANCO intact and close to the ANC is to prevent the organization from being used by opposition groups and parties. In fact, MP Sonto explained that "if we have splinter civics across the country, it's easy for those civics to turn against our liberation" (Sonto 2008). "I was convinced that if SANCO doesn't exist, you will then find people moving into that space that's counterrevolutionary," seconded a former national treasurer of SANCO (Jack 2008). If the ANC cannot coordinate the pockets of active civic units today, it still risks losing them to new political entrepreneurs. "[SANCO] mustn't die but remain weak because something else would pop up if it does" (Mayekiso 2008).

Today, given the power of ANC activists at all levels, many former civic leaders believe the organization remains redundant and irrelevant.

When his university-aged son asks him about the purpose of SANCO, SANCO's general secretary laughed, "I'll go and just say a whole host of things, and at the end I've realized that I haven't answered the question." So long as SANCO remains a stepping-stone to power, the organization will continue to attract members with more interest in dividing than in reviving the organization, leading SANCO's secretary general to adopt a wait-it-out approach. "It's not a good thing because there are people who will say 'SANCO is dying in your hands,'" he said. Nonetheless, refocusing SANCO in a way that would make it more relevant would necessitate an organizational restructuring that could mean stepping on the toes of SANCO's current leaders. "The crop of leadership that we have is not interested in that. It is interested in being in political office" (Mngomezulu 2008).

Summary

Over time it has become apparent that institutionally determined preferences have sufficient power to alter even the most stalwart allies of the pro-democracy movement even as these leaders claim to be working in the spirit of the organizations and in cooperation with the colleagues they have left behind. Preestablished ties are not irrelevant; they create openings for organization leaders to at least bring complaints or requests and may therefore increase feelings of inclusivity. Moreover, they can have real impact, at least with respect to the more mundane and limited policy debates. Ultimately, however, when these debates are ratcheted up a notch in terms of scope and the influence of state leaders on a particular policy, they are more likely to be fruitless and ultimately to sour relations. As in Poland, the crumbs offered to COSATU and SANCO (at least before the latter's virtual collapse) were often insufficient to hold back the tide of organizational anger, which in turn led to a cycle of deteriorating relations.

With Jacob Zuma's exuberant entry into the ANC presidency at a time when there was "more frustration than ever before" in COSATU, COSATU's leaders seemed to have learned their lessons and were only somewhat optimistic that Zuma would "engage and listen in the debate, whether he will agree or not." Ultimately, given the way in which

COSATU's experiences have shed light on the constraints of office, Ntshalintshali resigned himself to the understanding that "there is no guarantee. It is [only] a hope" (Ntshalintshali 2008). Indeed, within just two years of the fieldwork for this chapter, there was evidence that Zuma had been added to a long list of one-time activists whose policy priorities were transformed by the institutions they joined. Massive strikes over public-sector pay drew the customary accusations of personal largesse in Zuma's government, prompting the public services and administration minister, a former UDF activist, to retort, "Do they want ministers to ride on scooters when they do their work?" (Dugger 2010). Regardless of the answer, COSATU continues to feel frustration at its inability to gain significant influence without resorting to arm twisting—a measure that is sure to increase personal animosity and decrease the likelihood of state/labor cooperation.

The similarities between Poland's Solidarity and South Africa's COSATU may not be surprising since the organizations are essentially labor unions (despite Solidarity's historically wider reach). The fact that SANCO, a much more inclusive grassroots organization, also followed a very similar pattern in terms of influence is quite remarkable. The key difference in the case of SANCO was that senior leaders of the organization were confronted with new, institutionally based incentives even when they formally remained in SANCO. They alternated between raising and lowering their voices to climb the ladder and move into comparable government spots, from which their voices simply disappeared.

In the next chapter I move from a study of three massive social-movement organizations engaged in long and sometimes violent struggles to one of small, elitist, pro-democracy groups engaged in a brief period of mobilization to bring down an illiberal, corrupt regime.

5

The Struggle of NGOs After
the Rose Revolution

WHEN KOTE KUBLASHVILI BECAME THE HEAD of Georgia's
Supreme Court, it was another sign that Georgia's "Rose Revolution,"
the electoral uprising by opposition politicians and their pro-democracy
NGO counterparts against the incumbent nondemocratic regime, was
bearing fruit. Kublashvili seemed to personify the pro-democracy sector
in many ways. Most important, he was a highly educated lawyer who
cofounded and continued to remain on the board of one of the most influential pro-democracy organizations in the country, the Georgian Young
Lawyers' Association (GYLA).

It might seem odd, then, that years after Kublashvili took the helm
at the Supreme Court, GYLA's chairperson claimed that it was precisely
a lack of judicial independence that constituted the country's biggest
human-rights dilemma (Chkheidze 2007). Kublashvili neither resigned in
protest nor even spoke out against perceived shortcomings in his country's judicial system. Instead, he adamantly denied the charge, claiming
that, in fact, "the judicial system has really become independent" under
his watch. If the judicial system has changed for the better, Kublashvili
continued, GYLA has changed for the worse. "They left the ranks of
NGOs and started exactly the same activities as an opposition party
would," Kublashvili explained. "I had many disagreements with what they
were saying, so we went our separate ways."

The divergence of these paths was underscored when Kublashvili and other senior GYLA members who had moved on to the state appeared on national television to condemn GYLA, declaring that "these activities of GYLA now do not correspond to the principles, our goals which we established several years ago." Yet there is little evidence to suggest that GYLA, which has long functioned as both a service provider to and watchdog of incumbent governments, is any more oppositional today than it was under Shevardnadze. Rather, GYLA's leader from the immediate postrevolution period said, charges from ex-GYLA activists arise from their feelings of betrayal inasmuch as they "expected more loyalty from GYLA's chair than I exhibited" (Dolidze 2007).

A Movement from Above

From afar, the Polish and South Africa cases seem quite distinct from the Georgian one, where the pro-democracy social movement was composed of small, professional nongovernmental organizations whose members had opposed a relatively harmless but hopelessly corrupt regime for just a few years prior to breakthrough. It would be easy to assume that activists in Georgia had no grounds to expect that their ties would bear fruit.

Yet this perspective is a rational approach to a very emotional argument. In fact, Georgian activists were just as likely as their Polish and South African counterparts to calculate that bonds would remain strong under the new conditions. After all, the cohort that orchestrated Georgia's Rose Revolution was remarkably similar in terms of both age (with just a few years separating NGO leaders from their political counterparts in the United National Movement) and life-defining experiences (many of them had spent considerable time in the West). They were groups of friends who frequently predated their organizations. "We were always together—from the university," said one (Khidasheli 2007). "This was our generation," agreed a former civil-society leader, who emphasized that activists bonded through their involvement in a historic, life-defining event. "We fought together for freedom" (Kitsmarishvili 2007). The wave of state leaders with this very particular NGO background should have created a vast network of ties at various levels between the state and civil society. "All of us were in the NGO community before the Rose Revolution," noted one government official, with only a touch of hyperbole (GOG2 2007).

The man deposed during the Rose Revolution, Eduard Shevardnadze, began his career in the brutal Stalin years and eventually became the Georgian Republic's minister of public order at the young age of thirty-seven (in 1965) and then interior minister just a few years later (for a general discussion of the communist experience see Chapter 3). Shevardnadze came to power promising to root out corruption, an image he perpetuated throughout his rise in the Soviet Union's top communist structures during the 1970s, when, under the rule of Leonid Brezhnev, local leaders were given significant autonomy in return for obedience to the political hierarchy in Moscow. In many ways, Shevardnadze seemed to be going against the grain by standing up against graft when embezzlement, bribery, and falsified production records were increasingly what the system was built upon.

Shevardnadze's reputation would become an enormous political advantage when the tides turned following the 1982 death of Brezhnev and a brief schizophrenic period under two ailing leaders, Yuri Andropov and Andrei Gromyko, who alternated between fighting for systemic reform and championing the status quo. When Mikhail Gorbachev took control of the Soviet Union in the mid-1980s, he made Shevardnadze the country's foreign minister. As such, he would oversee the greatest thaw ever in relations with the West. Shevardnadze would not return to Tbilisi from Moscow until early 1992, at which point newly independent Georgia was in the throes of a civil war. Two regions, Abkhazia and South Ossetia, demanded independence from Georgia, and the cratered streets of the capital echoed with the sounds of gunfire.

Shevardnadze rose to power on the local Georgian scene through violence. Following a 1992 coup, he was made chairman of the Georgian state council, in which position he effectively ruled the country. Despite his less-than-democratic arrival in a period when, throughout the former Soviet Union, democracy was still seen as a feasible, if not likely, prospect, Shevardnadze was a welcome relief to those who were uncomfortable with the nationalist regime of Zviad Gamsakhurdia, frequently referred to by his opponents as a "fascist dictator" (Nodia 1995, 105). Shevardnadze was assigned the role of president by a freely elected parliament in 1992, however, and formally elected president in 1995, thus bolstering his democratic credentials. This formal recognition was partly responsible for and further strengthened by his ability to bring Georgia into major international organizations, including the United Nations and the Organization for Security and Cooperation in Europe. Shevardnadze also increased Georgia's value to the West by promoting a major energy corridor, the Baku-Tbilisi-Ceyhan gas pipeline.

The international legitimacy Shevardnadze bestowed on his country was prized by his constituents, who largely identified with Europe. Nonetheless, such legitimacy could be maintained only insofar as Georgia continued to democratize. In fact, Shevardnadze moved unevenly forward with democratization. For example, while he oversaw what were widely viewed as free and fair elections in 1992 and 1995 and allowed for relative freedom of the opposition, Georgia's system of strong presidentialism and its personalistic nature of power marginalized political parties and ensured that authority remained centralized. Similarly, though there was relatively little censorship in the mainstream media, which included a number of opposition outlets, state-controlled media functioned essentially as a government mouthpiece. Shevardnadze, however, provided conditions that allowed Georgia in the mid-1990s to become known as an "NGO heaven" in the region (Devdariani 2003, 13).

Georgian civil society had been activated in the late 1980s' glasnost period, when, as in other parts of the USSR, organizations formed to take up popular grievances unaddressed by the state (Broers 2005). These organizations at first focused on less overtly political issues, such as the environment and culture, but gradually took on clearly political demands, including political liberalization and autonomy. With Shevardnadze at the helm, NGOs became more involved in programs designed to increase the rule of law, further human rights, and ensure democratic accountability. In contrast to other nondemocratic states characterized by centralized power, the Shevardnadze government rarely fought off activist NGOs, instead encouraging them to, in the words of one activist, "take all responsibility for the problems in the country" (Saakashvili 2007).

Young, Western-educated individuals, who balked at working for a corrupt government locked in a downward spiral, often saw these organizations as their only option. NGOs were a tool through which they could apply their newly gained knowledge to effect incremental change. Many of these organizations focused on strengthening the rule of law and independence of institutions, such as the media and judiciary. Political leaders largely left NGOs and independent media alone and even paid lip service to them so long as they were perceived to present no real challenge. This budding civil society, fueled by Western assistance, created its own new elites, who strove to shape international and domestic public opinion.

In reality, while the state invented various commissions to create the appearance of cooperation with NGOs, they were usually designed to impress rather than implement. NGOs were endowed with a level of media freedom that would have made those in neighboring states envious, but the government readily ignored their litany of criticisms. When NGO-supported laws were passed, their implementation was usually half-hearted at best. Moreover, when the raucous civil-society sector seemed to pose a real threat to power holders, as in the case of the influential independent television station Rustavi 2, the authorities launched targeted crackdowns against the relevant group(s). NGO leaders often found themselves struggling to support reforms accepted and outwardly championed in some parts of the government without giving state leaders excessive and ultimately undeserved credit.

As the strength of the nongovernmental sector increased, especially in the capital, Shevardnadze began to see it—and democratization more broadly—as a threat. His dedication to democratic reform was especially tempered by political and economic challenges that steadily mounted in the 1990s. By 1997 economic growth had slowed, averaging only 2 percent from 1997 to 2002 (Cohen 2004). Unemployment rose, topping 17 percent during this period. In part, Shevardnadze's economic problems stemmed from the civil wars he did not start but could not end. Refugee flows and civil strife in Abkhazia and South Ossetia, which negatively affected Georgian exports to Russia, led to economic deterioration. But so, too, did rampant corruption, which emerged as a result of those vested interests in what one called "the informalization of Georgian politics" (Broers 2005, 334). Shevardnadze may have struggled against excesses during his rise to power, but so long as he was on top, influence was for sale at nearly every level.

The result was, not surprisingly, a perpetually failing state. Overall economic hardship and the state's failure to provide basic services and guarantee social welfare left Shevardnadze with miserable approval ratings and pushed him away from the democratic reforms that had gradually become a threat. The government began attacking independent media and then sought to drown out the voice of independent NGOs by creating and backing pro-governmental organizations. Shevardnadze used state media to portray NGOs as grant grubbers, promoting foreign values and weakening the state, and sought legislation to clamp down on organizational activities. Moreover, charges of foul play in the 1999 parliamentary and 2000 presidential elections increased his unpopularity at home and simultaneously damaged the reputation he had spent years building abroad. Although in 1999 Westerners continued to award Shevardnadze for his political leadership (Geyer 2000, 62), by 2000 he was increasingly viewed as empowered only as a result of electoral tricks and an extremely weak and fragmented opposition.

One reason for the opposition's fragmentation may well have been the source of its support. Nongovernmental organizations were almost exclusively backed by Western democracy promoters, who, along with various academics, had come to see them as vital to democracy because they create strong interpersonal networks that alter the shape of political discourse, facilitate citizen mobilization, and increase governmental responsiveness (Dryzek 1996, 481; Putnam, Leonardi, and Nanetti 1993; Kuran 1991; Olson 1971). Although these donors were happy to award hard currency to grant writers, the result was an outward-oriented rather than a homegrown, nongovernmental movement, with all the classic problems of resource dependency, including fraud (such as shopping a given project to a variety of Western organizations and then collecting from all of them), a focus on issues alien to the local population, and interorganizational competition for funding. None of these groups had particular resonance in Georgian society prior to the 2003 elections, when most citizens were more concerned with jobs and territorial integrity.

They may have been saved from obscurity by disgruntled colleagues they found within the state itself. Political opponents known as the "young reformers" (including Mikhail Saakashvili and Zurab Zhvania), who had spent their early political careers under Shevardnadze's personal tutelage, branded themselves the truly "Western," pro-democracy choice and joined in contentious NGO activities. Pro-democracy NGOs took advantage of these new networks of opposition political elites and other NGOs, learned new tactics, and grew more confident.

Over time, these organizations became the chief extraparliamentary political opposition under Shevardnadze. "This was the general understanding of NGOs and the media," explained one former NGO leader. "You should somehow oppose the government" (Ugulava 2007). While some of these organizations sided with one political party more than another (most notoriously, the Liberty Institute was connected to Saakashvili's National Movement, and GYLA was connected to the Republican Party), there was little concern about being charged with partisanship at the time. Nonetheless, by 2002 these two opposition parties had formed an alliance that would encompass five parties by the 2003 elections, when, according to one NGO activist, "we had a common view" (Guntsadze 2007). Shevardnadze had to go. To maintain an air of neutrality, the outward message was only slightly more nuanced: "We said we want a fair game—and are definitely against the ruling party," one said (Ugulava 2007).

NGOs thus formed a crucial pillar of opposition to the government and shared both ideological affinities and tight informal relations with opposition political elites. "We were very close. We were friends; we had common ideas, common visions, common objectives," Liberty Institute's Levan Ramishvili said (Ramishvili 2007). By early 2003 the situation in Georgia had become so dire that NGO leaders convened a meeting, in which they decided that the democratic process was irreparably broken; falsification in the upcoming elections was inevitable, and, as a result, these leaders "decided not to be just monitors but to be against the ruling party" (Ugulava 2007). One NGO leader explained the choice to ally with oppositionist politicians and shift to a revolutionary approach to change as a simple one: "We were in trouble," he said (Salamadze 2007). Another described a now-or-never feeling, adding that it was more despair than outright repression that drove Georgia's revolution: "People decided the [Shevardnadze] government was kind of hopeless" (Nodia 1995).

To mobilize from above, pro-democracy organizations engaged in a multipronged attack on the regime. This involved raising citizen awareness, organizing get-out-the-vote campaigns, monitoring the elections, and demonstrating to citizens that they were not alone in their disillusionment. NGOs put considerable legwork into preparing for the elections and engaged in a hectic schedule of bringing other NGOs on board and conducting election outreach. "We didn't sleep for four, six, eight months. We were traveling all around having meetings," said one NGO leader (Tsintsadze 2007). Nonmember-based organizations such as the Caucasus Institute for Peace, Democracy, and Development stoked support within broader civil society by holding debates before the elections and also assisted with voter-registration drives, while other relatively small organizations such as the Association for Legal and Public Education (ALPE) engaged in various types of voter outreach, including organizing politically oriented youth summer camps.

The Rose Revolution was a classic "electoral revolution" that followed the Serbian model and blazed the way for others to come. Following rigged elections, pro-democracy and human rights NGOs used their ostensibly more objective stature to bolster opposition claims against incumbents and helped coordinate mobilization efforts. The immediate catalyst was a series of voting irregularities—from improper voter lists and contradictory electoral commission instructions to attacks on election monitors—but these came on top of long-held, widespread allegations of corruption within the ruling regime. NGOs used their alliances with the media to amass evidence of fraud and inform the public that the status quo was rotten.

Two days after the elections, three core-opposition parties, including the National Movement, Burjanadze-Democrats, and Unity (Ertoba), came together in the United Opposition Front, and Saakashvili threatened mass demonstrations if the electoral commission did not recognize the opposition's victory. Again, NGOs, which were broadly aligned with opposition parties, gave cheated political candidates a credibility and distance from the old regime that they, the former reformers, might not have otherwise had (Karosanidze 2007; Meladze 2007; Zhvania 2007). "NGOs created the consensus that this government is going nowhere, that we should get rid of it," said a post-2003 government official. "I think this couldn't have been done by [any] party" (MVD 2007). "The trust toward [the] NGO sector, the trust toward the media was much, much greater than the trust of *any* political actors," added another (Tarkhnishvili 2007).

As with the events in Serbia, Shevardnadze did not capitulate in the first weeks after the election even as his country remained partially paralyzed. High-profile appearances on television allowed NGO leaders a chance to show the Shevardnadze government as not just corrupt but also vulnerable. "People believed they could change their lives, and they came" (Subari 2007). When Shevardnadze sought to convene his new parliament nearly three weeks after the elections, Saakashvili and his supporters— with around one hundred thousand protesters behind them—took over Georgia's parliament building with roses in their hands. Shevardnadze escaped via a back door and later officially resigned from his post. The Rose Revolution was over. It was, say NGO participants, the victory of "an NGO movement" that capitalized on palpable public anger (UNAG 2007).

It should be pointed out that many of the organizations that made up Georgia's pro-democracy social movement had been around for years, sometimes coordinating with one another but usually operating independently in the name of specific democratic reforms rather than democracy per se. This is especially true of GYLA and the Liberty Institute, which were among the most active groups and the most credited with the 2003 events. GYLA, for instance, was founded in 1994 with the aim of "teaching legal skills, defending human rights, encouraging the growth of civil society, and advancing the rule of law" (GYLA 2008). Critical GYLA functions included awareness-raising activities and election observation, as well as providing legal aid to organizations harassed for their election-related activities. GYLA and the International Society for Fair Elections and Democracy (ISFED) provided parallel vote tabulations and election monitoring that were instrumental in proving deception.

The Liberty Institute was founded just two years after GYLA by independent television (Rustavi 2) journalists to protect freedom of speech and independent media. Among its many functions, the Liberty

Institute has been largely credited with creating and serving as the base for the Kmara (Enough) youth movement, modeled on Serbia's successful Otpor youth movement, to broaden civic engagement. Just as in Serbia, where the organization used an array of tactics designed to demonstrate a popular membership that was in fact lacking, Kmara began as a kitchen-style organization of a few dozen students who before the elections would gather at Liberty and discuss the evening news (Mullen 2007). Those who came out after the elections marched in front of cameras to make lots of noise and create the image of a highly mobilized youth group. Liberty-supported Rustavi 2 also played an especially important part in the mobilization process by persistently showing citizens that they had been de-frauded in the elections and that their compatriots were in the streets.

It is also important to note that the pro-democracy NGO community had been split by the decision to engage more directly in politics and that not all pro-democracy organizations were active in the revolution. However, in a country where personalities dominate, even the em-phatically personal activity of an NGO leader supporting the 2003 events was sufficient to create the image that the individual was speaking for the entire organization. And many organizations that did not directly take sides considered the rise of the opposition a positive phenomenon. A representative from one such organization, which disseminated information about election violations, demonstrated the difficulty in staying non-partisan under the circumstances. "We supported the Rose Revolution in general, but we tried to keep some kind of distance from political parties" (Nanuashvili 2007). "We didn't actively take part in either the elections or the revolution," said a representative of another human-rights organization, who subsequently added, "We supported the revolution, expected changes, and waited for something better" (Chokheli 2007).

NGOs After the Revolution

Euphoric from their victory, confident in their colleagues, and inse-cure about their organizations' futures, those who remained in the NGO community the first year or so after the Rose Revolution exuded patience with the new government. With the notable exception of President Saa-kashvili's 2004 constitutional amendment, in which he increased the powers of the presidency and curtailed parliament's right to impeach the president, who could dissolve both parliament and the cabinet of ministers, NGOs watched with restraint as the new (and potentially volatile) political climate evolved. "At the beginning, our agenda, like the strategy of many other NGOs, was 'let's give some time to the new government; let's not start criticizing them right away,'" said Transparency International's executive director in Georgia (Karosanidze 2007). "I think it was a kind of grace period," added another NGO leader (Nodia 2007).

In part, this was a function of their faith in colleagues they had known so well. "There was this presumed vision that NGOs collectively are one kind of big actor with more or less the same values, perceptions," said one NGO leader (Nodia 1995). "We were always working for the same values, for the same issues," added another (Khidasheli 2007). The combination of personal bonds and grand visions gave the government plenty of breathing room. "We are all friends. Come on, let's get involved in politics. We'll be founders just like Jefferson, who established the new America," the founder of independent television station Rustavi 2 described the situation. "We had the chance to realize everything that we wanted to" (Kitsmarishvili 2007).

NGO leaders also took into consideration their country's fragile position. Despite the significant Western experience they and their colleagues brought to the new state, Georgia remained dangerously isolated. Not only did it share a border with three nondemocratic post-Soviet states, but one—Russia—was considered practically an enemy, with a long history of supporting Abkhazia and South Ossetia in their bids to secede. Many saw Georgia's entry into NATO and the European Union as the country's only chance for survival, and it was clear from the start that an unrepentant authoritarian state had no place in those Western structures. From this perspective it was best not to complain too much about small deviations from the ideal.

Finally, this respite was also a side effect of the profound reorganizations being contemplated throughout the NGO community. In the aftermath of the revolution the feeling in the NGO community was that "the era of NGOs" had ended and that, at last, "politics [had become] more serious" (Nodia 1995). As NGO leaders contemplated the long-term institutionalization process, recalled one leader who ultimately went on to the state, some felt that NGOs should permanently ease up on the new government. "Everyone realized NGOs had to be changed," the official said, adding that the old tactic of relentlessly pushing no longer made sense. "We had to find ways to cooperate with the new government" (GOG2 2007). The process was difficult for an NGO community that had since its existence taken a critical stance toward the state.

It was made more difficult by the fact that so many leaders were leaving for the state, convinced that they could do more in government than outside it. "After the revolution," explained GYLA's leader, who at the time of our interview had only recently returned from a stint with the prosecutor's office, "there was momentum for the young people to go into public service and change something" (Chkheidze 2007). The feeling was mutual. Those who took to the state turned around and saw NGOs as a "hub for human resources" (Ugulava 2007) for a new government in search of Western savvy, English-speaking professionals whom they could trust and who lacked a potentially embarrassing political biography.

As a result, said the former head of the National Democratic Institute in Georgia, "most of the brain trust of the NGOs [went] to government" (Mullen 2007). Between autumn of 2003 and spring of 2004 the once-powerful NGO sphere that had helped bring about change lost so many leaders to the state that it seemed impossible to replace them fast enough. GYLA, for instance, was jolted by the loss of 10 percent of its staff, and the Liberty Institute lost a majority of its founding members to the state (Dolidze 2007; Meladze 2007). Although many organizations were able to replace their exiting leaders in house, others simply ceased to exist (Nanuashvili 2007). Those that remained had to ask themselves why and how. "Their common goal was to stop the Shevardnadze regime," said one NGO analyst, referring to the first question. "When this regime was changed, NGOs did not know their new role" (Saakashvili 2007).

In the midst of their existential dilemma, NGOs were hit with yet another devastating reality: The hand that had fed them since inception was suddenly gone. Since many of the "well-known public personalities who were on TV all the time" (Nodia 1995) moved into the political sphere or state apparatus, it is no surprise that international observers involved in the funding of Georgian civil society suddenly saw the sector populated with a new generation of largely inexperienced unknowns (Representative 2007). With international actors feeling that watchdog NGOs had already accomplished their primary task, Western diplomats reduced their financial support and their political backing, which under Shevardnadze had ensured that their words did not fall on deaf ears. "This was a new world. The priority should be focused on supporting the government," one U.S. government official characterized the mood (USG2 2007). A significant chunk of what funding remained was poured into organizations that state authorities agreed to take on as partners, prompting many organizations to curtail their criticism of government policies they disagreed with (Dolidze 2007; Kitsmarishvili 2007; Tsintsadze 2007; Zurabishvili 2007).

In addition to financial constraints, those who were determined to remain behind felt continuing pressure from their ex-colleagues who had moved on to the state to give them a break. After November 2003 the government's perspective was that the rules of the game had changed and NGOs were expected to be "constructive" rather than critical (USG2 2007). "Reformer" politicians who pandered to the NGOs in the hope of winning their support before the Rose Revolution later criticized many of them as organizations paid to oppose the government. Government leaders tended to portray this need for restraint in stark terms, arguing that outspoken NGOs threatened Georgia's development and, by diminishing the likelihood of a successful NATO bid, its security. Moreover, while the old government feared the NGOs, the new one did not, thereby reducing their leverage. It seemed logical, said one government official, for NGOs to abandon their watchdog roles in the name of progress. "They should fill the gap between government and society. What government can't deliver can be delegated to this civil sector" (Ugulava 2007).

In their new institutions, ex-NGO leaders began to feel that they had personally represented the NGO sector before taking power and that they now remained its best and most capable representatives. These were leaders whose time working and studying in the West had endowed them with a "strong value base," said one (Tarkhnishvili 2007), and they felt prepared to represent the NGO sector at the highest levels (Getsadze 2007). Four years after the Rose Revolution state leaders disparaged the NGO community they had left behind, branding it a weak shell of its former self without the financial and human resources that had once made it so great (GOG2 2007; Kublashvili 2007; MVD 2007; Tarkhnishvili 2007). "Unfortunately, because these are kids, twenty, twenty-one . . . they don't know how to ask questions," Mayor Gigi Ugulava (who himself had worked as a journalist in his early twenties) said of Georgia's current stock of journalists (Ugulava 2007). Under the new conditions, governing elites believed the NGOs were no longer the "guardians of truth" they had once been and that there was no "moral obligation to cooperate" with them (Nodia 2007). "There is a general message that the government does not need NGOs anymore" (Saakashvili 2007) and that "this period when NGOs were so central is over" (Nodia 2007).

This message went beyond rhetoric into policy: "We know how to do the things. With or without your support, we'll do this," the head of public television characterized the stance (Tarkhnishvili 2007). Government officials and sympathetic NGOs also said that, since 2003, NGOs, long oriented to a slow, consultative approach, had failed to keep up with the fast pace at which their new government officials sought to deliver changes (Darchiashvili 2007; Guntsadze 2007; Ugulava 2007). They also attacked NGOs for acting on behalf of a constituency that did not exist, so their voices did not resonate (MVD 2007). "These organizations are self-appointed. They just represent themselves," Liberty Institute's head said ironically. "The government has democratic legitimacy—they represent their constituency" (Ramishvili 2007).

In the face of these attacks, after 2003 NGOs scrambled to adapt their missions to the new reality. The organizations included in this study, almost all of which were founded before 2003 by local elites wary of the Shevardnadze regime, consist of three basic types: service providers (which, even in the sphere of rule of law, focus more on technical assistance), watchdogs (charged primarily with publicly pressing the government for political liberalization and human rights), and hybrids (including elements of both watchdogs and service providers). In actuality, up until 2003 all of these organizations discussed carried out some watchdog functions, monitoring and vocally contesting state structures. Afterward, some of these organizations, including the Human Rights Information and Documentation Center, Article 42, the Egalitarian Institute, and Former Political Prisoners for Human Rights, remained watchdogs.

Others, including the Georgian Young Lawyers' Association, Transparency International, and the International Society for Fair Elections and Democracy, remained hybrid organizations, performing both watchdog and service-provider assistance.[1] However, after 2003 others largely abandoned their watchdog functions to focus almost exclusively on service provision: training, educational programs, technical assistance, and similar activities. The most notable of these is the Liberty Institute, but others include ALPE, the Caucasus Institute for Peace, Democracy, and Development, the Civil Society Institute, and the United Nations Association of Georgia.

Watchdogs and Their Ex-Colleagues

As watchdog NGOs over the course of 2004 got their bearings and grew concerned over what they saw as a deteriorating rather than an improving human-rights situation, they increased their monitoring activities and began speaking out first in private and then in public about their negative findings. The first signs of strain between former and continuing NGO activists occurred surprisingly soon, when President Saakashvili in early 2004 proposed constitutional amendments that strengthened the presidential office. The reaction was wide, if only brief, condemnation. NGO leaders did not hold back during this episode; in fact, Rustavi 2 reported talk of "dictatorship," and the head of GYLA accused the president of deception (BBC 2004). However, the amendments were soon passed, and most NGO leaders reverted to quiet optimism.

Another episode that illustrates that NGO leaders had put their gloves back on occurred later that year when they began raising a number of concerns with respect to judicial reforms, free media, and human rights (BBC 2004). When they were invited to meet with President Saakashvili, these concerns were apparently allayed with just a few words from their old friend. According to one NGO leader who attended the meeting, apparently the president had simply been unaware of the situation. A GYLA representative added optimistically, "We hope that Mr. President will react to this." In addition, an ex-NGO leader in parliament, Elene Tevdoradze, who would later become a fierce critic of Saakashvili, expressed satisfaction that "the president listens to what he is told."

NGO activists were soon frustrated again, however, as it became clear to them that the democratic deficits they raised showed no sign of remedy. By early 2005, about a year and a half after the "revolutionary" changes, journalists were complaining that the state had become increasingly obstructive, threatening the independent press that had contributed to the fall of Shevardnadze. Domestic and international observers similarly condemned prison conditions, which included severe overcrowding, unsanitary cells, and long pretrial wait times. These problems were compounded by allegations by international human-rights organizations that the government was routinely violating due process and continuing the practice of torture and ill treatment of detainees that its leaders had so vociferously condemned before taking power.

For activists on the outside, it was especially striking that old freedom fighters in their new state institutions actually favored the sorts of policies they had once decried. For example, GYLA leaders, who saw their senior members move into top positions in the justice ministry, prosecutor's office, Supreme Court, and Constitutional Court, were confronted with a set of legal reforms that they argued actually increased political pressure on the courts. These policies sometimes amended, overrode, or bypassed laws that these now state leaders had helped to create when they were in the NGO sector (Dolidze 2007). One aspect of the 2005 reforms, for example, included the conversion of district courts into appellate courts, which meant the automatic firing and optional rehiring of judges by the executive (BBC 2005). This reform, supported by GYLA's ex-colleagues in the state, was not only a politicization of the judiciary, GYLA's leaders said, but also unconstitutional. "This is unacceptable," the group's chair declared.

This was far from an isolated incident. That same year GYLA leaders attacked their former friends in the judiciary for illegally pressuring members of the Supreme Court to resign for allegedly taking bribes under the former regime. The accusations were informal since there was no evidence to back them up, and GYLA's head chose to legally defend a number of the accused judges, pitting the organization against its own members in the Supreme Court, Constitutional Court, justice ministry, and prosecutor's office. Government officials reacted to these and other attacks with speed and determination, purportedly denying GYLA members judgeships and launching a public assault on the organization by several top-level government and state leaders affiliated with GYLA (Chkhetia 2007; Dolidze 2007; Getsadze 2007; Papuashvili 2007). During the conference noted at the beginning of this chapter, GYLA member and Defense Minister Irakli Okruashvili condemned GYLA for becoming "an organization which organizes protests in support of criminal kingpins" (BBC 2006).

Successive reforms—or their conspicuous absence—prompted many activists in the NGO community to question the identities of their former colleagues, claiming that those who "used to be champions for human rights and liberalism" turned sharply away from their democratic ideals (Dolidze 2007). Those who were once adept at criticizing the government based on principle began reacting angrily to criticism, even eschewing "opposition" talk shows where they would be forced to openly discuss complaints (Chkheidze 2007; Chokheli 2007). "We have some elites in government who might have liberal values and follow this liberal reform agenda, but they're a really small group," said one. The rest, he added, "completely changed their shape" (Chkheidze 2007). Activists claimed that their former colleagues either abandoned the identity they had once had or subverted it for strategic reasons. In terms of human rights and democratization, said one Liberty Institute founder, ex-NGO leaders "turned out to be the main engine" behind the turn away from democratization that appeared imminent in 2003 (Zurabishvili 2007). The lesson, said one Eurasia Foundation official, is that "people from NGOs, as soon as they enter the government, unfortunately forget their NGO past" (Anjaparidze 2007).

Leaders of watchdog NGOs were obviously disappointed that their ex-colleagues would support illiberal policies, but they were also distraught by the propensity of these old friends to, like their Shevardnadze-era predecessors, blatantly disregard their appeals. "We'd go to the government and say 'These are the problems.' They would be like, 'Oh that's nothing, we don't really need to worry about it too much,'" recalled one activist. "At that point we just said it's time for us to start talking about these issues more openly" (Karosanidze 2007). As tensions began to surface, a "cold war" between the state and NGOs quickly emerged, complete with allegations of hypocrisy on both sides (Darchiashvili 2007).

"Cooperation now between NGOs and the government is illusionary," summarized the head of one human-rights organization four years after the transition began (Nanuashvili 2007).

Both sides chalked the new tensions up to institutional constraints. For those in the state, enormous public expectations for change could be met only with immediate and effective action (Chkhetia 2007; Tarkhnishvili 2007). One ex-minister and head of the Constitutional Court explained that whereas the old government feared but largely ignored NGOs, the new one had little fear of them but was rapidly implementing NGO-based policies (Papuashvili 2007). Before 2003, said another, "NGOs demanded reforms in all areas of life, but the government didn't want to do this. Now all these people moved [to the state], and we started all these reforms" (Ugulava 2007). These leaders prided themselves on results, and although they admitted to some mistakes (which they also claimed to be struggling to address), they argued that the overall direction is positive (Darchiashvili 2007; Kublashvili 2007; MVD 2007). "I am still idealistic," said one senior-level official, who added, "Of course, I have more information now" (GOG 2007).

Those remaining behind, these ex-NGO leaders say, have failed to adapt to a new era where the state is a source of good rather than evil. "To be a member of an NGO always meant to be an opponent of government. It didn't matter what the government did," a senior-level official said. "When the situation changed, they didn't change. They didn't want to see what the changes and the challenges were" (GOG 2007). "You define yourself in relation to the government," another high-level official agreed. "You're either pro-government or anti-government" (MVD 2007). Such critics say watchdog comments are often unfair and fail to take context into account, either lacking an understanding of or purposely looking away from the constraints of policymakers (Darchiashvili 2007; Getsadze 2007; GOG2 2007; Guntsadze 2007; Kublashvili 2007; Meladze 2007).[2] The classic governmental response to criticism has been broad, open accusations that the NGO community has gone to the opposition—a particularly painful charge for organizations rewarded for their objectivity. State leaders practically institutionalized the response that, in the words of another senior official, "those groups work with political parties. That's what our position is" (GOG 2007).

The rebuttal from these organizations was that they neither are nor support any particular party, "but we're part of politics because protections of human rights, efficiency of justice, and democratic developments are a part of politics" (Chkheidze 2007). Moreover, they say, state officials were quick to attack NGO activists as partisan merely because they disagree on key policy points. "If someone takes a stand on a particular issue—if they are critical in any way of the government—they are very, very easily marginalized by the government," said GYLA's former outspoken leader. "They have a very 'us' or 'them' attitude" (Dolidze 2007). Some say this is evidence of "authoritarian" personalities, characteristics the "reformers" inherited from their Soviet-era mentors. However, others see the problem as more a function of the institutional constraints facing their ex-colleagues, who feel that open criticism will inhibit the ability of ruling elites to deliver to voters key political goods such as security. One NGO leader more sympathetic to the government shared this perspective: "Okay, point out the problems, but don't exaggerate them because it harms us in Georgia-NATO relations" (Darchiashvili 2007).

The burden of governance has left what one sympathetic NGO leader called "visionary politicians" in a struggle "between rule-of-law principles and the necessities of national security." "In certain situations," Open Society Georgia's Darchiashvili continued, "these two imperatives were just impossible to balance" (Darchiashvili 2007). In defense of what critics of the government have called unjust policies, state leaders are quick to point to the massive scale of destruction, which impacted everything from infrastructure to public mentality, that they inherited from their predecessors. NGO leaders who were attacking without the perspective of power were "just too idealistic," said one high-ranking government official (MVD 2007). For these authorities, there was no time for the niceties they had once preached when "the public demands results today" (Chkheidze 2007). Thus, those criticizing the country's level of judicial independence, for example, must understand that Georgia's judiciary has never been independent and that to make it so involves aggressive tactics that may not always be seen as conforming to the rule of law (Kublashvili 2007; Papuashvili 2007). Those who complain about the heavy media campaign depicting mass arrests of individuals charged with corruption, another ex-NGO leader said, must understand that it is "very important to change society's attitude." "It's *so hard*, my God!" the official continued. "How can you make four million grown people act in a different way in one day, you know?" (GOG2 2007).

Opposition politicians and watchdog NGOs have been unsympathetic to these explanations. "That's not new to me," Liberty co-founder Zurabishvili said. "The Bolsheviks also tried to change people's consciousness" (Zurabishvili 2007). Nonetheless, state officials claim that such responses are symptomatic of information asymmetries and rely on the classic argument that if NGO leaders knew what they knew, they would act similarly. "When you're inside . . . you have more information. You start to look at these things a little bit more from the other side," said one. "Because I have more information, I'm not that critical" (Tarkhnishvili 2007). In particular, state leaders point to both internal and external security threats, praising the steps Saakashvili has taken to allay them. One official who said that, as an NGO leader, she had opposed the president's 2004 constitutional amendments said that in retrospect she "was too idealistic" (GOG2 2007). "Now I realize that it was the right political decision," the official continued. "I personally prefer to avoid huge political risks rather than have a theoretically balanced constitution." Such are the realities of governing in a postrevolution climate, conceded the Supreme Court chairman, who has been accused of heavy-handed tactics that decrease judicial impartiality. "There are questions [raised by NGOs] that I can never agree with because I know what the realities are here," he said, adding, "In this period there will be rights violations. We're not surprised" (Kublashvili 2007).

There is also a surprisingly widespread acknowledgment within the NGO community that institutional constraints are the cause of ex-activists' changed preferences. "When you come to the government, you take huge responsibility. This changes people," said the Civil Society Institute's Salamadze. "That's the real picture" (Salamadze 2007). According to this perspective, the government formulated a plan for how Georgia should look a few years into the future and began following the most direct path, aware that it would have to step on toes and civil liberties to get there. According to this perspective, those who protested government policies would also likely follow similar programs if they were in power, just as those government officials who attack NGOs would in all probability pursue the same path if they remained outside the state sphere (Guntsadze 2007; Salamadze 2007; Tarkhnishvili 2007; Tsintsadze 2007; UNAG 2007). With respect to the judiciary, mentioned earlier, it became clear that ridding Georgia of its corrupt judges required skirting elements of the rule of law, such as the presumption of innocence. Some, especially the more sympathetic NGOs, believed that the government's tactics were used merely to address "temporary, immediate needs" (Ramishvili 2007). But others were more cynical. "They started doing this little by little, and when they got away with it, they got spoiled," said one (Karosanidze 2007).

As noted earlier, government officials have dismissed these criticisms as naïve. "When you come to the government and when you have to do real work instead of [expounding on] theories, you see how hard [it is]" (GOG2 2007). However, in the view of this official's ex-colleague, who served with her first in GYLA and then in government before returning to direct GYLA, such simplifications are merely an excuse to tune out critics in what has become a debilitating cycle in Georgia. "Really good, honest public officials might, without control or supervision from civil society, follow the wrong path," GYLA's chairman said (Chkheidze 2007). This, in turn, has contributed to authorities' newfound distaste for civil society, which in the years after 2003 they began to see as an obstacle to the way they envision progress. The crackdown on the media also emerged from a newfound understanding that "openness is not always useful for them," said the former owner of Rustavi 2 (Kitsmarishvili 2007).

In the presence of the institutional divide that now separated them, watchdog NGO leaders claimed that personal networks actually spoiled relations more than they helped them. Some government officials with old friends back in the NGOs spoke of their criticism as resorting to "stereotypes," personal "anger" (GOG2 2007), and even "ridicule" (MVD 2007). In the Supreme Court bribery case, those in the state were "personally hurt" (Chkheidze 2007) and "insulted" at GYLA's attacks on them (GOG2 2007). This message was clear to those still in GYLA: "They say to our members that, when you're a GYLA member, an active member, and then one day you get criticism from your organization, it's not very good for you. It doesn't make you happy at all," GYLA's deputy chair added (Chkhetia 2007).

The case of Georgia's ombudsman, Sozar Subari, also highlights this unexpected role of personal connections. According to the network argument, Subari, a former reporter and Liberty Institute activist who was "very close friends" (Subari 2007) with many people in government, should have had excellent relations with the state, particularly since Liberty had become a government supporter organization. At the beginning of his tenure, Subari acknowledged, government officials used their personal relations to pressure him to be less critical. Despite claiming he was always outspoken about abuses, Subari admitted that at first he tried to maintain close relations with the government, which he felt would allow him to "better defend the rights of actual people." For instance, it would take only a couple of phone calls to have prisoners who were being illegally detained set free without further delay. "Sometimes it's very good to immediately resolve problems with very good connections," Subari said. "I very much want to keep these relations" (Subari 2007).

In effect, these networks led to the same self-censorship mechanisms other NGOs felt at the start of the transition, yielding an almost palpable silence from the ombudsman's office. By 2005, however, interviewees say Subari became much more outspoken in his criticisms of the government. From a purely institutional perspective, Subari's turnaround might have been expected since he was pressured from a number of sides to stand up for the rights his office proclaimed sacrosanct. Subari himself claimed he was motivated by a deteriorating rights situation. For others, Subari's reaction was as predictable as a pendulum swing and was seen as a visceral reaction to allegations in his first year of turning a blind eye to abuses in an effort to protect his government friends. "The reason he is so critical is that there are lots of people in government who are his personal friends," said one prison official, whose overcrowded and underfunded institution was a frequent target of Subari's attacks. "He is trying everyday to prove that he is independent" (Tsintsadze 2007).

Whatever the reason, the reaction was, as expected, swift and painful. Political leaders, despite being old friends from the pro-democracy movement, lashed out at Subari for a critical report he presented in parliament, in which he declared unconstitutional an accord between the state and the Georgian Orthodox Church, which he claimed would violate the rights of other faiths (BBC 2005). His report left politicians of all stripes enraged and led his old colleagues to tell Subari that "I discredited myself and the institution of the ombudsman" (Subari 2007). Others in the state condemned Subari for various declarations that are "not well argued" (Kublashvili 2007). "I don't like this. I take it to heart, and it hurts," Subari said. "I knew [when] taking this job [that] it was not going to be easy work. I didn't imagine it would be so hard, so painful."

Others who have crossed the government similarly described the ordeals in personal terms as very "emotional" conflicts. Rustavi 2's Kitsmarishvili, who claimed to have once been very close to Prime Minister Zhvania, said that his own preference to launch an amnesty for past corruption prompted Zhvania to organize "a very unpleasant campaign against me" (Kitsmarishvili 2007). Liberty cofounder Zurabishvili claimed that one of the other cofounders and a top National Movement official, Giga Bokeria, refused to even speak with him (Zurabishvili 2007). As GYLA's chair commented, "When some of the founders say this organization changed its values and became an opposition party, it really hurts" (Chkheidze 2007).

Unlike these examples, critical organizations whose leaders have not been drawn into the state have had much less strained relations with the authorities. For these watchdogs, including the Human Rights Information and Documentation Center and the International Society for Fair Elections and Democracy, 2003 was a relatively inconsequential blip on the radar screen with respect to their relationship to the state. In stark contrast to GYLA or the Egalitarian Institute, for example, Transparency International was frequently subjected to a private rather than a public tongue-lashing for its rebukes of the government. "They don't go radically against us, and they're not openly against us," said Transparency's Karosanidze. Instead, she added, "They try to create technical problems" (Karosanidze 2007). "In principal, our relationship has remained the same," said the head of another human-rights organization with no members in the state and which organizes up to three press conferences per month to protest specific cases of abuse. "We didn't have bad relations before, and there aren't bad relations today; neither were there very good relations with either the old or the new government" (Chokheli 2007).

Even organizations with a significant watchdog role (in addition to service provision) could find advantages in having empowered ex-colleagues, but in areas where they were the most outspoken this be-came difficult. GYLA leaders, for instance, have received especially little cooperation from those state bodies at which its (law-related) criticisms have been particularly targeted. So while they have maintained positive relations with the education ministry, they have encountered the most antagonism from judicial and law-enforcement bodies, precisely those places where their legal services should find a home. There, cooperation with the government was limited to the least domestically politicized top-ics with the greatest foreign interest, such as combating human traffick-ing. "The government understood that fighting against human trafficking was directly connected to funding from the United States government," explained the head of GYLA (Chkheidze 2007). It is clear, however, that personal connections have done more harm than good. As one former chair of GYLA explained with reference to those GYLA members who condemned the organization, "We don't have personal relations anymore, and we were very close friends. Very close" (Khidasheli 2007).

Service Providers: Limited Gains

Where NGO leaders moderated their agendas and took a supportive role in relation to the government, their usefulness was rewarded. These organizations received contracts and funding and, their leaders claimed, saw their organizational influence increase (Guntsadze 2007). "You have leverage to go to the government, knock on the door, use your personal relations to say, 'Hey, guys, this is not good—and this is what's better,'" said the Civil Society Institute's Salamadze. "They cooperate" (Salamadze 2007). These leaders readily admitted that they have had to curtail the public watchdog functions they once performed, but they were adamant that their private connections are more effective today. "When I thought they were doing something wrong, I didn't write the newspaper and make a statement," ALPE's leader said. "I'm not ashamed of this" (Guntsadze 2007). The Liberty Institute's Meladze similarly looked at self-censorship as a blessing, not a curse. "I think it opens doors for you to be more active in criticizing [in private] and also working with [the government] and co-operating" (Meladze 2007).

Beyond backroom influence, some organization leaders said that, because they are a known commodity, they are also better able to work more formally with the government—and thus attract donor support. Officials from the Liberty Institute, whose members or associates have occupied key positions in the National Movement, claimed to have found remarkable strength in their personal networks (Ramishvili 2007). "We don't just exist to exist," Liberty's director said. "We had certain ideas that we wanted to have implemented. In that way it was useful." "It helped in many ways," agreed another Liberty member. For example, Liberty's contacts enabled it to communicate with government officials and parliamentary leaders, thereby allowing them to take formal positions into account as they draft legislation (Meladze 2007). These contacts, coupled with their reputation for drafting legislation even before 2003, opened up additional doors, including requests from the state for Liberty to contribute its own draft laws (Ramishvili 2007). "If something is happening right now, we know it's happening and try to get involved" (Meladze 2007). In a country where the time from legislation initiation to adoption was extremely short (one human-rights leader calculated that on the last day of 2006 a bill was passed every three minutes and six seconds) (Chokheli 2007), leaders of other organizations agreed that Liberty has had a tremendous influence on Georgia's post-2003 development (Zhvania 2007).

Certainly the Liberty Institute, frequently alleged by international and local observers to have transformed itself from a highly critical watchdog into a government-organized nongovernmental organization, or GONGO, has had extraordinarily positive relations with the state. During interviews, Liberty officials repeatedly defended the government against accusations by (local and international) human-rights organizations (including a decline in media freedom and judicial independence), calling these charges "debatable" (Meladze 2007) and "a misunderstanding" or "misrepresentation of the facts" or "a problem with the facts and opinions." "You will find some people who will be disappointed with everything," Liberty's head reasoned (Ramishvili 2007).

While the Liberty Institute seems to be almost stereotypically placed in this category, leaders of similar organizations claimed that it was part of a deliberate strategy on their part, saying they held their tongues in the hope it would pay off in the long run. Among those that might fall under the "inclusion" label are Open Society Georgia, the Caucasus Institute, the UN Association of Georgia (UNAG), and ALPE. "There are many things I disagree with," the head of ALPE said. "But I don't make public statements because I know that, if I do, it will be very difficult to do other things that are much more important" (Guntsadze 2007). The director of the Civil Society Institute, which, like ALPE, engaged in watchdog activities under Shevardnadze but has since abandoned these, agreed. "Our vision is that we can make some improvements through cooperation, but if you're at the same time a watchdog, it's not possible," said the organization's leader. "Nobody likes biting" (Salamadze 2007). According to UNAG, NGOs that "don't know other methods . . . for how to advocate" apart from public criticism have suffered. "Our government is really quite sensitive to forms of criticism," he said. "In some cases for sure it might spoil relations" (UNAG 2007).

Those willing to bite their tongues and not criticize the authorities have been handsomely rewarded. Salamadze's Civil Society Institute, for instance, saw its revenues skyrocket, from $60,000 before the revolution (2002) to about $500,000 in 2006, primarily from state-related projects (Salamadze 2007). Since the revolution, another organization, UNAG, was awarded its largest project ever with the government. "Now we have more and more cooperative projects between government and civil society," one UNAG leader said, adding that governmental agencies actually called certain NGOs looking for assistance. "There was a tendency to work more closely with other NGOs, those that were, so to speak, more cooperative" (UNAG 2007).

Some governmental leaders (who must sign on to foreign-sponsored joint projects with the state) have reportedly made funding and cooperative opportunities available to NGOs in return for their more restrained tone. One government official, referring to the Liberty Institute's transition from watchdog to think tank, complimented that organization's leaders for having "a good sense of what's going on and what their most useful role can be" (Ugulava 2007). Other groups might find state cooperation if they focus on issues such as advising on how to streamline the bureaucratic process, helping with the inclusion of national minorities, or assisting with orphanage reform, this same official added. Organizations that have chosen this path are not GONGOs, their leaders emphasize, but rather represent one tactical niche through which they claim to "support something that will bring good changes to the country" (Guntsadze 2007). Such organizations may on occasion criticize the government in public as a last resort, but they have preferred to do so in private, providing measured expert advice during committee hearings or speaking to government colleagues in person. "We never publicize the issue. We present these arguments, we have these quarrels, but we do it inside," Salamadze said. "These are our techniques, and it works. I can tell you that we affect the policies" (Salamadze 2007).

However, these leaders also concede that their influence has been limited in two ways. First, their organizations have been able to influence the state primarily indirectly through their training programs and other services, a form of government outsourcing. Ultimately, however, their survival has come at the price of, in the words of one ex-NGO leader in the state, "saying what we would like to hear" (Tsintsadze 2007). Think tanks such as Liberty, for instance, have been afforded a voice that the government is comfortable with (Anjaparidze 2007).

Second, direct organizational influence is limited by policy level. While state officials have proven willing to hear conciliatory NGO leaders out in private, they have been swayed only with respect to finite policies. One interviewee from ALPE described his organization's influence in the case of a Tbilisi property improperly given away during the Shevardnadze period. When the local government suddenly attempted to reclaim it from hapless residents, "I went to [my friend] and said, 'Look, this is really ridiculous. Look at it from your old eyes,'" said ALPE's Guntsadze, referring to former ALPE leader and then Tbilisi mayor Gigi Ugulava. "He listened, and he changed some things" (Guntsadze 2007).[3] Other close observers said that NGOs were consulted on technical details rather than broad policy and, they wryly commented, only "if their positions coincide with the government's" (USG2 2007).

Still, the advantages these organizations have enjoyed have been especially great when compared to those of outspoken NGO leaders, described in detail earlier, who have found themselves isolated. Expectedly, GYLA and ex-GYLA officials claimed that at the start of the

transition—during the period when NGOs largely withheld criticism—
there were positive relations and cooperative efforts between the two
sides (Chkhetia 2007; Papuashvili 2007). After GYLA allegedly took a
turn toward the political opposition, the Supreme Court chair (then sitting on GYLA's board) said, "It turned out that there were no more of
these connections" (Kublashvili 2007). Even GYLA's chairman, who
worked in the prosecutor's office for six months before returning to head
his former organization, said that once he transitioned back to GYLA,
government officials largely cut off their ties with him, perhaps because
they were irked by his decision to return to such a critical NGO. "Maybe
it was viewed from their side as some kind of wrong or strange thing"
(Chkheidze 2007). High-ranking government officials who worked with
this individual while he was employed by the state agreed that such interpersonal connections have been insufficient to bridge the damage
done at an institutional level (GOG 2007; GOG2 2007).

GYLA, which dominates this category of the excluded, perhaps
best serves as a counterexample to Liberty, but it is not alone. "If they
don't like what you're doing, then cooperation won't happen," said Konstantine Kandelaki, head of the International Center for Civic Culture,
which focuses on local-government development and has been sidelined
for criticizing government-backed legislation (Kandelaki 2007). According to civil-society funders, once NGOs began engaging in watchdog
functions, including pressing for transparency, the opportunities initially
granted them were withdrawn. "They stop providing them with public
information, and they refuse to cooperate" (Anjaparidze 2007). The
publicly cautious head of Open Society Georgia, which also funds civil-
society projects, agreed that "when the government people feel that the
criticism is unfair, then of course it creates problems with them." He
continued: "But, objectively, what is fair and what is not is difficult to
judge" (Darchiashvili 2007). An internal affairs ministry representative
indirectly provided evidence in support of this assessment, commenting
that his regular invitation to meetings with the NGO community did
not "necessarily include all the opposition-minded and the radical [orga-
nizations]" (MVD 2007).

Transparency International is another organization that has watched
its opportunities fade away. After it published its first critical report, for

example, the government refused to sign memoranda of cooperation (making it more difficult to attract donor funding), curtailed access to senior-level officials, and closed the group's parliamentary office, essential to exercising influence in a country with such a fast-paced legislative process. "When we started writing critical reports, the government said, 'We're not going to cooperate with you,'" said Transparency's executive director (Karosanidze 2007). Instead, Transparency and others have sought to influence the government through what Keck and Sikkink refer to as a "boomerang" approach, lobbying international organizations to, in turn, put pressure on their own government (Keck and Sikkink 1998). "If you don't talk about these problems with NATO and other international institutions and structures, you have almost no influence in the government," Transparency's Karosanidze said. "They really don't care what NGOs or the media say" (Karosanidze 2007).

Summary

Georgia's new political leaders came to power in 2003 with little political experience but with "the values and the idea of how a normal country should look" (Tarkhnishvili 2007). They were revolutionaries out to build a new Georgia, armed with ideals and, they thought, the backing of society, civil society and all. Both old and new NGO leaders, long united in a principled struggle between what amounted to friendship networks and the state, were confident they had the backing of one another. "This is a special moment in history, and now this government is the center—where things are happening," as one civil-society leader summarized the spirit. "Morally you should be with us" (Nodia 2007). Yet within a year and a half formal alliances and informal relationships began to break down along the newly drawn state/nonstate boundary. Georgian elites, who had so recently been elated by victory, sank into a new era of mutual recriminations and competition for support.

Those NGOs who were willing to lie low and work quietly to see these objectives through have profited from the creation of opportunities in the new Georgia, especially where they have shared identities and personal networks with government leaders. Those outwardly opposed to these tactics, by contrast, have watched these relationships take a nosedive.

In these cases, identity has become a field of contestation— each side believes it is the one that has remained true to struggle-era objectives. Personal networks have only strengthened their feelings of betrayal. Not surprisingly, the opportunities afforded such groups are severely curtailed, igniting a vicious circle of accusations and interpersonal struggles that only further restricts available opportunities.

Just as in the context of mass-based organizations in Poland and South Africa, what appears to have separated yesterday's NGO leaders from today's in Georgia and what has as a result so often strained relations is tactics, not goals. "Let's just do anything we can do to get to that end goal," one NGO leader said of the government's attitude. "If we have to violate the law, that's okay for the time being" (Karosanidze 2007). Those in the state have claimed to be making the best choices they can under difficult conditions and take personal offense at the attacks leveled against them. "All of us were *founders* of the organization," one ex-GYLA government official said. "Time after time it became more evident that we were considered as bad people in the government" (GOG2 2007).

In the next chapter I reconsider the Georgia case in a broader, comparative framework, bringing together the three cases in this book in order to assess various factors that might influence the likelihood of any one of the arguments discussed in each case.

6

Implications and Conclusions

VICTORY FOR PRO-DEMOCRACY ORGANIZATIONS in Poland, South Africa, and Georgia was, as I have demonstrated, bittersweet. The old regime was gone—or at least safely contained by democratic institutions, but so, too, were many ideals and friendships that had formed during the struggle. Disappointment was almost palpable not only among the general public but also within the organizations that had led the pro-democracy struggle. After a brief period of euphoric optimism, one-time colleagues eventually found each others' actions to be incompatible with what the pro-democracy organization had long stood for. Organizations mobilized against their (former) friends now in office, and political leaders closed the doors to their (former) friends still in civil society. Many leaders who remained outside the state bureaucracy found themselves in an ironic position: Their influence was ultimately greater under the old regime, which had been run by their worst enemies, than under the new one, now run by their closest friends.

In Poland this occurred not just during the initial period of democratization (1989–1991 and 1991–1993) but also in the subsequent wave (1997–2001); in both instances, Solidarity leaders who went on to powerful positions with the state, regardless of their class background, claimed that their ties actually hindered cooperation with the organization they had left behind. In South Africa this phenomenon played out repeatedly for fifteen years in two different organizational contexts—the moderately inclusive union movement and the highly inclusive civic movement, neither of which was capable of using identities and networks to significantly influence the path of reform. Finally, in Georgia the same dynamics occurred with respect to those organizations that continued to function as watchdogs in the ostensibly new era.

However, to what degree are these cases distinguishable by the independent variables discussed in Chapter 2 (see Table 1, p. 32)? According to these variables, we should expect the network and identity arguments to be most salient in those pro-democracy organizations with the longest period of activity against the most abusive regimes. The logic, built upon a relatively scant but intuitively convincing literature, is that repression can reinforce feelings of group solidarity as activists huddle together against the storm and that the longer this storm lasts (and therefore the more intragroup interaction and collaboration), the more intense and enduring these feelings should be. As Aminzade and McAdam note, the collective identity becomes "an integral part of the individual's life and self-identity," where the stakes of group rejection and ostracism are elevated (Aminzade and McAdam 2001, 38).[1] Activists may strive to present an appearance of rationality, but social movements are characterized by strong emotions, where activists see their organizations as powerful "commitments or investments" that structure one's "orientation toward the world" (Goodwin, Jasper, and Polletta 2004, 418).[2]

If social movement–based identities and personal networks become stronger the longer the movement operates and the harsher its opponents are, then there should be clear disparities in the salience of these arguments among the chosen cases, which range from highly (South Africa) and moderately (Poland) repressive climates and long-lived social movements to relatively benign environments and brief movements (Georgia). According to the identity and network hypotheses, both factors should have played a greater role in postbreakthrough South Africa's politics, followed by Poland and then Georgia, enhancing the influence of pro-democracy organizations on their democratizing states.

Evaluating the Struggle's Impact on Identity and Networks

In practice, there is little evidence that identity created stronger state/nonstate bonds in any one of these cases, where activists who left the state and those who remained behind similarly claimed to uphold the values their movement had espoused. Rather than being an access point, identity quickly turned into a site of competition. In South Africa, for instance, those who remained in the organizations accused their ex-colleagues in the state of being "swallowed into a new thinking" (Ehrenreich 2008), while ex-activists in the state accused unionists of having a "crude sense of what constitutes Left and leftist policies and what government can and can't do" (Essop 2008). In Poland, the war over Solidarity's ownership continued for more than a decade and a half after the organization helped usher in democracy. Those who moved to the state questioned the level of altruism of an organization that had once fought for the good of Poland, and those who remained in the organization accused its ex-leaders of misunderstanding what Solidarity was (a worker's movement, they said) from the very beginning.

The result was a sentiment that offended organization leaders. "When I encounter them sometimes," said one Solidarity initiator of his successors, "I say, 'Gentlemen, remember that your legend comes from the founding fathers'" (Frasyniuk 2009). Not surprisingly, given this attitude, there is a perception among social-movement activists that, after their colleagues took power, they belittled the remaining organizations as deficient in both leadership and purpose. "People who left the union still felt they *were* the union," commented one longtime Solidarity activist (Osiński 2009). "The soda water went to their heads," added another (Borowczak 2009). This was certainly not unique to the extensive social movement that carried the day in Poland. South Africa's former unionists who took to the state saw their ex-colleagues preaching nothing more than "a whole lot of crap, which sounds flowery and exciting" (Copelyn 2008), and their ex-comrades in turn felt that "some [former COSATU leaders] would think that we were stupid" (Makwayiba 2008). "There is a general message that the government does not need NGOs anymore," echoed an NGO activist in Georgia (Saakashvili 2007).

If identities seem to have been generally unsuccessful in creating influence regardless of movement duration and the nature of the struggle, so were personal networks. It is, again, difficult to measure sentimental ties among individuals, but certainly whatever sentiments there were failed to translate into organizational influence on the state. While ex-leaders in the state felt that common ties with social-movement activists "helped us find a common language" (Kaminska 2009), leaders of the social-movement organizations complained that their ex-colleagues in the state helped—and sometimes only picked up the phone—only when they had relatively simple and isolated requests. In Poland and South Africa, organization leaders blamed a combination of personal ambition and new peer pressures for minimizing the utility of these networks. "He wants to make something of himself," one Polish unionist said of a colleague who accepted employment with the state, adding that this demanded listening to political voices and ignoring movement ones (Dubiński 2009). In Georgia, organization leaders who stayed on the power holders' good side by moderating their demands similarly found themselves able to meet with and influence ex-activists on finite issues but were largely ineffectual with respect to bigger issues.

The South Africa case, where identities and networks seem to have played a part in giving COSATU and SANCO seats in the ANC's governing Alliance, suggests that the independent variables evaluated may have been instrumental. Closer analysis, however, raises doubts. First, while these organizations sat at the governing table, their leaders felt sufficiently sidelined there that they continued to pursue contentious activities in order to have policy influence. Second, the Georgia case suggests that even relatively new movements that function in mild political climates can foster strong personal networks—particularly, according to Georgian interviewees, in small countries with tight, exclusive, elite networks in which cohorts were similar in, for example, age, Western experiences and general values. "The personal relationship can influence a lot in Georgia, which is a small country," said one NGO leader (Chkhetia 2007). "Everyone knows everyone else here," added another (Khaindrava 2007). Regardless, networks did not produce influence on their own.

In all three cases, some activists accused their ex-colleagues in the state of using their social-movement organization as a "trampoline" (in

Polish parlance) or "stepping-stone" (in South Africa) to more lucrative political positions, suggesting that identities and personal networks were much more fragile than one might have expected. Such accusations, more prevalent in Poland and South Africa than in Georgia (where they also occur), are obviously difficult to corroborate. But there are differences even in the former two. In Poland's Solidarity and South Africa's SANCO, activists accused ex-leaders of every microcohort of taking power for the sake of power, while South African unionists often explained the move as a function of limited opportunities for those unionists who had made it to the top. "The general secretary of the union, what do you do with him at the end of his term? Where does he go?" asked one unionist who moved on to the state (Mkhize 2008). In fact, senior officials from both COSATU and Solidarity mentioned this dilemma of having no place apart from the political sphere where senior unionists could make a "soft landing" from union activism. Whatever the reason, it became a source of dispute and resentment on both sides of the state line.

The Common Denominator: Institutions

Where identities became contentious and networks ranged from tepid to toxic, institutions were responsible. Activists in each state eventually realized that their initial assumptions—that strong bonds with new power holders or the unique qualities of their own organizations would be advantages—were utopian dreams in the face of stark realities. As their friends would repeatedly remind them, democratization came with a price tag both during the struggle and after.

It is important to emphasize that activists on both sides of the state/nonstate divide believed they were the ones paying the postbreakthrough tab. For the former, the burdens of governance necessitated putting off long-held policy preferences that from the helm suddenly seemed impractical. "It was time to come to the government and to do real work," said one Georgian official (GOG2 2007). Certainly, these ex-activists admitted, some policies could have been better, but hindsight is always twenty-twenty. "We are doing so many things so quickly that you end up making some mistakes," explained one senior Georgian official (MVD 2007).

The institutionally based incentives these new state leaders faced were both international and domestic in nature. By far the most striking emanation of the former was the tenacity with which (ex-)trade unionists and even self-proclaimed communists in Poland and South Africa pursued a neoliberal agenda upon taking power despite the local protests this action prompted. In Poland it is telling that even the postcommunist coalition that took back power between 1993 and 1997 continued along the free-market path, carved by the first post-Solidarity power holders and eventually opposed by the Solidarity organization, even as their own constituents and organized lobbies (OPZZ) attacked them. Certainly these actors were convinced by a slew of Western economists that rapid transformation was necessary, but they were also cognizant of the fact that such a transformation was a prerequisite to obtaining outside support from organizations such as the World Bank and the International Monetary Fund. Finally, they were motivated by a long history of political and economic weakness, both of which political elites believed could be resolved with their rapid—and conditioned—entry into the European Union and NATO.

In South Africa, even members of the Communist Party—which, unlike left-wing parties of Eastern Europe, continued to go by that name and profess a communist ideology—began supporting free trade against the wishes of their labor backers. As in Poland, elites in the state became convinced that they had no choice but to follow the dominant international line if they were to attract the Western assistance and investment that they felt they needed to turn their economies around. "I suppose as you become older, you become more pragmatic. You become more focused on what is accomplishable," explained one unionist who went to parliament in 1994 and into business in 1997 (Golding 2008). "It's not necessarily an ideological shift. It's an exposure to the reality of how the system functions," added another, a provincial minister (Godongwana 2008).

In Georgia, by contrast, neoliberal economic reforms received practically no attention from social-movement organizations, whose largely Western-educated leaders simply accepted this economic course. There, state leaders' institutional pressures, which prompted consternation in the movement organizations, were political in nature; new power holders felt that security concerns trumped the rule of law. While this may have been an effort to satisfy popular domestic demands for territorial integrity, it was certainly motivated by external factors, including the Russia threat and the apparent complacency of those same Western leaders who had helped Georgia's new principals take power to begin with.

Thus, those in policy positions went along with the course chosen either because they came to believe it was the only way forward or because they felt they had no choice but to accept that course if they hoped to keep their jobs and have their opinions heard in the future. These clearly institutionally shaped preferences left them open to attacks from their old colleagues. "If I take a platform in the public domain," laughed one prominent South African unionist who took ministerial jobs at both the state and local level, "I defend it in such a manner that you can think that I like it" (Godongwana 2008). Such longtime activists felt obliged to break not only with their own conscience but also with longtime friends since they now no longer represented the movement organization they had left behind but rather "the state, the society, the electorate" (Mosinski 2009). "This was an incredibly difficult situation for a union activist," said one Solidarity leader who accepted a parliamentary position. "But the union, of course, didn't elect me. Rather, society did" (Mozolewski 2009).

Such highly inclusive sentiment left activists feeling ironically disenfranchised. They had put their friends in power in order to influence the direction of the new state, and instead their voices were being drowned out in the name of some far-off greater good. Of course, their personal and ideational bonds gave them a degree of access others lacked, but what good was it when it amounted to "influencing" only those policies that were already "compatible with [the political leaders'] line" (Dubiński 2009)? Former friends talked past each other. In Georgia, for instance, the ombudsman claimed that for his one-time comrades "the ideal has become Pinochet, who had absolute power" (Subari 2007). Ex-activists who took to the state retorted, using the same words we saw in the South Africa chapter, that such critics "don't understand what's going on at the political level and . . . the threats of counterrevolution" (GOG2 2007). In all three cases activists were bitter not simply at having limited influence on the policy debate but also at being shut out almost entirely by their ex-colleagues, who no longer thought they were worth consulting.

Organization leaders who had spent the first year or two of reforms waiting patiently for their voices to be heard and their demands to be implemented finally returned to their prebreakthrough activities. The institutional barriers erected around their disloyal ex-colleagues seemed to offer no other alternative.

The problem was that this return to protest drew return fire when, as in other countries, "old friends" turned out to be "surprised and very unwilling to be monitored" (Bell and Keenan 2004, 346). Networks that had been useful for small favors at the beginning often became obstacles to cooperation after angry movement activists renewed their contentious activities. Activists and ex-activists in the preceding chapters described these relations using emotionally charged words such as "angry," "offended," "insulted," "personally hurt," "ridicule," and "stereotypes." As one Polish activist commented with reference to a Solidarity protest against its own colleagues' policies, "Our colleagues were even angry at us—'What are you doing?'" (Langer 2009).

Bridges were burned in all three states, but the blaze reached perhaps its greatest height in Georgia, where botched personal relations were the most lethal. In the other states, one might argue that the brute strength of the mass organizations served to check the instinctively negative response of state officials. Yet GYLA, with so many ex-leaders in power, is the most dramatic example of opportunities lost in Georgia despite the fact that this particular organization dwarfed most others in terms of both membership and proven mobilizing potential. Of course, GYLA could not have hundreds of thousands of protesters flooding the streets of the capital at the drop of a hat, as COSATU could. Nonetheless, relative to other Georgian organizations that received influence in return for moderation, it was the big kid on the block. Interestingly, in Georgia, personal animosity toward former colleagues was greatest, and, again, GYLA—with the longest history and thus arguably the closest personal networks—was the showcase for this rancor.

The reason relations went sour, as seen in each of the country chapters, was that the enormous expectations of support each set of actors had of the other were, given the contrasting institutional pressures, untenable. In all of the cases studied, it seems that both activists and former activists remained intoxicated by their monumental democratic victories and attempted to sustain that moment of nostalgia for months or even years, all the while in denial that they could ever let each other down. When reality hit, it hit hard. "They completely changed their shape," said one GYLA official of his former colleagues (Chkheidze 2007). Individuals on each side felt that they were the ones who were selflessly pursuing the dreams their organization had always espoused and found the others' actions a huge disappointment. "We did this pro publico, pro bono—for the public good," said one Solidarity activist who, having headed education reforms under AWS, became a target of anger from the union side. "This was a group of people that was thinking about Poland" (Książek 2009). That might apply to the rare "decent, honest union activists," commented one longtime activist (Marczak 2009), but, concluded another, "we were unhappy with a great many things" (Solidarity1 2009).

This important finding indicates not merely that these institutions changed their principal players but also that those who should have been empowered from a more emotionally-driven perspective, based on identities and networks, similarly lost out. Instead, identities and networks became poisonous under the new conditions, thereby undermining the organizations' ability to maintain constructive relations with their ex-partners no matter how strong the watchdog groups remained. Regardless of how, when, and where the struggle occurred, activists faced the same fate after breakthrough: Either accept the terms dictated by their former colleagues in the state or lose the chance to influence the country's new direction. In reality, a lack of influence on the most meaningful reforms was a foregone conclusion. The question was whether organizations would settle for crumbs or continue to fight in the hope of achieving more, no matter what the personal costs.

From Europe and Africa to Asia and America

The intra- and intercase comparisons described in the preceding pages clearly demonstrate the strength with which institutions can shape individuals' preferences in ways that cause former ties to buckle. It is important to emphasize that these cases are not isolated, as indicated in

Chapter 1. And with the spread of electoral revolutions in the last decade and a half, including in many parts of Europe and the Middle East, the list of cases is likely to grow. How representative are the cases relied upon here, and to what degree can we generalize from these findings?

A broad survey of the literature suggests that these cases are broadly representative of others around the world. Grassroots organizations similar to South Africa's civics have formed in numerous countries, usually with the initial aim of fighting for basic goods and services that weak or repressive states do not provide. These organizations can take on functions that range from helping the unemployed or those with housing problems to focusing on public health and education. As with the unions mentioned earlier, these organizations have eventually bridged into the political sphere largely out of protest against the nondemocratic state's economic mismanagement, but the transformation has marked a shift from concern about narrow economic interests to collective, politicized grievances. In the Philippines, Nigeria, Brazil, and Chile, for example, the growth of grassroots organizations around subsistence issues such as unemployment assistance, food distribution, and housing has been in part a function of political opportunities. Once these organizations appear, they can quickly become highly organized, autonomous actors capable of engaging in large-scale protest activity.

In other countries, including Serbia, Croatia, Ukraine, the Philippines, Nicaragua, Indonesia, Thailand, Peru, Mexico, Argentina, Brazil, and Chile, small nongovernmental organizations have played pivotal roles in voter registration, election monitoring, and popular mobilization prior to or after elections that ultimately yielded democratic breakthroughs. In the latter, for example, NGOs functioned as "key nodes in opposition networks" (Loveman 1991, 10) and through a variety of activities—from the provision of legal services and victim support groups to the monitoring of rights violations—helped bolster a rising opposition coalition. The Chilean Committee for Free Elections (CEL), created in March 1988, teamed up with the Roman Catholic Church–based CIVITAS foundation to engage in a massive voter-education and registration campaign prior to the 1988 plebiscite. Their activities included press campaigns, house-to-house visits, distribution of informational fliers, and voter drives. In the Philippines, a range of NGOs that had long been removed from political activity helped orchestrate daily demonstrations against the Marcos regime. As Aiyede notes in the case of Nigeria, small nongovernmental organizations may have had only weak links at the grassroots level, but they were successful in bringing large numbers of people into the streets in the name of democracy and human rights (Aiyede 2003, 11).

Union-backed movements have also wrested power from nondemocrats around the world. While the fact that unions tend to focus first and foremost on concrete, material issues may sometimes make them more susceptible to state cooptation, as in various Latin America states throughout the 1970s, unions in those same countries also have a history of forcing states to adopt transition projects or orchestrating protest movements that eventually help bring about full-scale transitions. The same is true for African transition states, such as Benin, Kenya, Nigeria, Ghana, and especially Zambia, as well as Asian states from Pakistan to South Korea, where trade unions in the twentieth century created strong pressures for change.

All of these organizational types are typically, at least early on, correlated with particular agendas and strategies that serve to further differentiate them. Pro-democracy NGOs often (though not always) focus on the most abstract issues, such as justice and rule of law, and limit their material support to individual, symbolic cases of concrete injustice. Their public message frequently targets the (independent or international) media in the hope of gaining high-level intervention rather than stirring up mass unrest. Unions, by contrast, normally fight on behalf of issues that are pertinent to workers, such as wages and safety, and organize their tactics around the workplace (e.g., strikes, slowdowns). Grassroots groups can focus on material issues (such as food or utility prices) or ideological ones, but they tend to do so in ways that are less abstract and thus more tangible to (potential) supporters than do NGOs.

Ultimately, though, these pro-democracy organizations all refocus their activities and tactics on a broad set of political demands—liberalization—that are seen as essential to the realization of everything else the group stands for. This is the period of broad-based mobilization and the birth of the social movement. Apart from country-specific nuances, in other words, the same phenomena of democratization that occurred in Poland, South Africa, and Georgia have also happened in scores of other states.

Unfortunately, there is little direct evidence from the postdemo-cratic breakthrough period in these other cases that might serve as evidence for or against the generalizability of this study. Here I present preliminary evidence from two cases, the Philippines and Chile, in which both massive and tiny social-movement organizations were instrumental in producing a democratic breakthrough and established their leaders in the new state bureaucracy in the belief that they would "strengthen and consolidate democracy after the transition" (Diamond 1992, 14). In both cases the outcomes appear to be very similar to what we have seen in Poland, South Africa, and Georgia.

The Philippines

Opposition to the moderately repressive Marcos regime in the Philippines included two major branches of civil society: nongovernmental organizations and "popular organizations" (POs). The former emerged from the student movement that began in the 1960s, and, as in Georgia, few observers at the time imagined that "small groups of young people" would ever be seen as "a vital component of civil society" (Constantino-David 1998, 26). However, also as in Georgia, the foreign-backed growth of this sector over time led outsiders to label the country an "NGO paradise" (Racelis 2000, 160). While these organizations frequently worked in cooperation with the state prior to the implementation of martial law in 1972, afterward they began working more with grassroots organizations and, to various degrees, sought to distance themselves from the state. By the 1980s they represented a political force that was capable of bringing about cooperation among students, labor, and the urban poor discontented with the Marco regime.

The organizations with which these Georgia-style NGOs cooperated were South Africa–style civic organizations or POs. The cooperation had begun as early as the 1970s, when, for example, NGOs and POs together launched a widespread educational campaign for the 1978 elections. However, it was not until the 1983 assassination of political opposition leader Benigno Aquino and the cheating against his widow, Corazon

Aquino, in the postassassination snap elections that the enormous potential of this cooperation became evident. The POs mobilized the population, staged regular demonstrations, and then organized electoral outreach in the face of the 1986 snap elections. Systematic fraud in those elections prompted a massive civil-disobedience campaign that helped mark the end of the Marcos regime that February.

Democratic breakthrough in the Philippines was characterized by the traditional weakening of the pro-democracy social movement as constituent organizations began transitioning from a grassroots base to more formal organizations capable of garnering donor support and conducting institutionalized pressure on the democratizing state. Unlike in Georgia, where many pro-democracy NGOs were created to press for democracy from the start, Philippine organizations often acquired these functions on top of their original missions of economic and social development. Democratization in the Philippines has thus long been equated with poverty reduction and empowerment. When Aquino came to power, it was easy for activists to revert to these positions, taking on service-provider functions in the process.

From Aquino's perspective, NGOs (and especially human-rights organizations) could play an instrumental role in improving her government's international image and help consolidate democracy. They were, Silliman and Noble write, "the vehicle by which political power would be democratized" (Silliman and Noble 1998, 288). To further this end and ensure NGOs were on board, Aquino brought a number of NGO leaders into the state, including in senior positions that ranged from the presidential spokesperson to the labor secretary. Of the forty-eight members of new constitution-drafting committee, to give another example, more than one-fifth came from the NGO community (Clarke 1998, 72–73). For many NGO leaders, the transition was natural; their members—like those of Georgian NGOs and South African civics—had often historically involved themselves in political activities. Aquino and then Ramos, after her, "opened their doors to NGOs, thereby providing spaces in the corridors of power" (Constantino-David 1998, 43).

The confluence of NGO professionalization and a leadership transfer to the state marked a decline in the level of pluralism within civil society and the elevation of a small number of networks over others (Silliman

1998, 68). The state took on a new and powerful role in determining the shape of the NGO community by providing an important new source of funding to those organizations that adopted service-provider functions, tasked mostly with education and economic/social-development projects.

The indirect evidence available suggests that what happened in Poland, South Africa, and Georgia had a precedent several years earlier in the Philippines. With their people in high positions, NGOs had occasional and "modest success" in influencing certain government policies, but by and large their interventions in the policy process were "unsuccessful in determining its outcomes" (Silliman and Noble 1998, 304). Those in the state were often loath to reach out to the well-funded and still-mobilized NGOs and POs, which they felt represented a threat to their policies and positions, and there is evidence that a schism developed between activists and ex-activists in the state (Silliman and Noble 1998, 298). The mechanisms that took root in the three cases described in this book seem likely to have been at play in the Philippines as well. Indeed, there is evidence that some NGO leaders who were given cabinet positions "were dismayed to discover that as government officials they frequently had to make unpopular compromises to retain their power" (Racelis 2000, 178). New institutional homes demanded unforeseen changes in policy preferences that would have left their ex-colleagues bitter.

Chile

Available evidence suggests that the Chile case played out similarly. There, as in Georgia, an active NGO community arose as "occupational alternatives" for those excluded from their professions (especially intellectuals) during the rule of Augusto Pinochet (Loveman 1991, 10). Apart from small organizations, which ranged from intellectual groups and human-rights organizations to other social, cultural, and religious associations, there were also well-organized, highly and moderately inclusive groups. These included a trade-union movement, which—in 1980s' Polish style—also worked in and with the support of the poor more broadly. It also included the Chilean shantytown movement, which, like South Africa's civics, was activated to deal with local problems resulting from state economic policies and assisted with everything from acquiring housing to group cooking. By the mid-1980s, in the face of an economic downturn, these groups engaged in mass protests, strikes, and demonstrations demanding an immediate end to Pinochet's rule. Throughout the mid-1980s, as South Africa's townships burned and Poland's Solidarity leaders struggled in the underground, Chile's protests gained steam. In contrast to South Africa, where a vast majority of the African community supported the ANC, and Poland, where political opposition parties were underdeveloped, Chile had a more salient and fractured political opposition structure that made long-term cooperation difficult. There were long-standing tactical rifts in the alliance, as some groups (namely the Democratic Alliance [AD]) preferred to negotiate with the regime, whereas others (especially the Popular Democratic Movement [MDP]) demanded ongoing protests until the regime collapsed. In 1986, when the military burned two protesters alive, the opposition, also under pressure from the middle class, became convinced that the costs of popular mobilization were too high. Soon after, politicians returned to the negotiating table and demanded the demobilization of grassroots organizations.

When a renewed round of mobilization occurred in 1988, the contentious approach abandoned a few years earlier was substituted by a grassroots electoral campaign orchestrated by Chile's three main political opposition parties, known as the Concertación Democrática de los Partidos Políticos por la Demokracia. The goal was to bring millions out to vote against what was in effect a plebiscite on Pinochet's continued rule. The plebiscite was the outcome of an elite-level pact in which the opposition abandoned its demands for an immediate end to Pinochet's rule in return for free and fair elections that would make this option a real possibility. Much like in the electoral revolutions that were common at the start of the next millennium, Chilean NGOs created organizations to conduct massive voter-education and registration drives, monitor the vote, and even provide advice as to legal aspects of the plebiscite. As in other cases, activists were harassed in various ways, from detentions and personal threats to the denial of permits to operate. Still, the campaign was a success and led the following year to new elections, in which opposition candidate Patricio Aylwin was victorious.

With democratic breakthrough, many of Chile's NGO leaders took to the state, attaining high-level positions in the first post-Pinochet government in part as a sort of payback and in part for their skills in areas such as foreign policy and assistance programs. At the same time, the new government promised to respect the autonomy of the NGO sector and provide it with material support. Chilean NGOs, in the words of one scholar, "had won recognition for their part in the campaigns of the transition, and appeared well placed to benefit from the new democracy" (Foweraker 2001, 849).

Despite this, NGOs saw several measures introduced by Aylwin, including the creation of a state fund that would coordinate NGO anti-poverty activities, as a threat to their own existence. Indeed, by controlling funding (foreign donors had diverted their support to the new government) Aylwin was able to speed up demobilization by pitting now competing organizations against each another. This may have been Aylwin's objective since, like Saakashvili almost two decades later, he had seen what NGOs could do to the old regime and knew they might do the same to new, democratically elected leaders. The state became a major donor, and, as acceptance of state funding necessitated certain compromises, the NGO sector became simultaneously a client and a policy facilitator of its new political benefactors.

Again, existing evidence suggests that the ex-leaders of Chile's social-movement organizations faced the same institutional pressures and motivations as have the others discussed here. Ex-NGO leaders who were struggling to remain loyal to their NGO role functioned in a government where they had to balance powerful forces from the old regime, including the military and political Right, with a commitment to the pro-democracy community. Although Aylwin's close ties to the popular sector helped him launch major market reforms, the adoption of neoliberal policies strained relations between the popular sector and political elites. Those who took to the state encountered "the daily stress of coalition management, office politics, and the need to respond publicly to popular demands for the first time. In each case, the immediacy of cries for social and economic programs to overcome years of authoritarian rule contrasted markedly with the relatively insulated, informal, forgiving, and unscrutinized routine of life in NGOs" (Loveman 1991, 13). The result was not the powerful push activists likely believed their colleagues would bring them upon taking power but rather a "within the possible" philosophy of policymaking (Loveman 1995, 312).

Clearly, these cases are incomplete. Nonetheless, they suggest that the dynamics detailed in this study are likely not limited to the specific contexts examined. Indeed, the diversity of cases in this book represents a determined effort to test competing arguments under a range of conditions described in Chapter 2. The preliminary evidence from the Philippines and Chile indicates the presence of two common themes: the migration of social-movement activists to the state upon breakthrough and the predictable transformation of their policy preferences once in these new positions. Old friends and ideas may have remained alive, but those ex-activists who were facing new, institutionally determined constraints and incentives felt forced to opt for policy options they once would likely have condemned.

Winning After Victory

The preceding discussion suggests that the findings in this study are likely to pertain to a much larger group of countries. In fact, anyone who follows politics knows there is nothing unusual about individuals taking to the state and failing to realize outside expectations. In advanced democracies, organizational leaders have found themselves sobered by how the institutions they enter transform their preferences and constrain their opportunities. Networks have been left with little staying power as, in the words of one set of scholars, "to the crude form of the 'Who you know versus what you know' question, the answer is 'What you know'" (Salisbury et al. 1989, 188). This particular conclusion leaves open an optimistic interpretation, in which leaders from nonstate organizations try to fit their experiences and goals shaped by the outside— aka identities—into the parameters defined by their new institutions. As the cases here indicate, though, identities are also challenged. In a grim assessment of another particular case in which identity might have been useful, Dryzek noted in reference to an environmental movement leader incorporated into the Clinton administration and subsequently pushed to the margins of policy debate, "What started out like a love affair turned out to be date rape" (Dryzek 1996, 480).

The scenario laid out in this study differs from that experienced in advanced democracies in critical ways. This study highlights how society's most outspoken leaders abdicated their watchdog responsibilities during arguably the most critical and formative periods in their state's recent history. As former leaders began carving a new political and economic face on the state, those remaining in social-movement organizations in all three cases essentially covered up rather than confronted the blemishes they saw forming. By speaking out against abuses early on, for example, Georgian watchdog organizations might have given their ex-colleagues pause by demonstrating that they would be held to the same scrutiny as their predecessors. Instead, by sitting on the sidelines during the first year of transition these organizations seem to have only emboldened their ex-colleagues to aggressively pursue the illiberal path they had begun to pave. The same can be said of Polish and South African organizations that, out of faith in and respect for their struggle-era comrades, initially watched in relative silence as politicians pursued economic reforms so painful to their societies and members.

This raises the critical question of what precisely the role of civil society is or should be in newly democratizing states. The very term *civil society* seems to be a catchall in the foreign policy and academic communities, but we might broadly define it as "an intermediary phenomenon, standing between the private sphere and the state" (Diamond 1999, 221).[3] Philosophers from Tocqueville to Locke have praised the ability of civil-society organizations to foster democratic values and community ties, simultaneously engaging with the state and positioning to counter it. Although Western policymakers involved in democracy promotion have over time tended to look at small nongovernmental organizations as the "building blocks of civil society" and frequently use the terms *NGO* and *civil society* interchangeably,[4] component organizations arguably include all of the organizations discussed earlier, from voluntary grassroots units opposed to the state to state-supported organizations with a full-time paid staff supporting state policies.

From the perspective of those who left social-movement organizations to join the state, there seems to be a near consensus that nonstate organizations should have played more of a supporting role for state policymakers by facilitating implementation or perhaps assisting with the development of policies and legislation in areas in which the government conceded its expertise was lacking. In Poland, there was an explicit expectation that Solidarity would shield the government from popular opposition to its reform programs. In South Africa, state leaders expected the civics to engage in service delivery and, where necessary, conspicuously alert the ANC to any policy shortcomings seen on the ground. COSATU was expected to at least, as in the Polish case, be openly supportive of the government, in which they technically had a say. In Georgia, state officials similarly felt that NGOs should transform themselves into policy facilitators. In all three countries, those who left the social-movement sector for the state questioned the credentials of those they left behind, particularly when it came to watchdog activities.

In short, new state leaders were confident they knew what was best for their respective population and felt a need to move quickly and to pursue the requisite policies unhindered. When organizations stepped in to contest these reforms, one-time colleagues derided them as lost, desperate, phony, and irresponsible. Watchdogs that had been praised before democratic breakthrough were subsequently portrayed as a burden to democratization by those who had given birth to these organizations in the first place. Meanwhile, those individuals who felt charged with keeping tabs on the new state justified their role as a prerequisite to successful democratic consolidation.

All of this, from afar, bodes poorly for democratic consolidation since civil society is traditionally assigned important roles such as checking and monitoring the state, stimulating political debate, organizing political participation, and fostering public-spiritedness. While there are cases of successful democratic consolidation despite the lack of an active civil society, including Spain and Chile, civil-society advocates argue that "third-wave" democracies that lack a strong civil society despite having adopted democratic institutions are "broken-back" democracies significantly weakened by this void (Rose and Shin 2001, 332).[5] As one scholar pointed out in the case of post-1989 Eastern Europe, "This migration left behind little or nothing in terms of oppositional public spheres. The gain was a liberal democratic state; the loss was a discursive democratic vitality" (Dryzek 1996, 485).

Indeed, while civil society was an important force in ushering in democratization, it has since suffered in the three countries studied. Polish politics, for instance, remains a largely top-down affair. According to one Polish sociologist, nearly twenty years after the transition began, the entire civil-society sphere was "still limping," and less than 2 percent of civil-society organizations were engaged in politics and human rights (Raabe 2008, 6). The SANCO case highlights this dilemma in particularly stark terms: More than 95 percent of the organization's six million members abandoned the organization during the first decade of transition, feeling it had become redundant, subordinate to the ruling political party, and useful primarily as a tool for personal enrichment. In addition, even the more institutionalized organizations in South Africa faced trouble in the new era as President Nelson Mandela, a symbol of democracy around the world, warned that many NGOs had "no popular base" and that, therefore, "as we continue the struggle to ensure a people-driven process of social transformation, we will have to consider the reliability of such NGOs as a vehicle to achieve this objective" (Mandela 1997).

Yet it is difficult to specify the degree to which these trends affected democratization in the cases here—and certainly only limited support for alarmists who claim that the abandonment of the civil sphere for the state really hurts prospects for democracy. Both Poland and South Africa quickly moved toward democratic consolidation, which they achieved within just a few years. In Poland, Solidarity leaders, under pressure from ex-activists in the state, constrained their organizations for the first year or two after breakthrough before pursuing a much more aggressive antireform stance. Yet during this initial period of restraint, according to Freedom House, the country moved from a nonfree to a free country (within a year of the 1989 elections).[6] In South Africa, where COSATU and SANCO followed an almost identical path (despite being members of the governing alliance), the country improved from a combined score of partly free (9) in 1993 to free (5) (lower is better) in 1994 and gradually improved in the decade since then.[7]

Still, it is clear from the voices of social-movement leaders that society paid a high price during this period, and one might wonder how these organizations could have reduced the cost to society. Of course, the pendulum eventually swung hard from one extreme to the other. In each case those quiet organizations subsequently became much louder, taking to the streets in marches, strikes, and protests that became almost routine. Democratic consolidation arguably demands some degree of contentious activity, as citizens come together occasionally to ensure their part in a process long denied to them. However, did Poland, the most contentious state in the region, democratize more fully or quickly than other less contentious states, such as Hungary, which witnessed just a fraction of the protest activity? Might civil society have had a more profound impact on the transformation if leaders of the social-movement organizations had not felt pressured to go along with changes implemented by their former colleagues early on?

Organizations in Poland and South Africa might have been lucky in that their new political elites chose policies that, while economically painful, led to a high level of democratic freedoms within just a year or two. In Georgia, by contrast, democratization faltered. According to Freedom House scores, Georgia's progress in democratization was nil in the first year after democratic breakthrough and, after very minor improvements that never brought it beyond a rating of "partly free," reverted to late Shevardnadze-era levels in 2008.[8] The Georgia case seems to justify concerns that the failure of these organizations to set constraints from the start can have disastrous implications on long-term development. "We have to violate the law," one NGO watchdog described the government's attitude at the start. "They started doing this little by little, and when they got away with it, they got spoiled" (Karosanidze 2007).

Perhaps one lesson from this study is that the type of pro-democracy movement has a potentially important impact on the success of democratization. In all three cases, civil society was weakened by democratic breakthrough, as easy external funding and certain levels of leadership expertise dried up. However, the weakness of Polish civil society after Solidarity came to power in 1989 and then again in 1997 did not lead to a soft authoritarianism. Nor did the collapse of South Africa's civics and the early acquiescence of COSATU mark a derailment of the democratic process. Only in Georgia, where social-movement organizations were the most limited in terms of public participation from the start, did a democratic deficit develop. Perhaps it was the Georgian public's general lack of participation in the opposition movement, save for a few short weeks surrounding the Rose Revolution, that set the stage for antidemocratic practices—ostensibly in the name of democracy—after breakthrough. Georgia's new political elites, ex-NGO leaders among them, saw themselves as the vanguard of society writ large. This might also help to explain reversals following "democratic revolutions" in countries such as Ukraine and Kyrgyzstan. And it may serve as a warning for those involved in the most recent revolutions in the Middle East.

An additional and somewhat related lesson common to each of these cases is that pro-democracy organizations would be wise to avoid complacency in the shadow of victory. More specifically, the assumption that colleagues and friends in the state will uphold the principles and long-standing demands of these organizations has proven flawed. Those who take to the state may be abundant in virtue, but they are also rational actors forced into a new and extraordinarily difficult balancing act. As they take their seats in new institutions, their policy preferences will almost invariably depart from those their organizations continue to espouse. If those associations believe these goals are still worth fighting for, then fight they must.

Apart from losing on concrete policies, those organizations that choose not to pursue this fight may face a devastating hit to their credibility. Poland's Solidarity, South Africa's SANCO, and Georgia's various NGOs were all considered complicit in the new system that they helped usher in precisely because they failed to aggressively hold the new government to account in the period immediately following democratic breakthrough. Where early interaction involves periods of undue deference to the state on the part of individuals historically charged with defending society, the result can be a broad social consensus that civil society is a mechanism by which political actors seek lucrative state positions or a last-ditch tool for use only during crisis. Although this observation is based primarily on the voices of elites, signs that civil society in all of these states remains weak are also indicative of this phenomenon.

International Actors, Social Movements, and Long-Term Success

All of these issues should be of concern to Western policymakers engaged in overseas assistance. In what Carothers calls the "transition paradigm" of the 1990s, foreign actors have increasingly sought to realize the goal of democratization abroad by supporting local civil society (Finkel, Perez-Linan, and Seligson 2007, 410). Throughout the 1990s, for example, USAID spent approximately $400 million per year on supporting advocacy-based NGOs, independent media, and labor unions, all of which have proven instrumental in mobilizing for political change. This funding frequently went to organizations around the world (including many noted in the previous section) operating in support of procedural democracy, including election monitoring, as well as voter registration, education, and mobilization. Such groups have proven capable of broadening civic engagement by demonstrating to citizens fraudulent techniques of the incumbent regime and working with opposition political party leaders to mobilize the population.

As the latter activity suggests, ostensibly neutral, local, foreign-backed organizations have usually stood for particular political alternatives. "In reality," Ottaway acknowledges, "these NGOs want to defeat the incumbent government" (Ottaway 2001). Although their tactics may appear low key, they often culminate in flashy displays of mass-based action. Protest movements have become increasingly frequent and have affected the speed and scope of democratization. Sometimes they are even the key catalyst for regime change. These so-called democratic revolutions are, Diamond says, "the cumulative achievement of tens and hundreds of thousands, sometimes millions of citizens who become actively involved in civic movements and independent media" (Diamond 1992, 6). Studies show that civil-society funding has had a "clear and consistent" impact on the process of democratization (Finkel, Perez-Linan, and Seligson 2007, 436).[9]

In fact, evidence indicates that Western state and nonstate donors played an important role in supporting each of the movements evaluated here. In Poland they provided everything from clandestine newspapers and broadcasting equipment to money and organizational assistance

(Frybes 2008, 65; Wedel 1998, 95; Bernstein 1992; Shevis 1981, 31). In South Africa donor funding played an especially important role during CO-SATU's early years, when it accounted for the lion's share of the union federation's revenue base, and throughout the entire period in which civics were functioning under apartheid (APHEDA 2007; Sellstrom 2002; MacKay and Mathoho 2001, 30; Adler and Steinberg 2000, 12; Kessel 2000, 24, 28; Landsberg 2000, 108; Seekings 1997, 10). Georgia's movement was almost entirely dependent on outside assistance. Donor support came from across Europe, but the United States played a particularly large role, spending $1.1 billion between 1992 and 2002 (Devdariani 2003, 13). As one political observer noted, Washington's NGO investments "seem to have paid off" (King 2004).

The long-term payoff in terms of civil-society capacity, however, was immediately in question in each of these states as members of organizations woke up bleary eyed the morning after their victory. First, these groups no longer faced the major opponent that had once kept their adherents committed and provided their organization its raison d'être. Second, they tended to see a net outflow of experienced personnel, especially to the (more lucrative) political sphere and state apparatus, where empowered political elites sought to heighten their legitimacy or capabilities by incorporating well-known names or leaders with particular skills, or simply engaged in payback. Third, their organizations' resource base was potentially threatened as foreign donors who were engaged in democracy promotion quickly moved on to the world's next hot spot.

All of these threats seem to spell demobilization, which is almost a foregone conclusion in the limited "What next?" portion of the social-movement literature. Demobilization from below can result from boredom, a perceived increase in costs of participation, or the feeling among participants that the movement is unable to provide the goods promised; demobilization from above can occur when politically empowered social-movement members or associates attempt to persuade their former organizations that their job is done. Often, especially in the case of victorious pro-democracy organizations, demobilization is simply a function of success—why keep playing when the game has already been won? Yet clearly some leaders consider it in their interest, whether out of political strategy or for tangible and intangible rewards, to maintain their organizations despite apparent victory. Many of these organizations continue to operate in the new environment, as the cases in this book demonstrate.

Organization leaders often adapt to this new environment by transforming their organizations into smaller, bureaucratic, and formalized units more capable of everyday interaction with new state institutions and external donors. Organizations that persist thus often do so in a slimmed-down version, as their leaders shift from mass mobilization to institutionalization, defined as the "creation of a repeatable process that is essentially self-sustaining" (Meyer and Tarrow 1998, 21). As they engage in conventional politics (and sometimes even create parties of their own), they may become more conservative, pragmatic, and less idealistic and place more of an emphasis on maintaining a broad, if latent, support base within society. This institutionalization can therefore lead to tensions in grassroots movements, where people are likely to feel alienated by the new way of doing things. Still, these organizations remain full of potential; just as social movements arose in the face of democratic lapses or economic pain earlier, they can do so again. This, in theory, should bolster the effect of any connections that are the focus of this book. The Polish, South African, and Georgian cases highlight the tumultuous nature of the transition for these organizations, and they raise questions about how long-time external supporters might help after transition begins.

In 2011, with a State Department budget request of $3.3 billion for democratization, U.S. government funding continued to be a major source of support for pro-democracy organizations around the world. Still, if the goal of the United States and other state and nonstate donors is to create strong civil-society organizations that are first the vanguard and then the guardian of democracy, ensuring that the postbreakthrough state remains accountable to the various concerns and demands of its citizens, then the cases here suggest a need to reconsider the almost habitual decision to rechannel support following breakthrough away from these organizations and into the new—and newly legitimate—government structures (Bell and Keenan 2004, 356). Organizations arguably need more, not less, support upon breakthrough to strengthen their standing in the new state and prepare them for the challenges they will face even when their members believe they can let their guard down as a result of the personnel transfer studied here. Maintaining support, both financial and diplomatic, can help ensure that these organizations play a role in not just democratic breakthrough but also consolidation.

Conclusion

Two decades after democratic breakthrough, Poland's first noncommunist president sat in a lavish office overlooking historic Gdańsk and recalled how, after breakthrough, his fight against communism turned into a battle against the very organization he had once led. "There are those who wave the banners and feel they are the [real] Solidarity," Wałęsa said. "I told them to come up with some clever name, maybe 'Reliability,' some nice name, but not Solidarity because Solidarity meant the period of struggle." Just blocks away Marian Krzaklewski, who headed Solidarity and the AWS coalition that came to power in 1997, declared that Solidarity had remained a social movement and that "the historic author of freedom and democracy . . . [had] completed its duty" under AWS. Asked about his own personal suffering and that of his organization as a result of Solidarity's 1997–2001 foray into politics, Krzaklewski looked to one side and unconvincingly replied, "You know, gradually, time heals all wounds."

That prospect seemed distant from the perspective of Georgian watchdogs who continued to contest the new state several years after breakthrough. In addition, it appeared similarly empty to those South African unionists who had helped in 2008 lead a virtual coup within the African National Congress in order to bring a populist, Jacob Zuma, to power. Zuma, it soon—and not surprisingly—turned out, was a Band-Aid on a gaping wound; his promises to backtrack on South Africa's neoliberal path had gotten lost somewhere during the move to his new institutional home. COSATU, in turn, remained militant in the face of its next lost comrade. One can surmise this has only further hurt relations and left COSATU outside South Africa's inner circle of political leadership.

The picture is not all dreary. The fact that, eventually, watchdogs in all of these cases have repeatedly stood up in the face of marginalization suggests that social-movement organizations can take root and survive in the tough postbreakthrough climate. Still, this book has demonstrated the challenges these organizations face as a result of their longtime ties with new state officials who surface from the social-movement sector. Social-movement leaders emerge from their struggles with confidence, skills, and a determination to bring about change at the state level. But the institutions they settle in have a profound impact on just how much the identities and personal networks they formed during the struggle will affect their postbreakthrough policies.

Appendices

Appendix 1

Methodology

MY METHODS, MEDIA ANALYSES AND INTERVIEWS OF LEADERS, were designed to uncover the evolving nature of the relationship between new state officials from the social-movement sector and their respective social-movement organizations, as well as those with organizations less personally affiliated with state officeholders. The media analysis, including both international and domestic reporting, is helpful in providing strong institutional knowledge (by locating the occurrence and intensity of possible rifts between particular organizations and the government) and information on key local players. I supplement the media review with a content analysis of the publications of social-movement organizations, which reflect their authors' stance toward the new government. Through media reporting and NGO documentation I establish a "relationship timeline" and illuminate core events that have led to warmer or cooler relations between specific organizations and the postbreakthrough state.

The media analysis targets both international and national media. For the former I conducted broad keyword searches on LexisNexis and included North American and European newspapers and wire services, as well as selected translations of national media. I narrowed the search terms to specific organizations, searching, for example, for "South Africa and COSATU" or "Georgia and Liberty Institute." The advantage of this approach is inclusivity, though I was also left with the large task of combing through superfluous material. Next I performed a more deliberate search of available local press, especially for my two more historical cases, and primarily chose publications based on their reputation for strong national coverage. For the South Africa case, this included an electronic search of *Mail and Guardian*, while for Poland it involved an extensive (physical) search of *Gazeta Wyborcza* (available at the Library of Congress). For the case of Georgia, in which the events were much more recent and heavily reported, I relied on articles from *Civil Georgia* (available online and with a significant focus on nongovernmental organizations). My formal media review focuses on the first several years after regime change: 1989–1999 in Poland, 1994–2000 in South Africa, and 2003–2006 in Georgia.

The media analysis is useful for establishing a general history of critical events, but the primary evidence for or against the arguments is based on leaders' perceptions. What are the core areas of conflict and cooperation between NGOs and government? How have various aspects of inclusion or formal exclusion influenced these relationships? To what degree are included NGOs perceived as independent or co-opted? What is the effect of this cooperation or noncooperation on the process of democratic consolidation? To answer these questions I conducted approximately 150 interviews with leaders who participated in the movements that were key to regime change, as well as close observers from the outside.

I must emphasize my methodological focus on the perceptions of these elites. My key interest is perceived organizational influence and access provided by personnel bridges. Attempting to evaluate influence is extraordinarily difficult. Success can be categorized in various ways, from whether an organization's goals are realized to personnel changes in the ranks of decision makers or state apparatus. As Clark cautions, though, "political *outcomes* do not necessarily reflect the preferences of any one actor, or group of actors, rather they are a product of many actors pursuing their interests" (Clark 1998, 247). For instance, if parliament passes legislation that appears to be pro-union, is that the influence of the one-time liberation labor union, other labor unions, or other forces entirely (such as, in the case of Poland, necessary legal changes in preparation for entry into the European Union)? While such data may be helpful in assessing the strength of claims made by either side, this book does not represent a fact-finding mission. Rather, it is an analysis of how these leaders view their own input and that of their former organizations. For this objective, observable conditions are less important than how leaders—the elites—interpreted them.

I selected my interviewees based on their activity in the former leading social-movement organizations. In Poland I concentrated on former and current Solidarity activists, a list that includes workers, as well as intellectuals. In South Africa most of my interviewees were one-time members of COSATU or one of the civic organizations, and I put a special emphasis on talking with activists who have been involved with the South African National Civic Organization, that alliance of civics created prior to democratic breakthrough. I also interviewed a few actors involved in small, local NGOs that played a supporting role in the pro-democracy movements in Poland and South Africa. In Georgia, by contrast, almost all of my local interviews took place with (former) NGO officials who had participated in some way in the Rose Revolution. Among the many organizations included were the Georgian Young Lawyers' Association, the Liberty Institute, the Kmara youth movement, the International Society for Fair Elections and Democracy, Transparency International, the ALPE Foundation, the Civil Society Institute, and the United Nations Association of Georgia. The varied nature of the pro-democracy organizations led to differences in the number of interviews. I carried out relatively more interviews in South Africa (56 in the summer of 2008) and Poland (45 in the winter of 2009), where mass-based organizations led to regime change, than in Georgia (33 in the summer of 2007), where small, elite organizations spearheaded the movement. As noted earlier, my interviewees were selected based on their functions. In each country I talked to pro-democracy activists who after democratic breakthrough took various state and political positions, as well as those who remained in the organization. In Georgia, where mobilization occurred primarily in Tbilisi, all of my interviews took place in the capital. In Poland and South Africa, by contrast, I traveled considerably. Site locations included Warsaw, Gdańsk, Katowice, Gliwice, Wrocław, and Kraków (Poland) and Cape Town, Port Elizabeth, Pretoria, and Johannesburg/Soweto (South Africa). These interviews generally lasted from forty minutes to three hours, with the average time one to one and a half hours.

The process of identifying, tracking down, and making contact with potential interviewees was at times extremely difficult. This is particularly true for the two historical cases, where many one-time leaders of the social-movement organizations from the immediate postbreakthrough phase had by the time of this study gone in very different personal, occupational, and literal directions. For instance, one potential interviewee in Poland was unwilling to speak due to what his peers described as an intense period of postrevolutionary bitterness and alcohol abuse; several South African interviewees had gone into business and were located only after much effort; and a few selected interviewees from Georgia were no longer residing in their country.

My formal interviews and media analysis build on a history of regional study and a familiarity with the political evolution in these countries (especially Poland and South Africa) that helped further clarify patterns in two ways. First, in Poland I was able to glean information from previous interviews with Polish elites on a different subject. Those interviews, conducted in 2003 and 2004 on transitional justice policies in that country, often suggested areas of state/nonstate conflict and cooperation that increased my awareness of the political environment. Second, my previous experience studying and living with a host family in South Africa proved extraordinarily useful as I corroborated information given to me under formal interview conditions with political leaders whom I knew and could speak with very informally (and off the record). In Georgia, while I had no such contacts, I was able to hit the ground running thanks to years spent working on events in the region.

My interviews were semistructured and based on a broad list of open-ended questions designed to probe interviewee perceptions of ways in which the pro-democracy organization had changed to adapt to the new (and still evolving) political environment and how the relationship between former freedom fighters has been altered as a result of new institutional divisions. Questions included topics such as motivations for leaving or remaining in the nongovernmental sphere and general perceptions of the evolving relationship between the government and various nongovernmental organizations. Many of my questions drew set and adamant answers, yet others elicited a much greater level of introspection. At times my interviews felt like a visit to a psychologist as interviewees became quite emotional when they stopped to consider the winding road from nondemocracy to democracy.

Most of my questions were context specific and indirect. Instead of asking respondents in Poland, "Do you identify with your (former) organization," for instance, I asked what Solidarity meant to them and how they believed other former activists perceived the organization. Similarly, rather than ask, "Do personal networks have a major influence on policy decisions" in South Africa, I questioned respondents about the degree to which their former peers actively solicited, sought to incorporate, or understood their policy preferences. Another indicator of whether former political elites continued to identify with their social-movement organization is whether they have considered returning to it, and another way of assessing the network argument is whether their peers claim they would take them back. I also asked much more direct questions: To what degree were you able to persuade these personal contacts to pursue your agenda? How did your preferences change over time? How would you describe your relations with your former partners?

One potential limitation of this study is its reliance on retrospective data (people's recollections). This is particularly true of the Polish case, where Solidarity activists migrated to the state in three waves, meaning that many of those who remained leaders in the organization and were disappointed by their first-wave colleagues subsequently went on to take power themselves. The result, in terms of interviewee assessments, appears to be a moderation of once-radical views and the contagion of "hindsight" references. "As I had the chance of experiencing this myself several years later," explained one longtime activist who became an MP in 1997, "one gets into parliament and sees that there are not two interests but twenty-five different interests, twenty-eight different groups, each with something to take care of" (Wasiński 2009). This limitation is minimized by the fact that many of my interviewees made their thought process clear. For example, with respect to one critical 1993 vote, in which Solidarity parliamentarians defied their organization's demands, a union leader from the time recalled being bitter but conceded that after 1997 "I was a parliamentarian, so I know how it is" (Denysiuk 2009).

After I collected my data, I, with the help of my research assistants, transcribed each interview. Research assistants transcribed a majority of the English-language interviews, as well as a few Russian- and Polish-language ones, in the original language. I transcribed the remaining ones and then translated all of them into English. Next I imported these transcriptions into a qualitative software program (NVivo) and went through each one in its entirety and coded relevant passages. I first coded responses in

free nodes, in which all of the statements concerning a given question were lumped together, and I then followed up by forming tree nodes, where I created subcategories
(e.g., positive or negative) for those particular responses. I also coded the respondent
with regard to basic variables, such as whether the individual held a leadership position
in the organization before and/or after democratic breakthrough, had accepted a political or state job, and had continued to be active in the organization after breakthrough.

With all of these variables coded I was able to run queries for questions such as
whether those who had moved to the political sphere or those who had stayed in the
social-movement organization were more satisfied with the relationship between the
two entities or whether those who had no personal relationship with new political elites
felt advantaged or disadvantaged by this relationship. Within each query I was able to
look at how the respondents in each of the categories had responded, which allowed me
to make a more nuanced interpretation. Because much of the information I acquired
was context specific, it was difficult to combine the interviews from all three countries.
Instead, I conducted a separate analysis for each case. For the same reason I have elected
to present this material by case, after which I conducted an explicit cross-case analysis.

Using country-specific chapters also allows me to flesh out the merits of each of
the three hypotheses in a detailed manner in a theory-confirming/refuting case-study
approach, which involves "an intensive study of a single unit for the purpose of understanding a larger class of (similar) units" (Gerring 2004, 342). In each chapter I begin
with a historical account of the movement's evolution, as detailed by key actors, and
then continue with a more pointed analysis emphasizing evidence for and against each
of the arguments. I then use replication logic to look for similar patterns in each case.

Appendix 2

Georgia Interviews

All interviews were conducted in Tbilisi unless otherwise indicated.

Anjaparidze, Zaal (program manager, civil-society programs), 2007.

Chkheidze, Giorgi (chair of the Georgian Young Lawyers' Association, 2007–2008), 2007.

Chkhetia, Lali (deputy chair, Georgian Young Lawyers' Association, 2006–2007), 2007.

Chokheli, Marina (executive director of Article 42 of the Constitution, an NGO), 2007.

Darchiashvili, David (executive director, Open Society Georgia Foundation), 2007.

Dolidze, Ana (former chair, Georgian Young Lawyers' Association, 2005–2006), telephone interview, 2007.

Getsadze, Gia (former GYLA chair, 1997–1998, and government deputy minister, 2003–2005), 2007.

GOG (senior government official, Georgia), 2007.

GOG2 (government official, Georgia), 2007.

Guntsadze, Zurab (director, ALPE Foundation), 2007.

Kakabadze, Nano (head of Former Political Prisoners for Human Rights), 2007.

Kandelaki, Konstantine (executive director, International Center for Civic Culture), 2007.

Karosanidze, Tamuna (executive director, Transparency International), 2007.

Khaindrava, Giorgi (former minister of conflict resolution, 2004–2006, and current head of the Egalitarian Institute), 2007.

Khidasheli, Tina (leader of Republican Party and former chair of GYLA, 1999–2001; 2003–2004), 2007.

Kitsmarishvili, Erosi (former head of Rustavi 2, 1994–2004), 2007.

Kublashvili, Kote (chair, Supreme Court of Georgia), 2007.

Meladze, Giorgi (member of the Liberty Institute and former member of Kmara, a political youth organization, 2003), 2007.

Mullen, Mark (former Georgia country director for the National Democratic Institute, 1997–2004), telephone interview, 2007.

MVD (internal affairs ministry representative), 2007.

Nanuashvili, Ucha (executive director, Human Rights Information and Documentation Center), 2007.

Nodia, Ghia (chair, Caucasus Institute for Peace, Democracy, and Development), 2007.

Papuashvili, George (chair of the Constitutional Court and former minister of justice and minister of the environment, 2005–2006), 2007.

Ramishvili, Levan (head of the Liberty Institute), 2007.

Representative, USG (U.S. government representative), 2007.

Saakashvili, Nino (executive director, Horizonti), 2007.

Salamadze, Vazha (chair of the Civil Society Institute), 2007.

Subari, Sozar (public defender [ombudsman] of Georgia), 2007.

Tarkhnishvili, Levan (head of Georgian public TV), 2007.

Tevdoradze, Elene (chair of the Human Rights and Civil Integration Committee, Parliament of the Republic of Georgia), 2007.

Tsintsadze, Irene (deputy head of the Department of Prisons, Republic of Georgia, and former head of Alternativa NGO, pre-2004), 2007.

Ugulava, Giorgi (mayor of Tbilisi and former founder/director of ALPE, an NGO, pre-2004), 2007.

UNAG (United Nations Association of Georgia representative), 2007.

USG1 (U.S. government official), 2007.

USG2 (U.S. government official), 2007.

USG12 (U.S. government official), Washington, DC, 2007.

Zhvania, Tamara (director, International Society for Fair Elections and Democracy), 2007.

Zurabishvili, David (independent member of Parliament, Republic of Georgia, and former founder/leader of the Liberty Institute, 1996–2003), 2007.

Appendix 3

Poland Interviews

Bartosz, Waldemar (head of Solidarity, Kielce region, and former MP, 1991–1993, 1997–2001), Gdańsk, 2009.

Borowczak, Jerzy (former head of Solidarity, Gdańsk Shipyard, 1991–1999, and MP, 2000–2001), Gdańsk, 2009.

Borusewicz, Bogdan (senator and former Solidarity MP, 1991–1993, and former vice chair of Solidarity, 1990–1991), Gdańsk, 2009.

Bujak, Zbigniew (former chair of Solidarity, Mazowsze region, 1989–1990, former MP, 1993–1997), Warsaw, 2009.

Denysiuk, Zdzisław (head of Solidarity, Chełm region, and former MP, 1997–2001), Gdańsk, 2009.

Dubiński, Waldemar (vice chair of Solidarity, Mazowsze region), Warsaw, 2009.

Frasyniuk, Władysław (former head of Solidarity, Dolny Śląsk region, 1989–1990, and MP, 1991–2001), Wrocław, 2009.

Janiak, Kazimierz (former vice chair of Solidarity, 1995–1997, and former AWS MP, 1997–2001), Gdańsk, 2009.

Jurczak, Stefan (senator and former head of Solidarity, Małopolska region, 1989–1995), Kraków, 2009.

Kamińska, Teresa (former head of Solidarity's national health division and minister charged with coordinating social reforms under AWS Prime Minister Jerzy Buzek, 1997–1999), Sopot, 2009.

Komołowski, Longin (head of Solidarity, Zachodniopomorze region, 1990–1997, and minister of labor, 1997–2001), Warsaw, 2009.

Kowalczyk, Zbigniew (member of Solidarity's regional presidium in Gdańsk), Gdańsk, 2009.

Kozlowski, Krzysztof (former internal affairs minister of Poland, 1990–1991, Kraków, 2004.

Krauze, Jarosław (treasurer of Solidarity, Dolny Śląsk, and local councilor), Wrocław, 2009.

Kropiwnicki, Andrzej (chair of Solidarity, Mazowsze region), Warsaw, 2009.

Krzaklewski, Marian (former chair of Solidarity, 1991–2002, and former chair of AWS, 1997–2001), Gdańsk, 2009.

Książek, Wojciech (head of Solidarity's education commission [Gdańsk region], and former vice minister of education, 1997–2001), Gdańsk, 2009.

Kulas, Jan (Solidarity parliamentary representative, 1991–1993), Warsaw, 2009.

Langer, Jerzy (vice chair of Solidarity), Gdańsk, 2009.

Lewicka, Ewa (former Solidarity vice chair, Mazowsze region, and AWS vice minister of labor), Warsaw, 2009.

Lipko, Andrzej (former head of Solidarity's mining department, 1990–1991, and then vice minister of industry, 1991–1992), Warsaw, 2009.

Lis, Bogdan (former vice chair of Solidarity's foreign relations committee and MP, 1989–1991), Warsaw, 2009.

Maj, Józef (Solidarity chaplain), Warsaw, 2009.

Mańko, Janina (former Solidarity activist, AWS vice minister of health, 1997–2001), Gdańsk, 2009.

Marczak, Henryk (secretary of Solidarity, Łódź region), Łódź, 2009.

Marszewski, Wacław (former head of Solidarity's national mining committee and Solidarity Dolny Śląsk region, 1998–2002), Gliwice, 2009.

Mietlicka, Aleksandra (former organizer, RS AWS, 1997–2001), Sopot, 2009.

Mosiński, Jan (head of Solidarity, Kalisz region), Gdańsk, 2009.

Mozolewski, Józef (chair of Solidarity, Podlaski region, and former AWS MP, 1997–2001), Gdańsk, 2009.

Niesiołowski, Stefan (former Sejm member, 1989–1993, 1997–2001), Łódź, 2004.

Osiński, Bogdan (chair of Solidarity, Łódź region), Łódź, 2009.

Pałubicki, Janusz (former national treasurer of Solidarity, 1990–1997, and AWS MP, 1997–2001), Poznań, 2004 and Gdańsk, 2009.

Pietrzyk, Alojzy (head of Solidarity, Śląsk region, 1990–1992, and MP, 1991–1993), Katowice, 2009.

Polmański, Eugeniusz (assistant to the chair of Solidarity, 1992–1998), Katowice, 2009.

Rulewski, Jan (senator and former representative of Solidarity in parliament, 1991–1993, and former head of Solidarity, Bydgoszcz region, 1980–1981, 1990), Warsaw, 2009.

Rybicki, Jacek (vice chair of Solidarity, 1993–1997, former AWS MP, 1997–2001), Gdańsk, 2009.

Smirnow, Andrzej (former vice chair of Solidarity, Mazowsze region, 1991–1993, and MP, 1991–1993, 1997–2001, 2006–present), Warsaw, 2009.

Śniadek, Janusz (chair of Solidarity), Gdańsk, 2009.

Solidarity1 (Solidarity regional officeholder), Gdańsk, 2009.

Stelmachowski, Andrzej (former senator, 1989–1991), Warsaw, 2004.

Szwed, Stanisław (MP, former head of Solidarity, Podbezkid region, 1992–1997, 2002–2005), Warsaw, 2009.

Tomaszewski, Janusz (former chair of Solidarity, Łódź region, 1992–1997, and former AWS interior minister, 1997–1999), Łódź, 2009.

Wałęsa, Lech (former chair of Solidarity, 1980–1990, and former president of Poland, 1990–1995), Gdańsk, 2009.

Wasiński, Włodzimierz (vice chair of Solidarity, Dolny Śląsk, and MP, 1997–2001), Wrocław, 2009.

Wójcik, Tomasz (former chair of Solidarity, Dolny Śląsk, 1990–1998, and MP, 1997–2001), Wrocław, 2009.

Wojtczak, Michal (senator, former chair of Solidarity, Toruń region, 1990–1998; former Solidarity member of parliament, 1991–1993, and AWS member of parliament (1997–1999) and secretary of state (2000–2001), Warsaw, 2009.

Wujec, Henryk (former MP, 1989–2001, and secretary of Solidarity's 1989 electoral commission, Komitet Obywatelski Solidarności), Warsaw, 2004.

Appendix 4

South Africa Interviews

Abrahams, Evan (provincial secretary of South African Transport and Allied Workers Union [SATAWU]), Cape Town, 2008.

Banda, Patrick (regional chair of the National Education, Health, and Allied Workers' Union [NEHAWU]), Port Elizabeth, 2008.

Cassiem, Ashraf (chair, Western Cape Anti-Eviction Forum), Cape Town, 2008.

Coleman, Neil (former parliamentary coordinator for COSATU, 1995–2007), Johannesburg, 2008.

Copelyn, Johnny (former head of Southern African Clothing and Textile Workers' Union [SACTWU], pre-1994 and MP, 1994–1996), Cape Town, 2008.

Councilor (municipal councilor and former civic member), Port Elizabeth, 2008.

Councilor2 (former municipal councilor, 1995–1996, and SANCO regional president, 1992–1995), Port Elizabeth, 2008.

Councilor3 (municipal councilor and civic activist, pre-1994), Port Elizabeth, 2008.

Dicks, Rudi (COSATU's former labor-market policy coordinator, 2005–2008, and current director of COSATU's National Labour and Economic Development Institute [NALEDI]), Johannesburg, 2008.

Doidge, Geoffrey (national MP and founding member/deputy chair of the Kokstad Civic Association, 1991–1995), Cape Town, 2008.

Dor, George (former SANCO coordinator, 1994–1996, and current general secretary of Jubilee South Africa), Johannesburg, 2008.

Ehrenreich, Tony (Western Cape provincial secretary of COSATU), Cape Town, 2008.

Essop, Tasneem (former trade-union activist and provincial minister, 2001–2008), Cape Town, 2008.

Godongwana, Enoch (former general secretary of National Union of Metalworkers of South Africa [NUMSA], 1994–1997, and member of the executive council [MEC] for finance in Eastern Cape Province, 1997–2004), Johannesburg, 2008.

Goduka, Phil (founding member of Port Elizabeth Black Civic Organization [PEBCO] and ANC member of regional executive), Port Elizabeth, 2008.

Golding, Marcel (former assistant general secretary of National Union of Mine Workers (NUM), pre-1994, and parliamentarian,1994–1996), Johannesburg, 2008.

Hlongwa, Brian (former Soweto Civic Association organizer and current, pre-1994, member of the executive council [MEC] for health, Gauteng province), Johannesburg, 2008.

Jack, Godfrey (former SANCO official), Johannesburg, 2008.

Leader, SANCO, local (MP, Port Elizabeth, former municipal councilor and SANCO regional president), 2008.

Madisha, Willie (former COSATU president, 1999–2008), Johannesburg, 2008.

Mahlatsane, Jonas (SACTWU regional secretary, Gauteng), Johannesburg, 2008.

Majadibodu, Edward (chief negotiator for the National Union of Mine Workers [NUM]), Johannesburg, 2008.

Makwayiba, Mzwandile (second deputy vice president of the National Education, Health, and Allied Workers' Union [NEHAWU] and former COSATU regional chair, 1997–2004), Johannesburg, 2008.

Mali, Aubray (ANC municipal councilor and SANCO national secretary), Port Elizabeth, 2008.

Masemula, Katishi (general secretary of the Food and Allied Workers' Union [FAWU]), Cape Town, 2008.

Maunye, Maggie (national MP and former union and civic official), Soweto, 2008.

Mayekiso, Moses (former MP, 1994–1996, general secretary of the National Union of Metalworkers of South Africa [NUMSA], 1987–1993, and SANCO president, 1993–1994), Johannesburg, 2008.

Mkhize, Herbert (executive director of the National Economic Development and Labour Council [NEDLAC], 2003–present), Johannesburg, 2008.

Mngomezulu, Linda (general secretary of SANCO), Johannesburg, 2008.

Mogase, Isaac Dank (national MP and former president of the Soweto Civic Association), Cape Town, 2008.

Mosunkutu, Khabisi (SANCO founder and former Post and Telecommunications Workers Association [POTWA] general secretary, pre-1994, national MP, 1994–1996, and provincial minister for agriculture, conservation, and environment, Gauteng province), Johannesburg, 2008.

Mtanga, Mandla (municipal councilor and SANCO provincial executive committee member), Port Elizabeth, 2008.

Naidoo, Jay (former COSATU general secretary, 1985–1993, Minister for Reconstruction and Development Program, 1994–1996, and Minister of Post, Telecommunications and Broadcasting, 1996–1999), Johannesburg, 2008.

Naidoo, Jayendra (former trade-union leader, 1981–1994, and first executive director of the National Economic Development and Labor Council [NEDLAC], 1995–1998), Johannesburg, 2008.

Ndungu, Kimani (senior researcher at COSATU's National Labor and Economic Development Institute [NALEDI]), Johannesburg, 2008.

Ngwane, Trevor (former municipal councilor, 1995–2000, and founder of the Anti-Privatization Forum and Soweto Electricity Crisis Committee), Soweto, 2008.

Ngwedzeni, Norman (former civic activist, 1989–1995, and municipal councilor), Johannesburg, 2008.

Ntshalintshali, Bheki (deputy general secretary of COSATU), Johannesburg, 2008.

Ronnie, Roger (former general secretary of South Africa Municipal Workers' Union [SAMWU], 2000–2007), Cape Town, 2008.

Rustin, Jonavon (provincial secretary of South African Democratic Teachers' Union [SADTU]), Cape Town, 2008.

SAGO (South African Government Official), Pretoria, 2008.

Sambatha, Madoda (former municipal councilor, 2000–2006, and lower-level official of the National Union of Mine Workers [NUM]), Johannesburg, 2008.

SANCO1 (former regional head), Port Elizabeth, 2008.

Sonto, Mzunani Roseberry (SANCO provincial chair, Western Cape, and MP), Cape Town, 2008.

Tsenoli, Lechesa Solomon (former SANCO president, 1994–1995, and current MP), Cape Town, 2008.

Unionist2 (union representative), Port Elizabeth, 2008.

Unionist5 (former union and government official), Johannesburg, 2008.

Unionist6 (provincial union leader), Johannesburg, 2008.

Wayile, Goodman (COSATU provincial chair and municipal ANC councilor), Port Elizabeth, 2008.

Williams, Donovan (member of SANCO's national executive committee), Pretoria, 2008.

Notes

Chapter 1

1. See, for example, Gershman 2004; Grugel 2000; Clarke 1998; Constantino-David 1998; Silliman and Noble 1998; Loveman 1995.

Chapter 2

1. In the Polish case, there was a difference between Solidarity leaders who took power (primarily intellectuals) and those who stayed behind (mostly workers) during the initial phase of democratic consolidation, but no such difference existed during subsequent phases (see Chapter 3).

2. See also Kilduff and Krackhardt 2008, 30; Whittier 2002, 291; Opp and Roehl 1990, 521; White 1989, 1289, 1291; Useem 1998, 218; Kitschelt 1986, 62.

3. See also Goodwin, Jasper, and Polletta 2004, 418; McAdam 1988, 216.

4. See also Eyerman 2005, 46.

5. For more, see Peters, Pierre, and King 2005, 1280; March and Olsen 1996, 252; Thelen and Steinmo 1992, 7–9.

6. See also Amenta and Caren 2004, 468; Allison 1969, 709.

7. See, for example, Diamond 1999, 251–52; Foweraker 1995, 70; Lanegran 1995, 105; Loveman 1995, 141; Terry 1993, 336.

Chapter 3

1. Despite this inclusivity, certain segments of society (namely nonwage earners, such as students, who still played a part in the anticommunist movement) were excluded from the union, rendering Solidarity moderately inclusive.

2. A similar sentiment was expressed by many others, including Borowczak 2009; Dubiński 2009; and Wojtczak 2009.

3. Polish Ministry of Health, www.mz.gov.pl/wwwmzold/index?mr=mo&ms=&ml=en&mi=535&mx=o&mt=&my=464&ma=5166.

Chapter 4

1. Others making the same claim, nearly word for word, include Abrahams (2008); Ehrenreich (2008); and Rustin (2008).

Chapter 5

1. Other organizations whose members were interviewed include Horizonti and the International Center for Civic Culture (organizations dedicated to the development of civil society); the Caucasus Institute for Peace, Democracy, and Development (an independent think tank); representatives from the independent TV station Rustavi 2; and representatives from various international organizations previously involved in opposition support (Open Society Georgia Foundation, Eurasia Foundation, National Democratic Institute).

2. For example, some liberties extended to NGOs under Western pressure during the Shevardnadze period, such as NGOs' unfettered access to prisons, were simply deemed irresponsible by the new government, which reversed them, to the chagrin of NGO activists (Getsadze 2007).

3. Ugulava, however, denied this, saying that rumors of ALPE's influence have made it more difficult for that organization to effectively raise money. "I have not been in touch with ALPE since I was appointed as deputy minister of justice in 2004," Ugulava said. "I did not have anything to do with them" (Ugulava 2007).

Chapter 6

1. See also Polletta and Jasper (2001, 285).

2. See also Eyerman (2005, 50); Goodwin, Jasper, and Polletta (2001, 2, 15); and Jasper (1998, 419).

3. Any effort to be more precise, however, becomes more problematic. If civil society is public in its activities (designed to facilitate collective action) and aims (focused on the commons) (Bratton 1995, 56), then what of organizations intent on providing private goods for their members (Olson 1971)? In his expanded definition Diamond refers to civil society as "the realm of organized life that is open, voluntary, self-generating, at least partially self-supporting, autonomous from the state, and bound by a legal order or set of shared rules" (Diamond 1999, 221). Critics might wonder, What, then, are the many organizations advertised by aid agencies as civil society but almost exclusively dependent on foreign donors? Is civil society reserved for the wealthy states that can afford it (Bienen and Herbst 1996, 29)? By concentrating on the "voluntary sector," according to Bratton, political aspects of the private, for-profit sector are not taken into account (Bratton 1995, 58). On the other hand, does civil society need to be involved in the political sphere?

4. See, for instance, Hachhethu (2007, 5); Encarnación (2001, 59); Grugel (2000, 90); Wedel (1998, 85).

5. The extent to which civil society is necessary for successful democracy is debatable. Some have warned that for this civil society to be beneficial, it must exist in the presence of strong democratic institutions (Berman 1997; Snyder and Ballentine 1996), whereas others have argued that simply a latent civil society, capable of organizing in periods of acute crisis, is an effective state constraint (Almond and Verba 1963).

6. Poland's scores improved from 5.5 before the Roundtable Talks to 4.3 the year of the first elections. A year later they dropped further to 2.2 (lower is better) and maintained that rating until 1995, when Poland scored 1.2, which rating it maintained until 2003, when it scored 1.1, the rating it has held ever since.

7. Keep in mind that a lower rating is better. South Africa's score went from 5.4 to 2.3 the year of the elections, after which it improved to 1.2 between 1995 and 2006, though it rose to 2.2 (still considered "free") afterward.

8. The scores were 4.4 from 2000 to 2004; 3.4 in 2005; 3.3 in 2006 and 2007; and 4.4 in 2008 and 2009.

9. For more see Herman (2006, 33); McFaul (2005); Ottaway (2001).

Bibliography

Abrahams, Evan. 2008. Provincial secretary of South African Transport and Allied Workers' Union (SATAWU). Interview, August 7, Cape Town, South Africa.

Adler, Glenn, and Jonny Steinberg. 2000. "Introduction." In *From Comrades to Citizens: The South African Civics Movement and the Transition to Democracy*, edited by G. Adler and J. Steinberg. New York: St. Martin's: 1–25.

AFP. 1994. "Labour Federation Demands Government Backing Against Employers." *Agence France Presse*, July 17.

———. 1996. "South African Minister Gives Some Ground on Macro-Economic Plan." *Agence France Presse*, July 26.

Aiyede, E. Remi. 2003. "The Dynamics of Civil Society and the Democratization Process in Nigeria." *Canadian Journal of African Studies* 37 (1):1–27.

Allison, Graham. 1969. "Conceptual Models and the Cuban Missile Crisis." *American Political Science Review* 63 (3):689–718.

Almond, Gabriel A., and Sidney Verba. 1963. *The Civic Culture: Political Attitudes and Democracy in Five Nations*. Princeton, NJ: Princeton University Press.

Amenta, Edwin, and Neal Caren. 2004. "The Legislative, Organizational, and Beneficiary Consequences of State-Oriented Challengers." In *The Blackwell Companion to Social Movements*, edited by D. A. Snow, S. A. Soule, and H. Kriesi. Malden, MA: Blackwell: 461–87.

Aminzade, Ronald, and Doug McAdam. 2001. "Emotions and Contentious Politics." In *Silence and Voice in the Study of Contentious Politics*, edited by R. Aminzade, J. A. Goldstone, D. McAdam, E. J. Perry, W. H. J. Sewell, S. G. Tarrow, and C. Tilly. Cambridge: Cambridge University Press: 14–50.

AN. 2001. "South Africa: Anti-Privatization Campaign Off to Flying Start." *Africa News*, August 17.

———. 2003a. "South Africa: ANC Sweetheart SANCO Wages War with COSATU." *Africa News*, March 9.

———. 2003b. "South Africa: Eskom Budgeted for R1,4bn Write-Off." *Africa News*, May 2.

Andrews, Molly. 1991. *Lifetimes of Commitment: Aging, Politics, Psychology*. New York: Cambridge University Press.

Anjaparidze, Zaal. 2007. Program manager, civil-society programs. Interview, Tbilisi, Georgia.

APHEDA. 2007. *20 Years of Working for Freedom*. Union Aid Abroad—APHEDA. Accessed December 30, 2010, http://apheda.org.au/projects/africa/history/1144624558_12643.html.

Art, Robert. 1973. "Bureaucratic Politics and American Foreign Policy: A Critique." *Policy Sciences* 4:467–90.

Ballard, Richard, Adam Habib, and Imraan Valodia. 2006. "Introduction: From Anti-Apartheid to Post-Apartheid Social Movements." In *Voices of Protest: Social Movements in Post-Apartheid South Africa*, edited by R. Ballard, A. Habib, and I. Valodia. Scottsville, South Africa: University of KwaZulu-Natal Press: 1–22.

Banaszak, Lee Ann. 2009. *The Women's Movement Inside and Outside the State*. Cambridge: Cambridge University Press.

Banda, Patrick. 2008. Regional chair of the National Education, Health, and Allied Workers' Union (NEHAWU). Interview, August 11, Port Elizabeth, South Africa.

Bartosek, Karel. 1999. "Central and Southeastern Europe." In *The Black Book of Communism*, edited by S. Courtois, N. Werth, J.-L. Panne, A. Paczkowski, K. Bartosek and J.-L. Margolin. Cambridge, MA: Harvard University Press.

Bartosz, Waldemar. 2009. Head of Solidarity, Kielce region, and former member of parliament (1991–1993, 1997–2001). Interview, January 20, Gdańsk, Poland.

BBC. 1994. "COSATU to 'Do All in Our Power' To Ensure ANC's Programme Is Not Blocked." *BBC Summary of World Broadcasts*, May 5.

———. 1995a. "South Africa: ANC Says 'Hidden Hand' Behind Latest Wave of Strikes." *BBC Summary of World Broadcasts*, October 6.

———. 1995b. "South Africa: COSATU Announces Plans for National Strike on 19th June." *BBC Summary of World Broadcasts*, May 30.

———. 2001. "SAfrica: COSATU Claims 'Huge' Success on Second Day of Strike." *BBC Monitoring Africa—Political*, August 30.

———. 2004a. "Expert Says Georgian President 'Not Fully Aware' of Media Restrictions." *BBC Monitoring Former Soviet Union—Political*, November 17.

———. 2004b. "Georgian NGOs Censure Proposed Constitutional Amendments." *BBC Monitoring Former Soviet Union—Political*, February 5.

———. 2005a. "Abolishing Georgian District Courts Ruffles Feathers of Judiciary." *BBC Monitoring International Reports*, November 2.

———. 2005b. "Georgian MPs Savage Human Rights Ombudsman Over His Stance on Religion." *BBC Monitoring Former Soviet Union—Political*, December 23.

———. 2006. "Georgian Government, Opposition Figures Clash Over Future of Influential NGO." *BBC Monitoring Former Soviet Union—Political*, January 9.

Bell, Christine, and Johanna Keenan. 2004. "Human Rights Nongovernmental Organizations and the Problems of Transition." *Human Rights Quarterly* 26:330–74.

Berman, Sheri. 1997. "Civil Society and the Collapse of the Weimar Republic." *World Politics* 49 (3):401–29.

Bernstein, Carl. 1992. "The Holy Alliance." *Time*, February 24. Available at www.carlber nstein.com/magazine_holy_alliance.php.

Bielasiak, Jack. 1985. "Solidarity and the State: Strategies of Social Reconstruction." In *Poland After Solidarity: Social Movements Versus the State*, edited by B. Misztal. New Brunswick, NJ: Transaction.

Bienen, Henry, and Jeffrey Herbst. 1996. "The Relationship Between Political and Economic Reform in Africa." *Comparative Politics* 29 (1):23–42.

Borowczak, Jerzy. 2009. Former Head of Solidarity, Gdańsk Shipyard (1991–1999), and member of parliament (2000–2001). Interview, January 13, Gdańsk, Poland.

Borusewicz, Bogdan. 2009. Senator and former Solidarity member of parliament (1991–1993), and former vice chair of Solidarity (1990–1991). Interview, January 12, Gdańsk, Poland.

Bratton, Michael. 1994. "Civil Society and Political Transitions in Africa." In *Civil Society and the State*, edited by J. W. Harbeson, D. S. Rothchild, and N. Chazan. Boulder, CO: Rienner.

———. 1995. "Civil Society and Political Transitions in Africa." In *Africa in World Politics: Post-Cold War Challenges*, edited by J. W. Harbeson and D. S. Rothchild. Boulder, CO: Westview: 51–81.

Broers, Laurence. 2005. "After the 'Revolution': Civil Society and the Challenges of Consolidating Democracy in Georgia." *Central Asian Survey* 24 (3):333–50.

Bujak, Zbigniew. 2009. Former chair of Solidarity, Mazowsze region (1989–1990), and former member of parliament (1993–1997). Interview, January 9, Warsaw, Poland.

Cassiem, Ashraf. 2008. Chair of the Western Cape Anti-Eviction Forum. Interview, August 4, Cape Town, South Africa.

CBOS. 1993a. "Ekonomiczna Samoocena Spoleczenstwa Polskiego u Progu Nowego Roku," edited by Centrum Badania Opinii Społecznej [CBOS]. Warsaw.

———. 1993b. "Sukces Wyborczy SLD: Oczekiwane Konsekwentcje: Komunikat z badan," edited by CBOS. Warsaw.

Chiledi, Accadoga. 1994. "South Africa Economy: Budget Broadly Welcomed." *IPS-Inter Press Service*, June 23.

Chkheidze, Giorgi. 2007. Chair of the Georgian Young Lawyers' Association (2007–2008). Interview, July 17, Tbilisi, Georgia.

Chkhetia, Lali. 2007. Deputy chair of the Georgian Young Lawyers' Association (2006–2007). Interview, July 17, Tbilisi, Georgia.

Chokheli, Marina. 2007. Executive director of Article 42 of the Constitution, an NGO. Interview, July 18, Tbilisi, Georgia.

Chong, Dennis. 1991. *Collective Action and the Civil Rights Movement*. Chicago: University of Chicago Press.

Clark, William Roberts. 1998. "Agents and Structures: Two Views of Preferences, Two Views of Institutions." *International Studies Quarterly* 42 (2):245–70.

Clarke, Gerard. 1998. *The Politics of NGOs in South-East Asia: Participation and Protest in the Philippines*. Politics in Asia series. New York: Routledge.

Cohen, Ariel. 2004. "Shevardnadze's Journey." *Policy Review* 124:75–85.

Coleman, Neil. 2008. Former parliamentary coordinator for COSATU (1995–2007). Interview, August 19, Johannesburg, South Africa.

Constantino-David, Karina. 1998. "From the Present Looking Back: A History of Philippine NGOs." In *Organizing for Democracy: NGOs, Civil Society, and the Philippine State*, edited by G. S. Silliman and L. G. Noble. Honolulu: University of Hawaii Press: 26–48.

Copelyn, Johnny. 2008. Former head of Southern African Clothing and Textile Workers' Union (SACTWU) (pre-1994), and member of parliament (1994–1996). Interview, August 8, Cape Town, South Africa.

Councilor. 2008. Municipal councilor and former civic member. Interview, Port Elizabeth, South Africa.

Councilor2. 2008. Former municipal councilor (1995–1996), and SANCO regional president (1992–1995). Interview, August 11, Port Elizabeth, South Africa.

Councilor3. 2008. Municipal councilor and civic activist (pre-1994). Interview, August 14, Port Elizabeth, South Africa.

Darchiashvili, David. 2007. Executive director, Open Society Georgia Foundation. Interview, July 23, Tbilisi, Georgia.

Denysiuk, Zdzisław. 2009. Head of Solidarity, Chelm region, and former member of parliament (1997–2001). Interview, January 20, Gdańsk, Poland.

Devdariani, Jaba. 2003. "The Impact of International Assistance." In *Building Democracy in Georgia*. International Institute for Democracy and Electoral Assistance (discussion paper).

di Palma, Giuseppe. 1991. "Legitimation from the Top to Civil Society: Politico-Cultural Change in Eastern Europe." *World Politics* 44 (1):49-80.

Diamond, Larry Jay. 1992. "Introduction." In *The Democratic Revolution: Struggles for Freedom and Pluralism in the Developing World*, edited by L. Diamond. New York: Freedom House: 1–27.

———. 1999. *Developing Democracy: Toward Consolidation*. Baltimore: Johns Hopkins University Press.

Dicks, Rudi. 2008. Former labor-market policy coordinator for COSATU (2005–2008), and current director of COSATU's National Labour and Economic Development Institute (NALEDI). Interview, August 20, Johannesburg, South Africa.

Dickson, Peter. 2000. "ANC Loses Sanco Support in Eastern Cape." *Mail and Guardian*, October 27.

Doidge, Geoffrey. 2008. National member of parliament and founding member/deputy chair of the Kokstad Civic Association (1991–1995). Interview, August 7, Cape Town, South Africa.

Dolidze, Ana. 2007. Former chair of the Georgian Young Lawyers' Association (2005–2006). Telephone interview, July 10.

Dor, George. 2008. Former SANCO coordinator (1994–1996), and current general secretary of Jubilee South Africa. Interview, August 27, Johannesburg, South Africa.

Dryzek, John S. 1996. "Political Inclusion and the Dynamics of Democratization." *American Political Science Review* 90 (3):475–87.

Dubiński, Waldemar. 2009. Vice-chair of Solidarity, Mazowsze region. Interview, January 6, Warsaw, Poland.

Dugger, Celia W. 2010. "Labor Unrest Empties South African Hospitals." *New York Times*, August 27.

Eades, Lindsay Michie. 1999. *The End of Apartheid in South Africa.* Westport, CT: Greenwood.

Eaton, Kent. 2003. "Restoration or Transformation? 'Trapos' Versus NGOs in the Democratization of the Philipines." *Journal of Asian Studies* 62 (2):469–96.

Ehrenreich, Tony. 2008. Western Cape provincial secretary of COSATU. Interview, August 4, Cape Town, South Africa.

Encarnación, Omar G. 2001. "Civil Society and the Consolidation of Democracy in Spain." *Political Science Quarterly* 116 (1):53–79.

Ensor, Linda. 1998. "Parliament Passes ESKOM Bill Despite Labour Threats." *Business Day* (South Africa), June 12, 3.

Essop, Tasneem. 2008. Former trade-union activist and provincial minister (2001–2008). Interview, August 8, Cape Town, South Africa.

Eveleth, Ann. 1997. "Council Smashes Squatter Shacks." *Mail and Guardian*, October 10.

Eyerman, Ron. 2005. "How Social Movements Move: Emotions and Social Movements." In *Emotions and Social Movements*, edited by H. Flam and D. King. New York: Routledge: 41–56.

Fine, Alan. 1994. "It's Crunch Time in South Africa." *Business Week*, June 27, 18.

Finkel, Steven F., Anibal Perez-Linan, and Mitchel A. Seligson. 2007. "The Effects of U.S. Foreign Assistance on Democracy Building, 1990–2003." *World Politics* 59 (3):404–40.

Foweraker, Joe. 1995. *Theorizing Social Movements: Critical Studies on Latin America.* Boulder, CO: Pluto.

———. 2001. "Grassroots Movements and Political Activism in Latin America: A Critical Comparison of Chile and Brazil." *Journal of Latin American Studies* 33 (4):839–65.

Frasyniuk, Władysław. 2009. Former head of Solidarity, Dolny Śląsk region (1989–1990), and member of parliament (1991–2001). Interview, January 18, Wrocław, Poland.

Frybes, Marcin. 2008. "French Enthusiasm for Solidarność." *European Review* 16:65–73.

Gerring, John. 2004. "What Is a Case Study and What Is It Good For?" *American Political Science Review* 98 (2):341–54.

Gershman, Carl. 2004. Democracy Promotion: The Relationship of Political Parties and Civil Society. *Democratization* 11 (3):27–35.

Getsadze, Gia. 2007. Former GYLA chair (1997–1998) and government deputy minister (2003–2005). Interview, July 23, Tbilisi, Georgia.

Geyer, Georgie Anne. 2000. "Conversations with Eduard Shevardnadze." *Washington Quarterly* 23 (2):55–66.

Giugni, Marco. 2004. "Personal and Biographical Consequences." In *The Blackwell Companion to Social Movements*, edited by D. A. Snow, S. A. Soule, and H. Kriesi. Malden, MA: Blackwell: 489–507.

Glaser, Daryl. 2001. *Politics and Society in South Africa: A Critical Introduction*. Sage Politics Texts. London: Sage.

Godongwana, Enoch. 2008. Former general secretary of the National Union of Metalworkers of South Africa (NUMSA) (1994–1997), and member of the executive council (MEC) for finance in Eastern Cape Province (1997–2004). Interview, August 20, Johannesburg, South Africa.

Goduka, Phil. 2008. Founding member of Port Elizabeth Black Civic Organization (PEBCO), and ANC member of regional executive. Interview, August 14, Port Elizabeth, South Africa.

GOG. 2007. Senior government official of Georgia. Interview, July 24, Tbilisi, Georgia.

GOG2. 2007. Government official of Georgia. Interview, July 23, Tbilisi, Georgia.

Golding, Marcel. 2008. Former assistant general secretary of the National Union of Mine Workers (NUM) (pre-1994), and parliamentarian (1994–1996). Interview, August 28, Johannesburg, South Africa.

Goodwin, Jeff, and James M. Jasper. 2006. "Emotions and Social Movements." In *Handbook of the Sociology of Emotions*, edited by J. E. Stets and J. H. Turner. New York: Springer: 611–35.

———. 2004. "Emotional Dimensions of Social Movements." In *The Blackwell Companion to Social Movements*, edited by D. A. Snow, S. A. Soule, and H. Kriesi. Malden, MA: Blackwell: 413–32.

Goodwin, Jeff, and Francesca Polletta. 2001. "Why Emotions Matter." In *Passionate Politics: Emotions and Social Movements*, edited by J. Goodwin, J. M. Jasper, and F. Polletta. Chicago: University of Chicago Press: 1–24.

Grodsky, Brian. 2009. "Lessons (Not) Learned: A New Look at Bureaucratic Politics and US Foreign Policy Making in the Post-Soviet Space." *Problems of Post-Communism* 56 (2):43–57.

Grugel, Jean. 2000. "Romancing Civil Society: European NGOs in Latin America." *Journal of Interamerican Studies and World Affairs* 42 (2):87–107.

Grzechowiak, Jan. 1993. "Niewdzieczny zwiazek." *Gazeta Wyborcza*, February 22, 2.

Guntsadze, Zurab. 2007. Director of ALPE Foundation. Interview, July 23, Tbilisi, Georgia.

GW. 1997a. "Marian Wybierz." *Gazeta Wyborcza*, November 24, 3.

———. 1997b. "Podwyżki bez konsultacji." *Gazeta Wyborcza*, December 2, 1.

———. 1997c. "Podwyżki bez wiedzy i zgody." *Gazeta Wyborcza*, December 2, 4.

———. 1997d. "Podwyżki pod pręgierzem." *Gazeta Wyborcza*, December 10, 3.

————. 1998a. "MEN wygrał z 'Solidarnością.'" *Gazeta Wyborcza*, March 18.

————. 1998b. "Obiecał, nie obiecał." *Gazeta Wyborcza*, April 2, 1.

————. 1998c. "Ursus Zwalnia." *Gazeta Wyborcza*, May 21.

GYLA. 2008. *GYLA Mission*. Georgian Young Lawyers Association 2008 (cited January 7, 2008). Available at www.gyla.ge/?id=43&lang=eng.

GYLA. 2010. *GYLA History*. Georgian Young Lawyers' Association 2008. Accessed December 27, 2010, http://gyla.ge/index.php?option=com_content&view=article& id=52&Itemid=144&lang=en.

Habib, Adam. 2005. "The Politics of Economic Policy-Making: Substantive Uncertainty, Political Leverage, and Human Development." In *Democratising Development: The Politics of Socio-Economic Rights in South Africa*, edited by P. Jones and K. Stokke. Leiden: Nijhoff: 39–53.

Habib, Adam, and Imraan Valodia. 2006. "Reconstructing a Social Movement in an Era of Globalization: A Case Study of COSATU." In *Voices of Protest: Social Movements in Post-Apartheid South Africa*, edited by Richard Ballard, Adam Habib, and Imraan Valodia. Scottsville, South Africa: University of KwaZulu-Natal Press: 225–53.

Hachhethu, Krishna. 2007. "Civil Society and Political Participation." *Democracy-Asia .org*. Accessed December 13, 2011, www.democracy-asia.org/countryteam/krishna /Civil%20Society%20and%20Polotical%20Participation.pdf.

Havel, Václav, and John Keane. 1985. *The Power of the Powerless: Citizens Against the State in Central-Eastern Europe*. Armon, NY: M.E. Sharpe.

Herman, Robert. 2006. "Advocacy in the Europe and Eurasia Region: Progress, Promise, and Peril." In *The 2005 NGO Sustainability Index for Central and Eastern Europe and Eurasis*, edited by USAID. Washington, DC: United States Agency for International Development: 26–39.

Hipsher, Patricia L. 1998. "Democratic Transitions and Social Movement Outcomes: The Chilean Shantytown Dwellers' Movement in Comparative Perspective." In *From Contention to Democracy*, edited by M. Giugni, D. McAdam, and C. Tilly. Lanham, MD: Rowman and Littlefield: 273–97.

Hirschler, Ben. 1996. "South African Policy U-Turn Spurs Dissension." *Financial Post*, August 21, 45.

Hlongwa, Brian. 2008. Former Soweto Civic Association organizer and current (pre-1994) member of the executive council (MEC) for health (Gauteng province). Interview, August 26, Johannesburg, South Africa.

Hunt, Scott A., and Robert Benford. 2004. "Collective Identity, Solidarity, and Commitment." In *The Blackwell Companion to Social Movements*, edited by D. A. Snow, S. A. Soule, and H. Kriesi. Malden, MA: Blackwell: 433–55.

Jachowicz, Jerzy. 1990. "Weryfikacja zweryfikowanych." *Gazeta Wyborcza*, August 24, 1.

Jack, Godfrey. 2008. Former SANCO official. Interview, August 22, Johannesburg, South Africa.

Janiak, Kazimierz. 2009. Former vice chair of Solidarity (1995–1997), and former AWS member of parliament (1997–2001). Interview, January 14, Gdańsk, Poland.

Jasper, James M. 1998. "The Emotions of Protest: Affective and Reactive Emotions in and Around Social Movements." *Sociological Forum* 13 (3):397–424.

———. 2006. *Getting Your Way: Strategic Dilemmas in the Real World*. Chicago: University of Chicago Press.

Jurczak, Stefan. 2009. Senator and former head of Solidarity, Małopolska region (1989–1995). Interview, Poland.

Kakabadze, Nano. 2007. Head of Former Political Prisoners for Human Rights. Interview, July 16, Tbilisi, Georgia.

Kamińska, Teresa. 2009. Former head of Solidarity's national health division and minister charged with coordinating social reforms under AWS Prime Minister Jerzy Buzek (1997–1999). Interview, January 13, Sopot, Poland.

Kandelaki, Konstantine. 2007. Executive director of International Center for Civic Culture. Interview, July 18, Tbilisi, Georgia.

Karosanidze, Tamuna. 2007. Executive director of Transparency International. Interview, July 19, Tbilisi, Georgia.

Keck, Margaret E., and Kathryn Sikkink. 1998. *Activists Beyond Borders: Advocacy Networks in International Politics*. Ithaca, NY: Cornell University Press.

Kerlin, Janelle. 2002. "The Political Means and Social Service Ends of Decentralization in Poland." Paper presented at the Annual Meeting of the American Political Science Association, Boston, August 29–September 21.

Kessel, Ineke van. 2000. *Beyond Our Wildest Dreams: The United Democratic Front and the Transformation of South Africa* (*Reconsiderations in Southern African History*). Charlottesville: University Press of Virginia.

Khaindrava, Giorgi. 2007. Former minister for conflict resolution (2004–2006) and current head of the Egalitarian Institute. Interview, July 24, Tbilisi, Georgia.

Khidasheli, Tina. 2007. Leader of Republican Party and former chair of GYLA, 1999–2001; 2003–2004. Interview, July 19, Tbilisi, Georgia.

Kilduff, Martin, and David Krackhardt. 2008. *Interpersonal Networks in Organizations: Cognition, Personality, Dynamics, and Culture*: *Structural Analysis in the Social Sciences*. Cambridge: Cambridge University Press.

King, Charles. 2004. "A Rose Among Thorns: Georgia Makes Good." *Foreign Affairs* 83:2.

Kitschelt, Herbert. 1986. "Political Opportunity Structures and Political Protest: Anti-Nuclear Movements in Four Democracies." *British Journl of Political Science* 16 (1):57–85.

Kitsmarishvili, Erosi. 2007. Former head of Rustavi 2, 1994–2004. Interview, July 23, Tbilisi, Georgia.

Kolarska-Bobinska, L. 1994. "Social Interests and Their Political Representation: Poland in Transition." *British Journal of Sociology* 45 (1):109–26.

Komołowski, Longin. 2009. Head of Solidarity, Zachodniopomorskie region (1990–1997), and minister of labor (1997–2001). Interview, January 21, Warsaw, Poland.

Korac, Zarko. 2005. Former deputy prime minister under Djindjic and member of parliament from the Social-Democratic Union. Interview, February 4, Belgrade, Serbia.

Koral, Jolanta. 1993. "Prezydent, Premier, Przewodniczacy." *Gazeta Wyborcza*, May 8–9, 1.

Kowalczyk, Zbigniew. 2009. Member of Solidarity's regional presidium in Gdańsk. Interview, January 14, Gdańsk, Poland.

Kozłowski, Krzysztof. 2004. Former internal affairs minister of Poland (1990–1991). Interview, January 21, Kraków, Poland.

Krauze, Jarosław. 2009. Treasurer of Solidarity, Dolny Śląsk, and local councilor. Interview, Wrocław, Poland.

Kropiwnicki, Andrzej. 2009. Chair of Solidarity, Mazowsze region. Interview, January 6, Warsaw, Poland.

Krzaklewski, Marian. 2009. Former chair of Solidarity (1991–2002), and former chair of AWS (1997–2001). Interview, January 12, Gdańsk, Poland.

Książek, Wojciech. 2009. Head of Solidarity's education commission (Gdańsk Region), and former vice minister of education (1997–2001). Interview, January 14, Gdańsk, Poland.

Kubik, Jan. 1998. "Institutionalization of Protest During Democratic Consolidation." In *The Social Movement Society: Contentious Politics for a New Century*, edited by D. S. Meyer and S. G. Tarrow. Lanham, MD: Rowman and Littlefield: 131–52.

Kublashvili, Kote. 2007. Chair of the Supreme Court of Georgia. Interview, July 23, Tbilisi, Georgia.

Kulas, Jan. 2009. Solidarity parliamentary representative (1991–1993). Interview, January 7, Warsaw, Poland.

Kuran, Timur. 1991. "Now Out of Never: The Element of Surprise in the East European Revolution of 1989." *World Politics* 44 (1):7–48.

Kurski, Jaroslaw, Przemyslaw Rot, and Wojciech Zaluska. 1993. "Ultimatum Solidarnosci." *Gazeta Wyborcza*, May 13, 1.

Laba, Roman. 1991. *The Roots of Solidarity: A Political Sociology of Poland's Working-Class Democratization*. Princeton, NJ: Princeton University Press.

Landsberg, Christopher. 2000. "Voicing the Voiceless: Foreign Political Aid to Civil Society in South Africa." In *Funding Virtue: Civil Society Aid and Democracy Promotion*, edited by M. Ottaway. Washington, DC: Carnegie Endowment for International Peace: 105–34.

Lanegran, Kimberly. 1995. "South Africa's Civic Association Movement: ANC's Ally or Society's 'Watchdog'? Shifting Social Movement, Political Party Relations." *African Studies Review* 38 (2):101–26.

Langer, Jerzy. 2009. Vice chair of Solidarity. Interview, January 12, Gdańsk, Poland.

Leader, SANCO, Local. 2008. Member of parliament, former municipal councilor, and SANCO regional president. Interview, Port Elizabeth, South Africa.

Levite, Ariel, and Sidney Tarrow. 1983. "The Legitimation of Excluded Parties in Dominant Party Systems: A Comparison of Israel and Italy." *Comparative Politics* 15 (3):295–327.

Levitsky, Steven, and Lucan A. Way. 1998. "Between a Shock and a Hard Place: The Dynamics of Labor-Backed Adjustment in Poland and Argentina." *Comparative Politics* 30 (2):171–92.

Lewicka, Ewa. 2009. Former Solidarity vice chair, Mazowsze region, and AWS vice minister of labor. Interview, January 8, Warsaw, Poland.

Lipko, Andrzej. 2009. Former head of Solidarity's mining department (1990–1991), and then vice minister of industry (1991–1992). Interview, January 8, Warsaw, Poland.

Lis, Bogdan. 2009. Former vice chair of Solidarity's foreign relations committee and member of parliament (1989–1991). Interview, January 6, Warsaw, Poland.

Lodge, Tom. 1994. "The African National Congress and Its Allies." In *Election '94 South Africa: The Campaigns, Results, and Future Prospects*, edited by A. Reynolds. New York: St. Martin's: 23–42.

———. 2003. *Politics in South Africa: From Mandela to Mbeki.* 2nd ed. Bloomington: Indiana University Press.

Loveman, Brian. 1991. "NGOs and the Transition to Democracy." *Grassroots Development* 15 (2):8–19.

———. 1995a. "Chilean NGOs: Forging a Role in the Transition to Democracy." In *New Paths to Democratic Development in Latin America: The Rise of NGO-Municipal Collaboration*, edited by C. A. Reilly. Boulder, CO: Rienner: 119–44.

———. 1995b. "The Transition to Civilian Government in Chile, 1990–1994." In *The Struggle for Democracy in Chile*, edited by P. W. Drake and I. Jaksic. Lincoln: University of Nebraska Press: 305–38.

MacKay, Shaun, and Malachia Mathoho. 2001. "Worker Power: The Congess of South African Trade Unions and Its Impact on Governance and Democracy." Research report 79. Social Policy series. Johannesburg: Centre for Policy Studies.

MacKinnon, Aran S. 2004. *The Making of South Africa: Culture and Politics.* Upper Saddle River, NJ: Pearson Prentice Hall.

Madisha, Willie. 2008. Former COSATU president (1999–2008). Interview, August 19, Johannesburg, South Africa.

Mahlatsane, Jonas. 2008. SACTWU regional secretary, Gauteng. Interview, August 18, Johannesburg, South Africa.

Maj, Józef. 2009. Solidarity chaplain. Interview, January 7, Warsaw, Poland.

Majadibodu, Edward. 2008. Chief negotiator for the National Union of Mine Workers (NUM). Interview, August 16, Johannesburg, South Africa.

Makwayiba, Mzwandile. 2008. Second deputy vice president of the National Education, Health, and Allied Workers' Union (NEHAWU), and former COSATU regional chair (1997–2004). Interview, August 16, Johannesburg, South Africa.

Mali, Aubray. 2008. ANC municipal councilor and SANCO national secretary. Interview, August 12, Port Elizabeth, South Africa.

Mandela, Nelson. 1997. *Report by the President of the ANC, Nelson Mandela, to the 50th National Conference of the African National Congress.* African National Congress. Available at www.anc.org.za/show.php?id=2461.

Mańko, Janina. 2009. Former Solidarity activist, AWS vice minister of health (1997–2001). Interview, January 11, Gdańsk, Poland.

March, James G., and Johan P. Olsen. 1996. "Institutional Perspectives on Political Institutions." *Governance: An International Journal of Policy and Administration* 9 (3):247–64.

Marczak, Henryk. 2009. Secretary of Solidarity, Łódź Region. Interview, January 5, Łódź, Poland.

Marszewski, Wacław. 2009. Former head of Solidarity's national mining committee and Solidarity Dolny Śląsk region (1998–2002). Interview, January 16, Gliwice, Poland.

Masemula, Katishi. 2008. General secretary of the Food and Allied Workers Union (FAWU). Interview, August 6, Cape Town, South Africa.

Maunye, Maggie. National member of parliament, and former union and civic official. Interview, 2008, Soweto, South Africa.

Mayekiso, Moses. 2008. Former member of parliament (1994–1996), general secretary of the National Union of Metalworkers of South Africa (NUMSA) (1987–1993), and SANCO president (1993–1994). Interview, August 25, Johannesburg, South Africa.

McAdam, Doug. 1988. *Freedom Summer.* New York: Oxford University Press.

McAdam, Doug, and Ronnelle Paulson. 1993. "Specifying the Relationship Between Social Ties and Activism." *American Journal of Sociology* 99 (3):640–67.

McFaul, Michael. 2005. "Transitions from Postcommunism." *Journal of Democracy* 16 (3):5–19.

McKinley, Dale T. 2001. "Democracy, Power, and Patronage: Debate and Opposition Within the African National Congress and the Tripartite Alliance Since 1994." In *Opposition and Democracy in South Africa*, edited by R. Southall. London: Cass: 183–206.

Meladze, Giorgi. 2007. Member of the Liberty Institute and former member of Kmara (political youth organization, 2003). Interview, July 17, Tbilisi, Georgia.

Melucci, Alberto, John Keane, and Paul Mier. 1989. *Nomads of the Present: Social Movements and Individual Needs in Contemporary Society.* Philadelphia: Temple University Press.

Meyer, David S., and Sidney G. Tarrow. 1998. "A Movement Society: Contentious Politics for a New Century." In *The Social Movement Society: Contentious Politics for a New Century*, edited by D. S. Meyer and S. G. Tarrow. Lanham, MD: Rowman and Littlefield: 1–28.

Mietlicka, Aleksandra. 2009. Former organizer, RS AWS (1997–2001). Interview, January 13, Sopot, Poland.

Millard, Frances. 1999. *Polish Politics and Society.* Routledge Studies of Societies in Transition. London: Routledge.

Mische, Ann. 2008. *Partisan Publics: Communication and Contention Across Brazilian Youth Activist Networks, Princeton Studies in Cultural Sociology*. Princeton, NJ: Princeton University Press.

Mkhize, Herbert. 2008. Executive director of the National Economic Development and Labour Council (NEDLAC) (2003–present). Interview, August 27, Johannesburg, South Africa.

Mngomezulu, Linda. 2008. General secretary of SANCO. Interview, August 21, Johannesburg, South Africa.

Mogase, Isaac Dank. 2008. National member of parliament and former president of the Soweto Civic Association. Interview, August 6, Cape Town, South Africa.

Mosiński, Jan. 2009. Head of Solidarity, Kalisz region. Interview, January 20, Gdańsk, Poland.

Mosunkutu, Khabisi. 2008. SANCO founder, former Post and Telecommunications Workers Association (POTWA) general secretary (pre-1994), national member of parliament (1994–1996), and provincial minister for agriculture, conservation, and environment, Gauteng province. Interview, August 20, Johannesburg, South Africa.

Mozolewski, Józef. 2009. Chair of Solidarity, Podlaski region, and former AWS member of parliament (1997–2001). Interview, January 12, Gdańsk, Poland.

Mtanga, Mandla. 2008. Municipal councilor and SANCO provincial executive committee member. Interview, August 12, Port Elizabeth, South Africa.

Mullen, Mark. 2007. Former Georgia country director for the National Democratic Institute (1997–2004). Telephone interview, June 26.

MVD. 2007. Internal Affairs Ministry representative. Interview, July 24, Tbilisi, Georgia.

Mvoko, Vuyo. 2000. "Alliance Leaders Discount Dissent." *Business Day* (South Africa), December 1.

Naidoo, Jay. 2008. Former COSATU general secretary (1985–1993), Minister for Reconstruction and Development Program (1994–1996), and Minister of Post, Telecommunications and Broadcasting (1996–1999). Interview, August 26 Johannesburg, South Africa.

Naidoo, Jayendra. 2008. Former trade-union leader (1981–1994), and first executive director of the National Economic Development and Labor Council (NEDLAC) (1995–1998). Interview, August 26, Johannesburg, South Africa.

Nanuashvili, Ucha. 2007. Executive director of the Human Rights Information and Documentation Center. Interview, July 16, Tbilisi, Georgia.

Ndungu, Kimani. 2008. Senior researcher at COSATU's National Labor and Economic Development Institute (NALEDI). Interview, August 15, Johannesburg, South Africa.

Ngwane, Trevor. 2008. Former municipal councilor (1995–2000), and founder of the Anti-Privatization Forum and Soweto Electricity Crisis Committee. Interview, August 17, Soweto, South Africa.

Ngwedzeni, Norman. 2008. Form civic activist (1989–1995), and municipal councilor. Interview, August 16, Johannesburg, South Africa.

Niesiołowski, Stefan. 2004. Former Sejm member (1989–1993, 1997–2001). Interview, January 6, Łódź, Poland.

Nodia, Ghia. 1995. "Georgia's Identity Crisis." *Journal of Democracy* 6 (1):104–16.

———. 2007. Chair of the Caucasus Institute for Peace, Democracy, and Development. Interview, July 19, Tbilisi, Georgia.

Ntshalintshali, Bheki. 2008. Deputy general secretary of COSATU. Interview, August 22, Johannesburg, South Africa.

Olson, Mancur. 1971. *The Logic of Collective Action: Public Goods and the Theory of Groups*. Rev. ed. New York: Schocken.

Opp, Karl-Dieter, and Wolfgang Roehl. 1990. "Repression, Micromobilization, and Political Protest." *Social Forces* 69 (2):521–47.

Orenstein, Mitchell A. 2001. *Out of the Red: Building Capitalism and Democracy in Postcommunist Europe*. Development and Inequality in the Market Economy. Networking Council Series. Ann Arbor: University of Michigan Press.

Osiński, Bogdan. 2009. Chair of Solidarity, Łódź region. Interview, January 5, Łódź, Poland.

Ost, David. 2001. "The Weakness of Symbolic Strength: Labor and Union Identity in Poland, 1989–2000." In *Workers After Workers' States: Labor and Politics in Postcommunist Eastern Europe*, edited by S. Crowley and D. Ost. Lanham, MD: Rowman and Littlefield: 79–96.

Ost, David. 2005. *The Defeat of Solidarity: Anger and Politics in Postcommunist Europe*. Ithaca, NY: Cornell University Press.

Ottaway, Marina. 2001. "Strengthening Civil Society in Other Countries: Policy Goal or Wishful Thinking?" New York: Carnegie Endowment for International Peace. Accessed December 13, 2011, www.carnegieendowment.org/2001/06/29/strengthening -civil-society-in-other-countries/5ucl.

Ottaway, Marina, and Theresa Chung. 1999. "Toward a New Paradigm." *Journal of Democracy* 10 (4):99–113.

Paczkowski, Andrzej. 1999. "Poland, the 'Enemy Nation.'" In *The Black Book of Communism*, edited by S. Courtois, N. Werth, J.-L. Panne, A. Paczkowski, K. Bartosek and J.-L. Margolin. Cambridge, MA: Harvard University Press.

Pałubicki, Janusz. 2004. Former national treasurer of Solidarity (1990–1997), and AWS member of parliament (1997–2001). Interview, January 7, Poznań, Poland.

———. 2009. Interview, January 10, Gdańsk, Poland.

Papuashvili, George. 2007. Chair of the Constitutional Court and former minister of justice and minister of environment (2005–2006). Interview, July 25, Tbilisi, Georgia.

Peters, B. Guy, Jon Pierre, and Desmond S. King. 2005. "The Politics of Path Dependency: Political Conflict in Historical Institutionalism." *Journal of Politics* 67 (4):1275–300.

Pietrzyk, Alojzy. 2009. Head of Solidarity, Śląsk region (1990–1992), and member of parliament (1991–1993). Interview, January 16, Katowice, Poland.

Polletta, Francesca, and James M. Jasper. 2001. "Collective Identity and Social Movements." *Annual Review of Sociology* 27:283–305.

Polmański, Eugeniusz. 2009. Assistant to the chair of Solidarity (1992–1998). Interview, January 16, Katowice, Poland.

Putnam, Robert D., Robert Leonardi, and Raffaella Nanetti. 1993. *Making Democracy Work: Civic Traditions in Modern Italy*. Princeton, NJ: Princeton University Press.

Raabe, Stephan. 2008. Transformacja i społeczeństwo obywatelskie w Polsce. Warsaw: Konrad Adenauer Foundation, Poland. Available at www.kas.de/wf/doc/kas_15103 -1522-8-30.pdf?081119041446.

Racelis, Mary. 2000. "New Visions and Strong Actions: Civil Society in the Philippines." In *Funding Virtue: Civil Society Aid and Democracy Promotion*, edited by M. Ottaway and T. Carothers. Washington, DC: Carnegie Endowment for International Peace.

Ramishvili, Levan. 2007. Head of the Liberty Institute. Interview, July 17, Tbilisi, Georgia.

Representative, USG. 2007. U.S. government representative. Interview, July 24, Tbilisi, Georgia.

Ronnie, Roger. 2008. Former general secretary of South Africa Municipal Workers' Union (SAMWU) (2000–2007). Interview, August 5, Cape Town, South Africa.

Rose, Richard, and Doh Chull Shin. 2001. "Democratization Backwards: The Problem of Third-Wave Democracies." *British Journal of Political Science* 31 (2):331–54.

Rulewski, Jan. 2009. Senator and former representative of Solidarity in parliament (1991–1993), and former head of Solidarity, Bydgoszcz region (1980–1981, 1990). Interview, January 8, Warsaw, Poland.

Rupnik, Jacques. 1988. Totalitarianism Revisited. In *Civil Society and the State: New European Perspectives*, edited by J. Keane. New York: Verso.

Rustin, Jonavon. 2008. Provincial secretary of South African Democratic Teachers' Union (SADTU). Interview, August 5, Cape Town, South Africa.

Rybicki, Jacek. 2009. Vice chair of Solidarity (1993–1997), and former AWS member of parliament (1997–2001). Interview, January 15, Gdańsk, Poland.

Saakashvili, Nino. 2007. Executive director of Horizonti. Interview, July 16, Tbilisi, Georgia.

SAGO. 2008. South African Government Official. Interview, August 26, Pretoria, South Africa.

Salamadze, Vazha. 2007. Chair of the Civil Society Institute. Interview, July 25, Tbilisi, Georgia.

Salisbury, Robert H., Paul Johnson, John P. Heinz, Edward O. Laumann, and Robert L. Nelson. 1989. "Who You Know Versus What You Know: The Uses of Government Experience for Washington Lobbyists." *American Journal of Political Science* 33 (1):175–95.

Sambatha, Madoda. 2008. Former municipal councilor (2000–2006), and lower-level official of the National Union of Mine Workers (NUM). Interview, August 22, Johannesburg, South Africa.

SANCO1. 2008. Former regional head. Interview, August 11, Port Elizabeth, South Africa.

Searing, Donald D. 1991. "Roles, Rules, and Rationality in the New Institutionalism." *American Political Science Review* 85 (4):1239–60.

Seekings, Jeremy. 1997. "SANCO: Strategic Dilemmas in a Democratic South Africa." *Transformation* 34:1–30.

Segarra, Monique. 1997. "Redefining the Public/Private Mix: NGOs and the Emergency Social Investment Fund in Ecuador." In *The New Politics of Inequality in Latin America: Rethinking Participation and Representation*, edited by D. A. Chalmers. Oxford: Oxford University Press: 489–515.

Sellstrom, Tor. 2002. *Sweden and National Liberation in South Africa*. Vol. 2. Uppsala: Nordic Africa Institute.

Sharman, J. C. 2003. *Repression and Resistance in Communist Europe, BASEES/RoutledgeCurzon Series on Russian and East European Studies*. London; New York: Routledge Curzon.

Shevis, James M. 1981. "The AFL-CIO and Poland's Solidarity." *World Affairs* 144 (1):31–35.

Sikkink, Kathryn. 1993. "Human Rights, Principled Issue-Networks, and Sovereignty in Latin America." *International Organization* 47 (3):411–41.

Silliman, G. Sidney. 1998. "The Transnational Relations of Philippine Non-Governmental Organizations." In *Organizing for Democracy: NGOs, Civil Society, and the Philippine State*, edited by G. S. Silliman and L. G. Noble. Honolulu: University of Hawaii Press: 49–74.

Silliman, G. Sidney, and Lela Garner Noble. 1998. "Citizen Movement and Philippine Democracy." In *Organizing for Democracy: NGOs, Civil Society, and the Philippine State*, edited by G. S. Silliman and L. G. Noble. Honolulu: University of Hawaii Press: 280–310.

Skipietrow, Natalia. 1993. "Kuron gani nauczycieli." *Gazeta Wyborcza*, May 7, 1.

Smirnow, Andrzej. 2009. Former vice chair of Solidarity, Mazowsze region (1991–1993), and member of parliament (1991–1993, 1997–2001, 2006–present). Interview, January 21, Warsaw, Poland.

Śniadek, Janusz. 2009. Chair of Solidarity. Interview, January 12, Gdańsk, Poland.

Snyder, Jack, and Karen Ballentine. 1996. "Nationalism and the Marketplace of Ideas." *International Security* 21 (2):5–40.

Solidarity. 1982. "The Solidarity Program." In *The Solidarity Sourcebook*, edited by S. Persky and H. Flam. Vancouver: New Star: 205–25.

Solidarity1. 2009. Solidarity regional officeholder. Interview, January 14, Gdańsk, Poland.

Sonto, Mzunani Roseberry. 2008. SANCO provincial chair, Western Cape, and member of parliament. Interview, August 7, Cape Town, South Africa.

Stelmachowski, Andrzej. 2004. Former senator (1989–1991). Interview, January 20, Warsaw, Poland.

Subari, Sozar. 2007. Public defender (ombudsman) of Georgia. Interview, July 18, Tbilisi, Georgia.

Szwed, Stanisław. 2009. Member of parliament; former head of Solidarity, Podbezkid region (1992–1997, 2002–2005). Interview, January 8, Warsaw, Poland.

Tarkhnishvili, Levan. 2007. Head of Georgian public TV. Interview, July 24, Tbilisi, Georgia.

Taylor, Rupert. 2002. "South Africa: The Role of Peace and Conflict-Resolution Organizations in the Struggle Against Apartheid." In *Mobilizing for Peace: Conflict Resolution in Northern Ireland, Israel/Palestine, and South Africa*, edited by B. Gidron, S. N. Katz, and Y. Hasenfeld. Oxford: Oxford University Press: 69–93.

Terry, Sarah Meiklejohn. 1993. "Thinking about Post-Communist Transitions: How Different Are They?" *Slavic Review* 52 (2):333–37.

Tevdoradze, Elene. 2007. Chair of the Human Rights and Civil Integration Committee, parliament of the Republic of Georgia. Interview, Tbilisi, Georgia.

Thelen, Kathleen, and Sven Steinmo. 1992. "Historical Institutionalism in Comparative Politics." In *Structuring Politics: Historical Institutionalism in Comparative Analysis*, edited by K. Thelen, S. Steinmo, and F. Longstreth. New York: Cambridge University Press.

Tomaszewski, Janusz. 2009. Former chair of Solidarity, Łódź region (1992–1997), and former AWS interior minister (1997–1999). Interview, January 5, Łódź, Poland.

Torres, Liv. 2005. "Labour and Politics in South Africa." In *Democratising Development: The Politics of Socio-Economic Rights in South Africa*, edited by P. Jones and K. Stokke. Leiden: Nijhoff.

Tsenoli, Lechesa Solomon. 2008. Former SANCO president (1994–1995), and current member of parliament. Interview, August 5, Cape Town, South Africa.

Tsintsadze, Irene. 2007. Deputy head of the Department of Prisons, Republic of Georgia, and former head of Alternativa NGO (pre-2004). Interview, July 25, Tbilisi, Georgia.

Ugulava, Gigi. 2007. Mayor of Tbilisi and former founder/director of ALPE, an NGO (pre-2004). Interview, July 21, Tbilisi, Georgia.

UNAG. 2007. United Nations Association of Georgia representative. Interview, July 26, Tbilisi, Georgia.

Unionist2. 2008.Union representative. Interview, August 13, Port Elizabeth, South Africa.

Unionist5. 2008. Former union and government official. Interview, August 14, Johannesburg, South Africa.

Unionist6. 2008. Provincial union leader. Interview, August 18, Johannesburg, South Africa.

USAID. 2007. USAID official. Interview, January 25, Washington, DC.

————. 2010. *USAID: Democracy and Governance—Civil Society and Media.* U.S. Agency for International Development. Accessed March 15, 2010, www.usaid.gov /our_work/democracy_and_governance/technical_areas/civil_society/.

Useem, Bert. 1998. "Breakdown Theories of Collective Action." *Annual Review of Sociology* 24:215–38.

USG1. 2007. U.S. government official. Interview, July 24, Tbilisi, Georgia.

USG2. 2007. U.S. government official. Interview, July 24, Tbilisi, Georgia.

USG12. 2007. U.S. government official. Interview, January 5, Washington, DC.

Valpy, Michael. 1997. "Big Labour Becoming Big Business." *Globe and Mail* (Canada), May 13, A16.

Wałęsa, Lech. 2009. Former chair of Solidarity (1980–1990), and former president of Poland (1990–1995). Interview, January 13, Gdańsk, Poland.

Wasiński, Włodzimierz. 2009. Vice chair of Solidarity, Dolny Śląsk, and member of parliament (1997–2001). Interview, January 17, Wrocław, Poland.

Wayile, Goodman. 2008. COSATU provincial chair and municipal ANC councilor. Interview, August 12, Port Elizabeth, South Africa.

Wedel, Janine R. 1998. *Collision and Collusion: The Strange Case of Western Aid to Eastern Europe, 1989–1998.* 1st ed. New York: St. Martin's.

White, Rober W. 1989. "From Peaceful Protest to Guerrilla War: Micromobilization of the Provisional Irish Republican Army." *American Journal of Sociology* 94 (6):1277–302.

Whittier, Nancy. 2002. "Meaning and Structure in Social Movements." In *Social Movements: Identity, Culture, and the State,* edited by D. S. Meyer, N. Whittier, and B. Robnett. Oxford: Oxford University Press: 289–307.

Williams, Donovan. 2008. Member of SANCO's national executive committee. Interview, August 18, Pretoria, South Africa.

Wójcik, Tomasz. 2009. Former chair of Solidarity, Dolny Śląsk (1990–1998), and member of parliament (1997–2001). Interview, January 16, Wrocław, Poland.

Wojtczak, Michal. 2009. Senator, former chair of Solidarity, Toruń region (1990–1998), former Solidarity member of parliament (1991–1993), AWS member of parliament (1997–1999), and secretary of state (2000–2001). Interview, January 7, Warsaw, Poland.

Worth, Robert F. 2011. "Egypt's Next Crisis." *New York Times Magazine,* May 11.

Wujec, Henryk. 2004. Former member of parliament (1989–2001), and secretary of Solidarity's 1989 electoral commission, Komitet Obywatelski Solidarności. Interview, Warsaw, Poland.

Wydra, Harald. 2000. *Continuities in Poland's Permanent Transition.* Houndmills, Basingstoke, Hampshire: Macmillan.

Zald, Mayer N., and Roberta Ash. 1966. "Social Movement Organizations: Growth, Decay, and Change." *Social Forces* 44 (3):327–41.

Zhvania, Tamara. 2007. Director of the International Society for Fair Elections and Democracy. Interview, July 18, Tbilisi, Georgia.

Zuern, Elke. 2006. "Elusive Boundaries: SANCO, the ANC, and the Post-Apartheid South African State." In *Voices of Protest: Social Movements in Post-Apartheid South Africa*, edited by R. Ballard, A. Habib, and I. Valodia. Scottsville, South Africa: University of KwaZulu-Natal Press: 179–201.

Zurabishvili, David. 2007. Independent member of parliament, Republic of Georgia, and former founder/leader of the Liberty Institute (1996–2003). Interview, July 20, Tbilisi, Georgia.

Index

Aeschylus, 7
African National Congress (ANC), 19;
   armed resistance declared by, 31;
   banning of, 31, 74; briefing notes 2001,
   83; on budget deficit, 79–80; civic
   community functions usurped by, 92;
   cooptation by, 93; delegates to, 71;
   establishment of, 73–74; exile of, 31,
   74; NEDLAC disregarded by, 80;
   SANCO incorporated as junior
   partner to, 87; SANCO threatening,
   92; ward committees established by,
   92–93
Afrikaners, 73
agency-centered approach, 20;
   institutions in, 21
All-Poland Alliance of Trade Unions
   (OPZZ), 59, 61, 66
analysis unit, 27–32
Andropov, Yuri, 105
apartheid: formal existence of,
   73; unsustainability of,
   76
Aquino, Benigno, 144–45
Aquino, Corazon, 144–45
Arab Spring, 1
Arkuszewski, Wojciech, 54
Article 42, 116
Association for Legal and Public
   Education (ALPE), 110, 117; Ugulava
   on, 178n3
Aylwin, Patricio, 147–48; measures
   introduced by, 148

Baku-Tbilisi-Ceyhan gas pipeline,
   106
balance, 22, 23–24
Balcerowicz, Leszek, 43
Balcerowicz Plan, 43; costs of, 44
Banaszak, Lee Ann, 5, 14
Bantustans, 73
Benford, Robert, 16
betrayal, 13
Black Sash, 75
Bokeria, Giga, 125
Bonaparte, Napoleon, 13
boomerang approach, 131
Borusewicz, Bogdan, 52, 54
Brazil, 5
Brezhnev, Leonid, 105
broad policy goals, 23
broken-back democracies, 151–52

case selection, 27–32
Caucasus Institute for Peace,
   Democracy, and Development, 110,
   117, 128, 178n1
Chile: NGOs in, 146–49; protesters
   burnt in, 147
Chilean Committee for Free Elections
   (CEL), 142
Chilean pobladores, 29, 146–47
Civic Parliamentary Club (OKP), 42–43,
   49; split in, 52–53
civics: factionalism within, 98;
   hierarchal structure of, 86–87;
   historical focus of, 86; labor unions

The authorized representative in the EU for product safety and compliance is:
Mare Nostrum Group
B.V Doelen 72
4831 GR Breda
The Netherlands

www.ingramcontent.com/pod-product-compliance
Lightning Source LLC
Chambersburg PA
CBHW030330270326
41926CB00010B/1564